CONCEPTUAL THINKING

A LOGICAL INQUIRY

BY

STEPHAN KÖRNER

Professor of Philosophy in the
University of Bristol

Dover Publications, Inc.
New York

Published in Canada by General Publishing Com-
pany, Ltd., 30 Lesmill Road, Don Mills, Toronto,
Ontario.
Published in the United Kingdom by Constable
and Company, Ltd., 10 Orange Street, London
WC 2.

This Dover edition, first published in 1959, is an
unabridged and corrected republication of the work
originally published by the University of Cambridge
for the University of Bristol in 1955.
This edition also contains a new Preface by the
author.

Library of Congress Catalog Card Number: 59-10442

Manufactured in the United States of America
Dover Publications, Inc.
180 Varick Street
New York, N. Y. 10014

PREFACE TO THE DOVER EDITION

The first edition of this book was exhausted soon after it appeared and I am glad that the Dover Publications has agreed to re-issue it in unchanged form.

I have always been aware of the need for taking further some of the points I have sought to make. In particular, anyone interested in a fuller exposition of the logical relations between inexact concepts will find this in an article entitled "Reference, Vagueness, and Necessity" (*Philosophical Review*, vol. LXVI, No. 3, July 1957).

S. K.

1958

PREFACE

In this book I propose to try to exhibit in outline the ways in which different types of concept are related to one another; the manner in which they are linked to experience; and some of the purposes for which they are employed. To trace these connections is a philosophical task, and in pursuing it a writer is unavoidably confronted by the traditional problems of philosophy—epistemology, theory of value, metaphysics—as also by the expectation that he should be able to throw light on some of them. How far such expectation is here fulfilled must be left to results to declare.

As to presentation, since the work to be done had to include an exploration, however cursory, of the field of contact between exact logical, mathematical and scientific concepts on the one hand and the inexact characteristics of everyday experience on the other, I have found myself unable to adopt either of two highly attractive ways of expression. One of these is to use the exact language of some ready-made system of mathematical logic and ignore, on the whole, the incurable vagueness of ordinary empirical concepts. The other is to use the language of ordinary discourse and abjure all conscious use of technical terms. For my part I have had to follow, as I could, the practice of the majority of philosophers and employ both technical and non-technical language, defining new terms as and when it became necessary.

The first draft of the manuscript was finished in August 1952. Professors Ryle, Field and Braithwaite have been kind enough to read it and have made helpful suggestions. I have used the summer vacation of 1954 for a thorough revision of the manuscript without, however, changing its substance and without, therefore, considering any publications which have appeared since the completion of the first draft. In the task of revision, I have had the generous help of Professor J. W. Scott and I am deeply grateful to him for the patience and care with which he advised me on questions of style and formulation. Mr Basil Cottle has very kindly given his time to help me read the proofs.

PREFACE

My thanks are due to the editors of *Mind* and of the *Proceedings of the Aristotelian Society* for permission to use some previously published material. It gives me great pleasure to thank both the Publications Committee of the University of Bristol for having made possible the publication of the work and in particular the Vice-Chancellor, Sir Philip Morris, for the kindness he has shown me on this and many other occasions.

S.K.

BRISTOL
March 1955

CONTENTS

vii

CONTENTS

INTRODUCTION

CHAPTER I

THE NATURE AND SCOPE OF THE INQUIRY

THE meaning of the term "conceptual thinking" must ultimately be conveyed by exemplification. Examples are easily given and readily understood. The person who expounds a mathematical proof and equally the person who follows the exposition is thinking conceptually. So is the person who is engaged in any kind of classification; as also the judge who applies a legal statute to a state of affairs. Any child who uses a colour-word correctly proves himself thereby a conceptual thinker.

As is the case with all notions whose meaning is given thus, the notion of conceptual thinking admits of borderline cases. Indeed, by speaking of conceptual thinking one implies that other kinds are possible and that presumably some or all of us think at times non-conceptually. I am further prepared to admit the applicability of the notion of degree here; not only are there other kinds of thinking, but instances of the kind called "conceptual" shade off into instances of kinds of thinking which are not conceptual.

But, whether all thinking is conceptual or not, I believe that any attempt to distinguish between thinking and other kinds of activity without admitting borderline cases must fail. Most people who reflect on the point would, I think, agree that instances of conceptual thinking shade off into instances of intelligent doing, and further into all sorts of more or less automatic behaviour.

These considerations suggest a certain vagueness in demarcating the field of our inquiry. The same impression becomes stronger when we consider the distinction between acts and dispositions, between occurrences of conceptual thinking and dispositions to think conceptually. Here the line is again, to say the least, not easily drawn. Our policy for the present, however, must be to acknowledge these difficulties and to pass on.

That the border-regions must be indefinite between conceptual and non-conceptual thinking on the one hand, and between thinking and doing on the other, need not deter us from our undertaking. Rather it might be some reassuring evidence that we are not from the start replacing conceptual thinking, as it is found in examples, by some idealised model which owes its neatness to postulates. Moreover, as with all notions whose meaning is given by exemplification, some instances are perfectly clear. Indeed just as the meaning of "green" can be exemplified by satisfactory examples, so one can easily point, as we have in fact pointed, to a nucleus of examples of conceptual thinking which are not borderline cases.

To come now to the subject-matter of this inquiry. We are to consider the rules of conceptual thinking; relations between these; and some contexts in which they can be accepted or satisfied. Such an inquiry is not empirical, but it is at least undertaken with an eye to certain empirical facts: for what lends interest to its definitions is that they are not empty, and the possibilities which will claim our attention are possibilities often realised.

It is to be observed that the aim of a logical inquiry into conceptual thinking is not the discovery of natural laws. It makes no claim to be looking around to see how the performances of conceptual thinkers vary with variations of emotional strain, of illness, of senescence or other such conditions. The experimental psychologist who tries to discover the natural laws of conceptual thinking may safely assume that the rules of conceptual thinking which his subjects accept are clear enough for his purposes. He certainly need not be, and in fact is not, concerned with explicitly exhibiting and discussing those rules of conceptual thinking which he himself accepts and tries to satisfy when designing and interpreting his experiments.

While an empirical inquiry aimed at discovering the natural laws of conceptual thinking would have little connection, if any, with the present undertaking, another inquiry, likewise empirical, in the field of conceptual thinking is highly relevant to it. I mean that which aims at discovering what rules of conceptual thinking are in fact accepted, either by all people or by certain groups or even certain individuals. It makes little difference whether we regard such an inquiry as psychological, anthropological or as belonging to some other branch of science. I am sure it would even be in accordance with philosophical tradition to regard it as belonging to critical philosophy, in so far at least as the latter consists not in inventing or constructing propositions, but in making universally accepted but hidden intellectual commitments explicit.

Before discussing this last empirical inquiry in its relation to our purpose, we must consider it for a little on its own account. It is necessary to distinguish, first of all, between the empirical proposition that a person accepts a rule (whether of conceptual thinking or anything else) and the other empirical proposition that he behaves in accordance with a law of nature. The difference can be clearly illustrated by an example. Consider, on the one hand, the empirical proposition that if a policeman signals to the driver of a car, then as a matter of scientific or causal necessity, the driver always stops; on the other hand, the empirical proposition that all car-drivers *accept the rule* to the effect that at a policeman's signal to them they have to stop. The difference between these two is seen from the relation which each of them bears to the further statement—also an empirical statement—that on a certain given occasion a policeman signalled and the driver did not stop. This last is incompatible with the statement of scientific necessity. It is *not* incompatible with the statement about the car-driver's acceptance of the rule. It is, indeed, by no means self-contradictory to assert that a person who accepts a rule is nevertheless found breaking it.

It is further necessary to distinguish between the empirical proposition that a rule is accepted by somebody and the rule itself. To discover that somebody or everybody accepts a certain rule is to discover an empirical fact. But no rule, as such, is an empirical proposition, whether it is or is not accepted by anybody. Rules differ from empirical propositions, and, equally, from logical propositions such as entailments. A rule can be accepted, and then satisfied, or violated. Indeed, only a rule can be so treated. An empirical or logical proposition cannot. I am not denying here that the words "accept", "satisfy", "violate" may occur also in talk about empirical and logical propositions. It will, however, be agreed in these cases, that though the words are the same, their rules of use are different.

The method by which the acceptance of a rule by a person is discovered may differ in different circumstances, and there exists no one procedure which unfailingly leads to the discovery of what rules are accepted. A person accepts a rule if he satisfies it intentionally—or at least has the intention to satisfy it. Of the presence of this intention there are various more or less reliable indications. Thus it may be evidence of the intention if the accepter can formulate his intention (and therefore also formulate the rule which he intentionally satisfies or intends to satisfy). The intention to satisfy a rule may also be indicated by less impressive evidence, for example, by the fact that on the occasion of the breaking of the rule the accepter of it notes, however vaguely, that some rule has been broken.

Any rule which follows logically from accepted rules is also accepted, even if its accepter is unaware of it. The role played by deduction in our discovering what rules are accepted is similar to the role it plays in other fields. Deduction does not provide premisses but it makes hidden consequences obvious. It can yield accepted rules, but only from premisses which are themselves accepted rules. Unlike the mathematician, the discoverer of rules which are accepted, whether he be anthropologist, psychologist or critical philosopher, must establish some empirical propositions non-deductively. This ultimately involves observing what people say or do, including himself, and imagining what he or they would say or do in various sets of circumstances. A particularly effective way of establishing the acceptance of a rule consists in charging its presumed accepter with having really accepted its contrary.

I have remarked that although a logical inquiry into conceptual thinking is not directly concerned with empirical facts, there are facts about conceptual thinking which are relevant to it and lend it interest. These consist, as we have said, in the acceptance of certain rules of conceptual thinking, and they are brought to light by the kind of empirical inquiry just described. To see the relevance of such empirical inquiry to our undertaking we have only to note that the number of different rules of conceptual thinking capable of being accepted is practically unlimited. The need is thereby indicated for some principle or principles of selection, if an account of them is not to become unbearably amorphous or trivial.

I propose the following: that we first discuss (as far as possible) those rules of conceptual thinking which are universally or almost universally accepted by human beings; and secondly, say something of those which although not universally or even widely accepted, are linked with philosophical problems in such a manner that their discussion may throw some light on these problems.

Rules of the former kind can be discovered only by an empirical inquiry such as we have called anthropological or critical. We should find, I believe, that all or almost all human beings (after a certain stage in their development) accept what I propose to call "ostensive rules". A very simple example of such a rule would be conveyed if anybody said (with appropriate pointing gestures) that this and this and this and everything like it is to be called "green", the term being thereafter referred to as an ostensive predicate, and the particulars to which it is applicable as its bases.

To consider ostensive rules is thus to consider the relation of ostensive predicates to their bases. Moreover, the fact that conceptual thinkers accept more than one ostensive rule raises the question of possible relations between different ostensive predicates. We shall, furthermore, have to discuss to some extent the purposes for which ostensive rules are applied or accepted. Although discussion of these last will often take us outside the first of our proposed topics—the universally accepted rules—it is easily brought within the limits of the second—rules philosophically important—since considerations of certain purposes in the service of which we apply and accept ostensive rules may be found to throw light on some philosophical questions, in particular questions of ethics and aesthetics.

Apart from the ostensive, we shall have occasion to discuss certain other rules of conceptual thinking—and so other kinds of predicate, their relations to their bases (in so far as they have bases), their relations to other predicates of the same type and of different types, and some broader contexts of their satisfaction. In all this, however, we shall still be moving within at least one of the two territories above proposed for exploration, and often we shall find ourselves within both.

In concluding this chapter it may be well to remark explicitly that the proposed explorations cannot at the outset promise to be exhaustive. Some relevant subjects may simply have been over-looked. About others—and here I would mention in particular the entire subject of probability-theory—I have nothing to say which I do not know to have been adequately said by others already.

CHAPTER II

SOME QUESTIONS OF TERMINOLOGY

THE recent remarkable developments of formal logic and the philosophy of language have rightly emphasised the importance of a clear and consistent terminology. Some philosophers, however, have gone so far as to assert that all philosophical problems can be settled by terminological decisions and even that a proposition is meaningful if, and only if, it can be formulated in some specific terminology. Before explaining a few terms which will be used later in the inquiry, some remarks on the role of terminology in philosophy are called for, if only in order to show that our choice of terminology involves us in no grave commitments.

There are philosophers for whom a linguistic confusion lurks behind every philosophical question. Their search for this has often been successful and their discoveries illuminating. They have shown that philosophical difficulties are not necessarily difficult philosophical questions; and that some philosophical questions merely express the need for terminological decisions. Terminological decisions which settle philosophical difficulties may range from some simple adjustment of a natural language to the construction of an elaborate deductive system. There are, nevertheless, philosophical questions which cannot be settled in this manner. In philosophy, as elsewhere, one often does not know, and wishes to know, what is entailed by clearly formulated assumptions, or how requirements which are perfectly clearly formulated can be fulfilled. No examples are necessary to show that not every terminological innovation is an answer to a philosophical question. The impression to the contrary and the false appearance of novelty is often merely due to the fact that it takes time to recognise translations from one terminology into another for what they are.

The view that some more or less elaborate terminology can be used as a test of the meaningfulness of all propositions is another over-hasty generalisation of important discoveries. Russell and later formal logicians have shown us that certain "meaningless" propositions—in particular certain logical antinomies which are generally regarded as meaningless—cannot be formulated in the language of *Principia Mathematica* and other formal languages. This was an important discovery. But it does not justify the conclusion that no proposition is other or better than meaningless unless it can be formulated in a particular formal language. Nor does it justify the conclusion that a language is discoverable, though not yet discovered, which could be used as a test of meaningfulness. Either of these conclusions presupposes a criterion to decide whether, if a proposition cannot be expressed in some language, it is the proposition which is defective and not merely the language. Such a criterion has not been provided, and it cannot be dispensed with by decreeing that a particular language be the standard of meaningfulness. What applies to formal languages applies also to so-called "ordinary language". Here again we cannot decide in general whether, if a proposition cannot be expressed in it, the proposition or the language should be blamed.

It is surprising how vaguely the term "ordinary language" is used by those who appeal to it as the ultimate authority in philosophical matters.[1] It can hardly mean some inextendable set of sentences and rules which are used, or are likely to be used, by the men in certain streets. For we may include the street in which the analysing philosopher lives; and then his sentences will be meaningful by definition! If, on the other hand, we exclude this street, then even so much extension of the set as is involved in a clarification of "ordinary language" might easily be inadmissible.

"Ordinary language" more often seems to refer to a set of sentences or rules which can be changed. It can be changed by adding more rules or by replacing some by others. If the term is used to refer to such a changeable system, then, unless the principles of permissible extension and replacement are indicated, the meaning is too vague to be of much use.

It is not difficult to think of philosophical questions and answers which can remain the same and yet be formulated differently—

[1] See, for example, the Introduction to *Essays on Logic and Language*, edited by A. G. N. Flew (Oxford, 1951).

that is, by using different sets of predicates. If a philosophical theory can be thus variously formulated, then, as far as the theory is concerned, the choice of any of these sets is in the familiar phrase a "matter of terminology". An obvious and traditional example of a merely terminological choice is the theory of the syllogism which, as Porphyry already recognised, can be formulated equally well in nominalist or realist terms. It is, so to speak, neutral with respect to a choice between nominalism and realism, or invariant with regard to translation from a nominalist to a realist terminology.

The preference of one particular set of predicates to another, with which to formulate a theory neutral to either, is often grounded in the conviction that the set recommended is "less misleading". No exception need here be taken so long as it is realised that no terminology is *as such* misleading; that it is only misleading in so far as persons are misled by it. Whether one is misled by a terminology depends on many circumstances and they vary from person to person. To guard against being victimised by a misleading terminology, people should become familiar with more than one. It seems highly unlikely that any one should be found which could not mislead anybody.

An inquiry of the type now before us cannot, I believe, proceed without, sometimes, using unusual words or using common words in an unusual way. The terminologies which suggest themselves, and have in fact been used, for our purpose, are variants of what might be called either the terminology of "meaningful sentences and words", that of "judgments and their parts", or again the terminology of "concepts and propositions", and there are others. My own choice is for the terminology of "concepts and propositions"—I shall explain the key-terms presently. With respect to the questions to be asked and the answers proposed all these terminologies will be neutral. The impression that they are not, and that one of them is preferable to others, will be found to be due to the intrusion of metaphysical or ontological questions which are alien to this inquiry.

We do not at any stage presuppose an answer, either affirmative or negative, to the question whether, and if so in what manner, propositions and concepts "exist". For every statement about concepts or propositions will be regarded as an elliptical and easily completable statement about users of concepts and users of propositions, that is, about persons behaving or being disposed to behave in certain observable ways. If in thus assuming the existence of persons I seem to be indulging in an unwarranted and over-daring hypothesis, I can only assure the reader that the nature of questions and statements about existence, whether they concern that of physical objects and persons, or that of propositions, belongs to the subject-matter of the present essay and will come up for discussion in due course.

It is usual to characterise propositions as being true-or-false. A disadvantage of this is that it links the notion of propositions with those of truth and of falsehood. The latter notions are ambiguous. As is well known, none of the many different theories of truth has found general acceptance.

Another way of defining the notion of propositions is to point out that they are the only objects of belief, of doubt and of other so-called "propositional attitudes". This is to link the notion with disputes about mental acts and dispositions. Here again there is much less agreement about the adequacy of the different theories than about the use of the term "proposition" itself, at least in contexts of logic. I shall therefore presently propose a definition of "propositions" which is independent of the notion either of truth or of propositional attitudes.

In satisfying certain rules in the use one makes of words and other signs, one is using these signs as statements and as predicates. Thus in using the sign ‹this is green›[1] as a statement and the sign ‹green› as a predicate one is satisfying rules—and, among others, an ostensive one, that is, a rule to the effect that ‹green› is to be assigned to any particular which resembles certain well-identified objects and does not resemble certain others. To make statements is to use signs governed by ostensive rules and a great variety of others.

A sign is used as a statement, in the same way as a piece of iron is used as a tool. We call a certain object "a tool" not only when

[1] Single French quotes are used in mentioning signs considered apart from any rules for their use.

12

it is actually being so used but also when we wish to indicate its possible use. Exactly so I shall call such a sign as ‹this is green› a "statement" not only when it is actually being used as such, but also when I wish to indicate such possible use of it.

In order to identify a particular statement it is necessary to mention the sign (the statement-sign) *and* to specify the rules which govern its use. I shall use as statement-signs either the small letters ‹*p*›, ‹*q*›, ‹*r*›, or statement-signs of the English language. It will usually not be necessary to specify the rules which govern the use of a statement-sign. In such cases, when mentioning one, I shall indicate that it is used as a statement by putting it within double quotes. Thus "this is green" and "*p*" are statements.

There is a set of rules for the use of any statement-sign. Let us call this set "synonymous" with the set of rules governing another and different statement-sign if the rules differ only in that they govern the use of different signs. Let us also call the signs themselves, in that case, "synonymous signs". Lastly, let us call any rule which permits the arbitrary replacement of a sign by any one of its synonyms, a "synonymity rule". If we add to the rules for the use of a sign as a statement a synonymity rule we shall say that it (the statement-sign) is now being used not as a statement but as a proposition. In sum: if the arbitrary replacement of it by any of its synonyms is allowed, the statement sign (for example, ‹this is green›) is being used as a proposition; if this liberty may not be taken it is being used as a statement.

In order to identify some particular proposition it is necessary on the one hand to mention one of the synonymous signs which can be used as this proposition (one of the synonymous propositional signs) *and* on the other to specify the rules governing its use. These rules, of course, include a synonymity rule. Again I shall use when indicating propositional signs the small letters ‹*p*›, ‹*q*›, ‹*r*›, etc., or statement-signs of the English language. Instead of specifying the rules for the use of a propositional sign I shall often, when mentioning the sign, indicate that it is used as a proposition by putting it in single quotes. Thus '*p*' and 'this is green' are signs used as propositions—briefly they are propositions.

My use of 'predicate' and 'concept' is analogous to my use of the terms 'statement' and 'proposition'. In order to identify a particular predicate it is necessary to mention the sign (the predicative sign) which is used as the predicate *and* to specify the rules which govern its use. I shall use as predicative signs capital letters or predicative signs of the English language, and when mentioning them I shall indicate their being used as predicates by putting them within double quotes. Thus "green" and "*P*" are used as predicates, or, as we may say more briefly, they are predicates.

By adding a synonymity rule to the rules which govern the use of a sign as a predicate we again change its use. The sign is then being used no longer as a predicate but as a concept. If we are not free to substitute for the sign any of its synonyms that we please, then we are using the sign as a predicate. If we are so free we are using it as a concept. In order to identify a particular concept it is necessary to mention one of the synonymous conceptual signs and to specify the rules governing its use. As conceptual signs I shall, as in the case of predicative signs, use capital letters or predicative signs of the English language, indicating their use as concepts by putting them into single quotes. Thus '*P*' and 'green' are used as concepts in accordance with certain unspecified or not fully specified rules, or, as we may say again more briefly, they are concepts.

For the sake of brevity and for want of a better name we shall call the use of signs in all these ways—as statements, propositions, predicates or concepts—"discursive". For, indeed, without the use of signs in this manner intelligent discourse would be impossible.

So far we have considered, and considered only cursorily, the discursive use of signs whose use is governed by (among others) ostensive rules. If we define the discursive use of signs as being their use in accordance with ostensive and similar rules, we admit a large border-region between the discursive and the non-discursive use of signs.

We can greatly contract the border-region by assuming familiarity with the concept of logical deducibility—the concept 'entails'. For in using this concept we mention concepts, propositions, predicates or statements as antecedents or consequents. Examples are "'green' entails 'coloured'", "'being triangular' entails 'being trilateral'", and so forth. Now it is a necessary and sufficient condition for the discursive character of a sign that, according to the rules which govern its use, it can occur as antecedent or consequent of the concept 'entails'. In other words discursively used signs and only such can entail or be entailed. This will be found, so I believe, to characterise not only my own use of "concept", "proposition", "predicate" and "statement", but that of many other philosophers and logicians, even of some who seem to imply that their use is different.

By showing concepts and propositions to be signs whose use is governed by certain rules we do not in any way answer the question whether and how far concepts and propositions "exist" apart from people using them, but this is as it should be. Moreover, we are not concerned to deny that other definitions of "concept" and "proposition" and altogether different terminologies may have the same merit of neutrality, and might prove equally suitable equipment for our undertaking.

In talking to each other people often satisfy rules of conceptual thinking. They do, however, sometimes satisfy these rules without talking to each other or even to themselves. How far non-verbal signs including possibly incommunicable signs (for example, private body feelings which can be produced at will) can be used in conceptual thinking is a matter for empirical inquiry.

If we remember that people frequently think without talking, no harm can be done by considering in the first place the verbal and audible satisfaction of rules for the use of concepts, extending the results thus obtained later to the non-verbal and inaudible.

CHAPTER III

A CLASSIFICATION OF PROPOSITIONS

So far we have distinguished the discursive from the non-discursive use of signs. The only examples we have offered of those discursively used, that is, used as statements, propositions, predicates and concepts, have been signs whose use is governed by ostensive rules, and by the concept 'entails' which latter concept we have provisionally assumed to be familiar. The discursive use of signs is our main topic and other examples will be given later. About the non-discursive use of signs little will fall to be said here. Examples are the logical connectives such as 'and', 'or', 'not', etc., all of them devices for combining discursively used signs. They connect discursively used signs in such a manner that from the rules for the connectives and the rules for the unconnected signs the rules for the connected signs follow. Thus the rules for 'and', 'p' and 'q' imply the rules for 'p and q'.[1] Other devices which mediate the combination of discursively used signs according to rules, such as word order, inflection, intonation, deserve to be and have been given attention by descriptive linguistics.

All these non-discursive uses, though we shall not be treating of them, are clearly relevant to a full understanding of conceptual thinking. Other uses of signs fall entirely outside the scope of a logical discussion of conceptual thinking. An example is their use in poetry and art in general. The little that will be said about this is intended only to shed some light on the discursive use of signs by way of contrast, and it had best be postponed until the latter has been discussed more fully (Chapter XXIV).

Within the discursive use of signs we have already distinguished statements and predicates on the one hand from propositions and concepts on the other by pointing out that the use of propositions and concepts, but not of statements and predicates, is governed by synonymity rules. No explicit distinction has been made between

[1] Any text book of symbolic logic discusses the use of logical connectives.

concepts and propositions, or between predicates and statements. We are hardly ever actually in doubt about a discursive sign as to whether it is being used as a concept or as a proposition. It is none the less not obvious how to formulate general criteria for this distinction, and for our purpose such criteria are necessary.

The distinction is easily made for concepts and propositions whose use is governed by ostensive rules. It is fairly obvious that in uttering the words <this is green> we are often satisfying an ostensive rule. In that case we are using <green> as a concept, but the complete utterance as a proposition. Here we *apply* the ostensive concept to some basis and we *state* the ostensive proposition. To distinguish between the ostensive concept 'green' which is applied to some basis, and the ostensive proposition 'this is green', which is stated, is not, I believe, to be guilty of pedantry, but to articulate different features in a familiar situation.

The distinction between concepts and propositions is less easily formulated when we pass from signs the use of which is governed by ostensive rules to other discursively used signs such as 'perfect triangle' or 'electron', since the latter cannot in any straightforward manner be regarded as applicable to anything. The notion of applicability to something will eventually have to be defined more closely if we wish to be clear how non-ostensive, for example mathematical, concepts (though not non-ostensive propositions), are applicable or "quasi-applicable". At present we can only make the general distinction by noting that, in the case of every concept, *either* the concept itself *or its negation* is applicable to some ostensive basis, that is, some basis of an ostensive concept. On the other hand, no proposition or negation of a proposition is applicable to any ostensive basis. Thus 'being a perfect triangle' is a concept because 'not being a perfect triangle' is clearly applicable to whatever I see in front of me. On the other hand, neither 'all perfect triangles are bounded by perfect straight lines' nor its negation is applicable to any ostensive basis.

These remarks should be sufficient to characterise propositions for the purposes of convenient classification. A proposition and only a proposition is characterised by the following features. First, it entails or is entailed. Secondly, neither it nor its negation can be applied to ostensive bases. Thirdly, among the rules for its use is a synonymity rule. The first feature distinguishes propositions from signs which are not used discursively; the second from predicates and concepts; and the third from statements and predicates.

Propositions can be classified into rules, logical propositions and factual propositions. Like every theoretical discussion the present inquiry proceeds by (a) stating factual propositions, (b) drawing attention to logical propositions and (c) proposing the acceptance of rules. It differs from other theoretical discussions in that factual and logical propositions and rules are part of its subject-matter. It was said at the outset that a rule, and a rule alone, could conceivably be, in an obvious sense of the word, accepted, violated, or satisfied by people's behaviour. This was already a consideration of the nature of rules. We have had to emphasise the difference between a rule itself and the fact, if it is a fact, of its being accepted, satisfied or violated. We might have added that a rule must also be distinguished from the manner in which a person tries to impose it (or rather to impose its acceptance) on somebody else. A rule, therefore, is not a command, proposal or recommendation, although, of course, its acceptance can be commanded, proposed or recommended.

Remembering the above characterisation of propositions we have now to ask whether rules are propositions. First, rules clearly entail or are entailed by other rules. This hardly requires illustration. Secondly, a rule is not a concept, since no rule (or negated rule) is applicable to any ostensive basis. This may seem obvious, yet there is some danger of confusing a rule governing the use of a concept with the concept itself. For example, Kant does not always clearly distinguish the two. However, to apply a concept or its negation to an ostensive basis is to satisfy a rule, and not to apply the rule to a basis. If we remember to distinguish rule-propositions from rule-statements according as their use is governed or not by synonymity rules, and if we reserve the term "rule" for rule-propositions, then rules have all the three characteristic features by which we distinguished propositions from other discursively used signs.

Of all propositions it must be said that they either are rules or are not. Assuming familiarity with the concept 'entails', we find entailment-propositions among propositions which are not rules. To state an entailment-proposition is to state a logical relationship between discursively used signs. Entailment, as will become apparent, is only one of a number of logical relationships which have to be discussed. If to state a logical relationship is to state a logical proposition, then some propositions that are not rules are logical propositions and some are not. Those that are not logical propositions, we shall call "factual".

The classification of propositions as rules, logical and factual propositions is not, of course, the only classification. But it is convenient for our purpose. Its special recommendation is its enabling us to apply to rules the results of our discussion of logical and factual propositions. It thus shortens presentation and simplifies it. An inquiry into the nature of logical and factual propositions yields corollaries concerning rules, and to show why and how this is will occupy the remainder of this chapter.

Since a rule and only a rule can conceivably be satisfied by people's behaviour, there corresponds to every rule a number of factual propositions describing such behaviour. Of a proposition which describes behaviour satisfying a rule, we shall say that it *fulfils* the rule. Thus the rule 'Income tax should be paid before the end of the month' is fulfilled by the factual propositions 'Income tax is paid before the end of the month', 'Income tax is paid before the middle of the month' and others.

If the consequent of an entailment-proposition fulfils a rule then so also does its antecedent. This principle shows the fundamental interrelation between factual propositions, logical propositions and rules. It can be expressed schematically as follows: that ('p' entails 'q') and ('q' fulfils 'r') entails that ('p' fulfils 'r').

An important notion, if we wish to make clear how factual propositions and rules are related, is the notion of the *indicative* of a rule. By means of this notion we establish a correspondence between every rule and *one* of the factual propositions fulfilling it. The indicative of a rule is a proposition which fulfils the rule and which is entailed by every other proposition which fulfils the rule. (It follows that if there are two indicatives of the same rule, they entail each other. However, we may assume for convenience that synonymity-rules exclude the possibility of more than one indicative, though whether or not we make this assumption is of little importance.) Every rule has an indicative.[1] To give an example, the indicative of 'Income tax should be paid before the end of the month' is 'Income tax is paid before the end of the month'. The indicative of a negative rule is the negation of the indicative of the corresponding affirmative rule. The indicative of a conjunction of two rules is the conjunction of their indicatives. The indicative of an alternation of two rules is the alternation of their indicatives. Lastly, all logical propositions relating rules correspond to exactly similar propositions relating their indicatives. To illustrate this last point, the rule 'r_1' entails the rule 'r_2' if, and only if, the indicative of 'r_1' entails the indicative of 'r_2'.

Using the notion of indicatives we can say that a factual proposition fulfils a rule (or that the state of affairs described by the factual proposition satisfies the rule) if, and only if, it entails its indicative. Similarly, a factual proposition discredits a rule (the state of affairs described by the factual proposition violates the rule) if, and only if, it entails its negated indicative. A factual proposition is neutral with regard to a rule if, and only if, it neither fulfils nor discredits it, that is, entails neither its indicative nor its negated indicative.

The notion of a factual proposition's fulfilling or discrediting a rule is useful in making obvious the following two characteristic features of every rule, which otherwise might be easily overlooked and which will prove relevant to the discussion of certain types of metaphysical proposition. The two features are that, in a sense to be given to these terms, no rule can be "comprehensive" and none can be "perfect".

Let us call a rule (or conjunction of rules) "comprehensive" if no proposition describing an action can conceivably be neutral with respect to it. Writing 'r' for the rule, '$i(r)$' for its indicative, 'r' is comprehensive if, and only if, we can say that for every factual proposition 'p' which describes an action—'('p' does not entail '$i(r)$')' entails '('p' entails '$not\text{-}i(r)$')'. Since this is—for any sense of entailment—obviously incorrect, no rule can be comprehensive.

---

[1] In fact it could be regarded as the alternation of all propositions fulfilling the rule.

Let us call a rule or conjunction of rules "perfect" if it is fulfilled only by factual propositions which are mutually consistent. Putting the assumption that a proposition is perfect into the entailment-idiom, this means: if a rule '*r*' is perfect and fulfilled, say, by '*p*' and '*q*' then '('*p*' entails '*i(r)*')' and '('*q*' entails '*i(r)*')' together entail that '*p*' does not entail '*not-q*'. This again obviously is incorrect. Two propositions which separately entail a third are not necessarily consistent with each other. No rule can be in this sense perfect.

Every proposition fulfilling a rule is a factual proposition, although many factual propositions, namely those which do not describe human behaviour, neither fulfil any rule nor discredit any. As a result of the correspondence which we have established between rules and those factual propositions which are indicatives of rules, whatever is said about the logic of factual propositions which fulfil rules has an obvious parallel in the logic of rules.

Some final remarks on the trichotomy of propositions into logical propositions, factual propositions and rules may be of use at this point. By calling some propositions "factual" I imply no more than that they are neither logical propositions nor rules. In particular, I do not imply that they are empirical propositions in any of the many senses of that term. On the other hand, all propositions usually called "empirical" are, in my sense of the word, factual.

Concerning rules, especially those for the use of concepts, it should be clear that although we may choose to accept, violate or satisfy them, it does not necessarily depend on our choice whether or not the rules are satisfiable. To assume that it is we ourselves who make satisfiable all satisfiable rules for the use of concepts, and that it is thus we who make the concepts *applicable*, is a mistake. Such a mistake might well, for all I know, be implied in the view of writers who declare, somewhat vaguely, that language is wholly a matter of convention. We can, of course, choose to accept, and either satisfy or violate, the rules governing the use of, say, 'cat' or 'dog'. That these rules are satisfiable, however, in any particular case, and that the concept is applicable, does not entail that these rules ever have been, are, or ever will be satisfied. It does not even entail that anybody ever satisfies a rule.

CHAPTER IV

CONCEPTS, BASES AND INSTANCES

THE last of our preliminary tasks is a discussion of concepts, bases and instances. We have already distinguished the notion of concepts from that of propositions by noting that only concepts and their negations, not propositions or their negations, can be applied to ostensive bases. We introduced the notion of ostensive bases together with that of ostensive rules. In the present section we proceed to discuss the applicability and inapplicability of concepts to bases, different kinds of these relations, and different kinds of bases. Lastly, I shall try to contrast the bases of concepts with their instances.

The "analysis" of propositions which rests on the distinction between concepts and bases is not the only possible one. Many others have been proposed by writers on logic and theory of knowledge. By distinguishing between concepts and bases, however, and considering their relations, we emphasise, though we do not therefore hypostatise, certain features of conceptual thinking, that is, of people's discursive use of signs. The recognition of these features will prove relevant to philosophical problems—some of them even as seemingly remote from our inquiry as justification for the belief in an external world, or explanation of how pure mathematics applies to experience.

Our understanding of the relation between concept and basis in a proposition, say 'p', is greatly helped by considering logical relations between 'p' and other propositions. I therefore propose, first of all, to compare schematically 'p' with entailments such as '('p' entails 'q')' or '('p...' entails 'q')' (where the dots are intended to indicate that 'p' is a component part in a compound proposition which is formed from 'p' and other propositions by means of the connectives 'and', 'or' and 'not').

Consider, for example, in the presence of something that is pointed out (for example, by gestures and by means of "this" and "that"), the factual proposition 'this is to the left of that' and the entailment-proposition '("this is to the left of that' entails 'this is on one side of that')'. It should not be difficult to imagine a situation in which one quite naturally states both these propositions, the factual one and the entailment one. In considering them we assume agreement about the conjunction of rules, say 'r', which governs the use by English-speaking people of ‹to the left of›, ‹on one side of› and ‹entails›.

Let us assume, then, that a person in making the statement 'this is to the left of that' would not be violating the conjunction of rules 'r'. I propose to indicate this by calling the statement in question "theoretically appropriate" or, briefly, "appropriate" and by saying that 'to the left of' is applicable to its basis in the proposition. Of the person who in fact applies 'to the left of' to this basis, I shall say that he applies the concept appropriately.

Let us say similarly that 'this is to the left of that' is inappropriate if a person, by stating it, would violate 'r'. In that case we shall also say that 'to the left of' is inapplicable to its basis in the proposition and of a person who in fact applies 'to the left of' to this basis that he applies this concept inappropriately. Lastly, we shall say of the entailment '("this is to the left of that' entails 'this is on one side of that')' that it is appropriate if stating it *would not*, and that it is inappropriate if the stating of it *would* violate 'r'. As it happens, it does not; the entailment is appropriate.

It is necessary here to interpolate two remarks. First, in speaking of the applicability and inapplicability of concepts to bases there is no need to distinguish between properties and relations. Although we often make use of properties to identify the bases of relations there is not any need to do this. We may, for instance, identify the basis of 'to the left of' as a complex pattern without first identifying its terms separately, for example, as this table and that chair.

Secondly, while the appropriate application by anyone of a concept to a basis entails the applicability of the concept to the basis, the converse does not hold. Application implies applicability, but not applicability application. Similarly, while the inappropriate application of a concept to a basis by a person entails its inapplicability thereto, the inapplicability again does not entail the non-application.

An important relation between the factual 'this is to the left of that' and the entailment '('this is to the left of that' entails 'this is on one side of that')' can now be formulated in a simple manner. The appropriateness of the entailment-proposition is compatible with both the appropriateness and the inappropriateness of the factual. Using the term "concept-basis relations" for the relations of applicability and inapplicability between concepts and their bases we can also express the point by saying that the appropriateness of the entailment does not depend on the concept-basis relation in the antecedent (or, of course, the consequent). In other words, by stating the entailment we *suspend* the concept-basis relation in the antecedent or, very briefly, the entailment suspends the concept-basis relation in the antecedent.

A further point about the entailment between two propositions, for example, 'this is to the left of that' and 'this is on one side of that': the entailment is appropriate if, and only if, that between the corresponding concepts, for example, 'to the left of' and 'on one side of', is also appropriate. If the logical relations of concepts be characterised by the adjective "concept-concept", we can say that the entailment '('this is to the left of that' entails 'this is on one side of that')' suspends the concept-basis relation and exhibits a concept-concept relation of its antecedent.

The question about a proposition, 'what is its basis?', can at times have its difficulty. In the fact that some entailments, as, for instance, that of our example, suspend concept-basis relations and exhibit concept-concept ones we have provided a good means of identifying the bases of propositions, namely by putting them, so to speak, into entailments. It must be noted, however, that this method of separating concept and basis is subject to certain limitations. First, it is possible that an entailment, for example, '('p' entails 'p')' or '('p and q' entails 'p')', while it does suspend the concept-basis relation, does not at the same time exhibit any concept-concept relation of its antecedent or a component thereof —this is because the antecedent or its component is *inessential* to the entailment. (A proposition 'p' is essential to an appropriate entailment, if an inappropriate entailment results from replacing '*p*' by '*not p*', wherever it occurs in the original appropriate entailment.) If we wish to use our device for separating concept from basis in, say, the proposition '*p*' we must, therefore, ensure that '*p*' is put into an entailment to which it is essential.

A second limitation to this device concerns relational properties. To illustrate it let us apply the relational property 'to the left of the Town Hall' to some basis *b* (let us say some tower or chimney). Let us now put the resulting proposition '*b* is to the left of the Town Hall' into an entailment to which it is essential, say, '('*b* is to the left of the Town Hall' entails '*b* is on one side of the Town Hall')'. It is clear that this entailment suspends the concept-basis relation not only between 'to the left of the Town Hall' and *b*, but also between 'to the left of' and a basis which includes, besides *b*, that which we indicate by ⟨the Town Hall⟩. To put it generally, our device separates, as it were, pure concepts, such as 'to the left of', but not also impure concepts, such as 'to the left of the Town Hall', from their bases.

It is plausible to assume that bases are of different types. A possible classification of them would follow the lines of the trichotomy of propositions into rules, factual propositions and logical propositions; of which last, entailments are the only representatives we have so far considered. Of this triad, rules obviously have no bases. Consider, for example, 'Income tax should be paid before the end of the month'. Clearly, no concept-basis relation is discernible here. As to factual propositions, they are either ostensive or non-ostensive. The bases of ostensive propositions, which might be called "ostensive bases", are, as we shall see later (Chapters XIV, XV), either directly given, and so such as can be pointed out without the use of concepts, or else they are indirectly given. Indirectly given bases, that is, those which are spatially or temporally remote, cannot either be given without the use of concepts or be given by using concepts only. (In identifying a spatially remote mountain, we must point out verbally or by gestures some directly given object as a basis, and apply some spatial relation, for example by saying "it is three miles west from there".)

Coming to non-ostensive factual propositions, their bases, like those of factual propositions about, say, nuclei of atoms (or, if we may believe some philosophers, even factual propositions about perfect triangles), are what we may call "*postulated* bases". This, however, is provisional. We shall see later that the function of non-ostensive propositions, or rather of non-ostensive concepts, can be understood without recourse to such postulated bases.

Comparing an entailment, say, '('p' entails 'q')' with another entailment in which it occurs and to which it is essential, say, the entailment that '('p' entails 'q') and ('q' entails 'r')' entails '('p' entails 'r')', we note that the latter suspends the concept-basis relation between the concept 'entails' and its basis 'p' and 'q', while exhibiting a concept-concept relation of 'entails'. The bases of entailments are propositions and discursively used signs in general. All of these, as has already been pointed out, are identified (see pp. 12 ff. above) by indicating signs and by specifying the rules for their use.

It will prove convenient to distinguish a basis of a concept from an instance thereof. That a basis is not necessarily an instance of a concept appears plausible even before attempting a more precise definition of "instance". We may note first of all that, for example, "this is *a chair*" and '(this is an instance of 'chair')' are used either synonymously or at any rate as logical equivalents. If to point to a basis of 'chair' were necessarily to point to an instance, and vice versa, we could always, instead of saying "(this is an instance of 'chair')", say '(This basis of 'chair' is an instance of 'chair')' and also "(this instance of 'chair' is an instance of 'chair')". Since, however, the former proposition is factual and the latter is a tautology, "instance" and "basis" are used differently.

Another way of showing that it is desirable to distinguish between "basis" and "instance" consists in briefly considering the position of a philosopher who denies that the ordinary concept 'physical object' (or one of its refinements) has any instances whatever. Our philosopher's denial that, for example, his fountain pen is an instance of 'physical object' does not imply that he does not know how to conform to the rules governing this concept.

True, he does not himself accept these rules or recommend their acceptance by others; but he knows very well that anybody who applied 'physical object' to the fountain pen *would* thereby not violate the rules governing this concept. One might describe his position by saying that although the fountain pen is, even for him, a *basis* of 'physical object', the concept 'physical object' has yet no *instances* for him—in a sense of the term which has yet to be made clear.

These remarks were required in view of our next task, the definition of "instance". We are now able to define "instance" in terms of "basis" without doing violence to the customary uses of the term. We shall say, then, that a basis *b* of a concept '*P*' is *for a certain person* an instance of '*P*' provided (1) '*P*' is applicable to *b* and (2) '*P*' has been accepted by this person—acceptance of '*P*' meaning here as usual acceptance of the rules governing it. In the customary contexts of thinking and talking, the person *for whom* a basis is an instance of a concept need not be specified and is not. The person is usually the thinker or speaker, and in most cases his identity is clear from the context.

When anyone states that a certain basis *b* is a chair or an instance of 'chair', he does not merely state that 'chair' is applicable to *b*. In other words, he does not merely state that anybody who did apply 'chair' to *b* would not be guilty thereby of violating the rules governing the use of 'chair'. He intimates, in addition, that he has in fact applied 'chair' to *b;* in other words, that *b*, besides being a proper basis of 'chair' (that is, a basis to which this concept is applicable), is, *for him*, an instance as well.

What has just been said of instances and bases has some consequences which, if only for future reference, are worth mentioning. It is always possible that a basis *b* should be an instance of a concept '*P*' for one person and not for some other—the other person having conceivably neither applied '*P*' to any basis nor even accepted the concept '*P*' at all.

To state that a basis *b* is an instance of '*P*' is, we have seen, to state a relation between a basis, a concept which is applicable thereto, and a thinker who has so applied it. The proposition that '*P*' is applicable to *b* (or inapplicable) is compatible both with the proposition that a person has applied 'P' to b and that he has not done so. It is further equally compatible either with the proposition that a person has accepted 'P', that is, intends to satisfy the rules for 'P', or with the proposition that he has not accepted 'P'.

Let us take "concept-basis-thinker relation" as convenient shorthand for the relation between (1) a person who applies (accepts, does not apply, or does not accept) a concept, (2) the concept, and (3) a basis of the concept. We may then observe that we, as it were, suspend any concept-basis-thinker relation which may or may not hold between a concept, a basis and a thinker, whenever we state about any concept that it is applicable to a certain basis or is inapplicable to it, that is, whenever we state a concept-basis relation.

We can now briefly summarise results for this chapter. By asserting concept-concept relationships, that is, logical propositions relating concepts or propositions, we suspend the concept-basis relations of these concepts and therefore their concept-basis-thinker relations. By asserting concept-basis relationships, we suspend the concept-basis-thinker relations of these concepts and their bases. By proceeding from the consideration of concept-concept relations, to that of concept-basis relations and further to that of concept-basis-thinker relations, we gradually broaden the field of inquiry. The possibility and convenience of this procedure suggests a plan for the rest of the present essay.

In Part I, I hope to consider mainly concept-concept relations or the "logical content" of concepts and propositions. Most of the topics treated in this part belong traditionally to logic in a wide sense, or to the philosophy of logic, in a narrow sense of the term "logic".

Part II will be mainly concerned with concept-basis relations. Many of the topics there considered have been treated traditionally under the headings of epistemology and ontology.

Part III will be devoted to concept-basis-thinker relations, both by themselves, and in some broader contexts, which include the thinker's desires and purposes. Some of the topics in this last part furnish frequent matter of discussion for what have been traditionally known as aesthetics, ethics and philosophical method.

PART I

THE LOGICAL CONTENT OF
CONCEPTS AND PROPOSITIONS

CHAPTER V

ON THE PRIMITIVE LOGICAL RELATIONS BETWEEN OSTENSIVE CONCEPTS

WE have argued that the meaning of the term "conceptual thinking" is ultimately given by examples, and typical examples of it are the application and acceptance of ostensive rules. We have, moreover, assumed as an empirical fact, which we are not concerned to establish, that all conceptual thinkers accept ostensive rules and thus ostensive concepts. This fact suggests a minimal definition of 'conceptual thinker' as 'accepter of ostensive concepts'. It also lends plausibility to a further assumption concerning concepts, namely, that the acceptance and application of ostensive ones is in some ways fundamental to the use of all other concepts. The mere possibility of this demands that more attention be given to ostensive concepts and their logical relations than has been usual. For logicians in particular have with few exceptions regarded such concepts as hardly deserving separate consideration.

I have defined ostensive concepts as those the use of which is governed by ostensive rules. We shall call ostensive concepts "purely" ostensive if their use is governed *only* by ostensive rules. It may well be that the ostensive concepts in question are concepts hardly ever used, but it is not difficult to produce examples of them. One need only consider the ostensive concepts one accepts, regarding them in abstraction from the *non-ostensive* rules which, with the ostensive, actually govern their use. Thus if a concept 'P' is used in accordance with an ostensive rule along with other rules, there will correspond to it a concept 'P_1' which is used in accordance with the ostensive rule only—*not* with the others. I shall say, in that case, that 'P_1' is the purely ostensive derivative of 'P'. It is convenient to regard every purely ostensive concept as being its own purely ostensive derivative.

The principal subject of this chapter will be the general logical relations which purely ostensive concepts (and again which the purely ostensive derivatives of ostensive concepts) have to one another. These we shall call the *primitive* logical relations (and so distinguish them from the *full* logical relations) between ostensive concepts. Our position will be that there may well be a difference between (*a*) the primitive logical relation between concepts '*P*' and '*Q*', that is, the relation between the purely ostensive derivatives of them, and (*b*) the full logical relation between these two concepts. Whenever, hereafter, we speak of logical relations without qualification, we shall mean full logical relations.

Apart from ostensive concepts and their primitive logical relations, I shall also consider in this chapter those compound concepts the components of which are ostensive concepts connected by means of 'not', 'or' and 'and'. I shall then try to show how imperfectly Boolean algebra and similar mathematical systems reflect the use of ostensive concepts. Although our discussion will profess to provide a standard of adequacy for any formal theory of ostensive concepts, the actual construction of such a theory will not be undertaken.[1]

To apply an ostensive concept like 'white' or 'shrill' to a basis, that is, to state an ostensive proposition like 'This piece of paper is white' or 'The noise I heard was shrill', is to satisfy (or violate) an ostensive rule. As has been said, the most familiar way of formulating an ostensive rule is to say, with appropriate pointing gestures, that this and this and this, and everything like it is to be assigned a certain label. Any such rule involves (1) the choice of a word (or other sign) as ‹white› above, (2) a set of examples or exemplifying set (the set of white things pointed to) and (3) a comparing clause—a 'like-it' clause, as we may say.

(1) What sign is chosen is for our purposes unimportant, since any two ostensive rules which differ only in their sign are synonymous. To satisfy either is to apply the same concept; for example, whether ‹yellow› or ‹gelb› is chosen makes no difference as long as the rules governing these signs do not differ in other respects.

---

[1] The mathematically minded reader will find such a construction in *A Mathematical Theory of Ostensive Predicates* by Dr A. Fröhlich and myself which, it is hoped, will appear in the near future. It will contain detailed developments, some of which are out of place in the present context, while others require a specialised mathematical equipment which I make no claim to possess.

(2) The exemplification—the operation providing the exemplifying set—need not necessarily be performed by pointing gestures or by the use of demonstrative pronouns, but can be achieved in many different ways, sometimes with the help of other concepts, sometimes without. Thus one might occasionally exemplify an ostensive concept without pointing, by saying that the series of appearances which will face a person after opening successively a certain series of doors will constitute the exemplifying set for the concept. Many so-called "operational definitions" are exemplifications for ostensive concepts.[1]

In the case of compound ostensive concepts the components of which are connected by 'and', 'or', 'not', etc., we can sometimes explain the use of the concept without exemplifying it, simply by indicating its components and the manner of their connection. This, however, is possible only if these component concepts themselves (or their components in turn) have been exemplified. It is thus proper to say that the use of every ostensive concept is ultimately given by exemplification.

(3) We show that we understand an ostensive rule when we are competent to give further instances or to give "anti-examples", that is, to indicate bases, to which to apply the ostensive concept would violate the rule. The indication of anti-examples may indeed be part of the ostensive rule, which then involves not only an exemplifying set but also a set of anti-examples—an "unlike-it" clause, as well as a "like-it" clause. This complication can, however, be safely neglected here. It is often difficult to convey an ostensive rule to another person, but like the problems of communication in general, this makes no difference as regards our purpose. For our purpose everybody might limit himself to the consideration of ostensive rules formulated by himself for himself. This is not, of course, to prejudge the question of the extent to which the facts and needs of human co-operation and of communication have shaped the conceptual thinking of man in general and of different men in different societies. I am even prepared to

---

[1] A detailed discussion of different methods which may be pursued in the exemplification of ostensive concepts is to be found in Chapter v of R. Robinson's *Definition* (Oxford, 1950).

grant that every type of conceptual thinking, from higher mathematics, which almost certainly presupposes an intellectual tradition, and so communication, down to the simplest application of ostensive concepts, is in some way dependent on previous communication between the conceptual thinker and other people. All this is still quite consistent with the possibility of considering ostensive rules apart from their being communicated.

The exemplifying set of any ostensive rule, and the comparing clause (for which we have used the words ‹and everything like it›), involve the familiar notion of resemblances—of discovering and stating them. In satisfying an ostensive rule we state a likeness between some basis *outside* the exemplifying set, and the members of that set. We can, but of course need not, thereupon incorporate the new instance into the exemplifying set. If we do this, and so extend the set, we have replaced the original ostensive rule by another. The two differ, however, only in that the exemplifying set of the new rule is an extension of that of the original one. It is, in a sense, a refinement of the original rule. The comparing clause indicates that the number of further instances, and consequently the possibility of refining the ostensive rule by extending its exemplifying set, are not limited.

If we consider the possible logical relations between different ostensive rules, then the nature of these, and consequently of ostensive concepts and propositions, will become clearer than if we only considered ostensive rules in isolation. It is best to start with the *primitive* logical relations between ostensive concepts, that is, those which hold between their purely ostensive derivatives.

Purely ostensive concepts (and therefore purely ostensive derivatives of ostensive concepts) may stand to each other in one of the following logical relations which, however, do not exhaust all possibilities: (1) inclusion,[1] (2) exclusion and (3) overlap. For example, the logical relation between the purely ostensive derivative of ‘red’ and that of ‘coloured’ (and so the *primitive* logical relation between ‘red’ and ‘coloured’) is clearly inclusion. Assuming, as it is legitimate to do, that the exemplifying sets of ‘red’

---

[1] There are of course three cases of inclusion: two unilateral (‘P’ in ‘Q’; ‘Q’ in ‘P’) and one bilateral (‘P’ in ‘Q’ and ‘Q’ in ‘P’).

and 'round' overlap, the primitive logical relation between 'red' and 'round' will then be overlap. Lastly, the primitive logical relation between 'being a sound' and 'being a colour' is clearly exclusion. I shall call the relations of inclusion, overlap and exclusion the *exact* logical relations. Classes and "concepts" which are given by enumeration, for example, 'being a book on this shelf', can stand only in exact logical relations to each other: and the same holds for non-ostensive concepts and most classes which are the concern of mathematicians. Reasons for this will occupy us later. Only the exact logical relations between ostensive concepts can be expressed as affirmative and negative entailments. Thus if, and only if, '*P*' is included in '*Q*', does '*P*' entail '*Q*'. If, and only if, '*P*' excludes '*Q*' does '*P*' entail '*not-Q*'. Lastly, if, and only if, '*P*' overlaps with '*Q*', does '*P*' not entail '*Q*' *and* not entail '*not-Q*'. If by 'entailments' we understand, over and above affirmative ones, their negations, and also combinations of them by 'and', 'or', 'not', then we can say that all exact logical relations are entailments.

As just stated, however, the exact logical relations of inclusion, overlap and exclusion do not exhaust all possible relations between purely ostensive concepts. This can best be seen by considering particular cases. Let us assume that the signs ⟨ black ⟩ and ⟨ raven ⟩ are governed *only* by ostensive rules; and that the exemplifying set for 'black' consists of, say, the objects *a*, *b*, *c*, *d*, *e*, *f*; while that for 'raven' consists of *a*, *b*, *c*. It is clear that 'black' and 'raven' here cannot be exclusive of each other. The first exemplifying set includes the second. But this neither entitles us to regard the logical relation between the exemplified concepts as inclusion; nor to regard it as overlap. What, then, is the logical relation between the two concepts?

The customary answer would be, I take it, that (*a*) 'raven' and 'black', as defined by the ostensive rules, stand either in the relation of inclusion or in that of overlap and (*b*) that we do not know which of the two does hold between them. But this answer must be rejected. It is not warranted by the content of the ostensive rules. It depends on certain further assumptions which go far beyond them.

Thus the assumption is being made that ostensive rules permit us to decide for *any and every* object that it either does, or does not, sufficiently resemble the members of an exemplifying set, that is, that any and every object is or is not a raven, is or is not black. But not all objects fall thus clearly either under a purely ostensive concept or outside. There are marginal objects, which so long as we do not change or supplement our original rules must remain marginal. It makes no sense to say that the "set of marginal ravens" either is included in or overlaps with "the set of marginal black objects". To say that one of these alternatives must be the case—even if we do not *know* which—makes, if possible, still less sense. But even if we granted the quite unrealistic first assumption we should, it seems to me, still not be justified in holding that our two purely ostensive concepts stand in the relation of either overlap or inclusion. For this the further assumption would be needed that all things in the universe can be divided into clearly demarcated sets. In other words, the position requires the assumption that the number of things in the universe is either finite, or in such a convenient manner infinite, that such classification becomes possible. Whether we accomplish this by means of the Russellian axiom of infinity or by some other postulate, the result is not anything that the two ostensive rules which we are considering do, as such, imply.

By themselves, then, our ostensive rules governing 'black' and 'raven' do not imply that these concepts stand in any of the three exact relations; or that their relation is either inclusion or overlap. The relation in which they do stand is of a different type. I shall call it "inclusion-or-overlap", indicating by the hyphen that it is not an alternation of inclusion and overlap. (The reason for choosing this name will be clear when we come to consider supplementary rules which allow us, as it were, to superimpose by convention either inclusion or overlap upon the relation of inclusion-or-overlap.) As distinct from the exact relations we shall call inclusion-or-overlap "inexact".

One other inexact relation may hold between ostensive concepts: I shall call it "exclusion-or-overlap". It, too, can be explained by means of particular cases. Let us take again a purely ostensive concept 'black', exemplified by a, b, c, d, e, f; and a purely ostensive concept 'sheep', exemplified, say, by k, l, m. Here the exemplifying sets exclude each other. For reasons exactly similar to those given above, we cannot conclude from the ostensive rules alone that the two concepts stand in the relation of either exclusion or overlap. What we have is a new simple relation, namely, exclusion-or-overlap.

No third inexact logical relation, of inclusion-or-exclusion-or-overlap can hold between ostensive concepts. To see this we only need to remember that the exemplifying set of an ostensive concept is given by enumeration, and that therefore any two exemplifying sets can only stand in one of the three exact logical relations. Clearly, both inclusion and exclusion between the exemplifying sets would be incompatible with an inclusion-or-exclusion-or-overlap between the concepts; while an overlap between the exemplifying sets implies an overlap between the concepts.

The inexact character of, for example, the *primitive* logical relation between 'black' and 'raven', that is, their being in the relation of inclusion-or-overlap, is irremediable. We might, of course, decide to consider rules other than such as are ostensive. In particular, we might consider a further rule to the effect that to be a raven is "by definition" to be black. In that case we should, however, no longer be considering a primitive logical relation. We should behave like a doctor who proposes to cure a patient by substituting another patient for him. Similarly, if we tried to achieve exactitude by extending the exemplifying sets of our concepts, we should again be only replacing them by others.

Having discussed purely ostensive concepts in isolation, and further, the possible logical relations between them (which are at the same time the possible primitive logical relations between ostensive concepts in general), we must next consider negations and compounds of ostensive concepts.

We note, first of all, that the negations of purely ostensive concepts are no longer ostensive. Thus while in applying the concept 'green' we satisfy an ostensive rule—this and this and this and everything like it to be called 'green'—we do not satisfy any such rule by applying 'not-green'. There is no rule for the use of 'not-green' which involves an exemplifying set and a comparing clause. It has often been pointed out that negation signs are not always a reliable guide for deciding whether a proposition is affirmative or negative. For some propositions and concepts, however, the distinction can be expressed by saying that if of two contradictory concepts or propositions one is ostensive and the other, therefore, non-ostensive, the ostensive one will be affirmative, the non-ostensive negative, however the negation sign is placed.

In considering those concepts which are (1) conjunctions (connections by means of 'and') and (2) alternations (connections by 'or', used non-exclusively), we note that not every logical conjunction of ostensive concepts and not every logical alternation of them is itself an ostensive concept. Thus although 'green' and 'shrill-sounding' are clearly ostensive concepts, the necessary exemplifying set and "like-it" clause are not available for either 'green and shrill-sounding' or 'green or shrill-sounding' which thus are not ostensive concepts. This distinction, namely between ostensive and non-ostensive compounds of ostensive concepts, is relevant to any attempt at classifying so-called "natural kinds" and to the formalisation of classificatory systems, in, for example, zoology and botany.

No ostensive proposition or concept, whether compound or not, is internally inconsistent, for an internally inconsistent concept cannot be exemplified and cannot therefore be ostensive. A concept or proposition is usually defined as internally inconsistent if it entails a conjunction one of whose members excludes another member. From this definition, together with the internal consistency of ostensive concepts and prepositions, it follows that the internal consistency of a concept or proposition can be established in three ways, namely, by showing that it does not entail a conjunction; or by showing that although it does, none of the latter's members excludes another; or lastly, by showing that it is ostensive.

Now it is never certain whether a seemingly simple concept is not really compound or whether a concept which can be "decomposed" into an internally consistent conjunction cannot also be decomposed into another conjunction one of whose members does exclude some other. Hence of the three methods of proof only the last is absolutely safe. Unfortunately, in mathematics, where the need for consistency-proofs is greatest, the last method—by establishing ostensiveness—is not available for the good reason that the concepts and propositions of mathematics are not ostensive at all. Many of the so-called consistency proofs of mathematics assume that arithmetic is internally consistent, and proceed by showing the conjunction of the theorems to a given theory to be consistent *if* the theorems of arithmetic are internally consistent. A proof of the internal consistency of arithmetic is still a long way off. It might possibly be brought nearer by a thorough consideration of the relations between ostensive propositions and the non-ostensive propositions of arithmetic. (A few tentative remarks on these relations will be made in Chapter VII).

Our discussion of the five primitive relations between ostensive concepts, and of the ostensive and non-ostensive compounds of ostensive concepts, is in itself sufficient to show that Boolean algebra is not the algebra of ostensive concepts; for the former represents only the exact logical relations between such concepts. To the difference between ostensive and non-ostensive concepts and to the difference between the ostensive and the non-ostensive compounds of ostensive concepts it is insensitive. This can be seen very clearly by considering a principle of Boolean logic which I shall take the liberty of calling the "complement-thesis". According to it every class-inclusion has a complement. More precisely if 'α' and 'β' are two classes such that 'α' is unilaterally included in 'β', then, according to the thesis, *there exists* a class 'γ' which is the complement of the inclusion. It consists of all members of 'β' which are not also members of 'α'. The complement, for example, of the inclusion of 'the class of fathers' in 'the class of males' is 'the class of males who are not fathers'.

In spite of its apparent clarity the complement-thesis is obscure. Mainly, this is due to the occurrence of the phrase "there exists" in its formulation. Its air of self-evidence derives from a trivial piece of interpretation which one must be aware of. I mean the interpretation according to which to assert the existence of a complement is merely to assert its being postulated.

Let us assume that 'α' is an "ostensive class", say the class consisting of the members of the exemplifying set of an ostensive concept 'P' and of everything like them; that 'β' is similarly an ostensive class corresponding to the ostensive concept 'Q'; and that 'α' is unilaterally included in 'β'. (Although there is no need to distinguish between the inclusion of 'α' in 'β' and of 'P' in 'Q', we make this distinction to emphasise the similarities and differences between ostensive concepts and Boolean classes.) Now, if the complement-thesis for ostensive concepts implies that the inclusion of 'α' in 'β' has a complement 'γ' *which is an ostensive class*, then it is certainly false.

Beginning with 'α' unilaterally included in 'β' we may without contradicting ourselves proceed to assert that no sign, say $\langle C \rangle$, can be used as an ostensive concept in such a manner that the corresponding ostensive class is the complement of the inclusion of 'α' in 'β'. This might seem ludicrous to those who regard all classes as Boolean, and consequently all class-relations as exact logical relations which can be visualised by means of Euler's diagrams. A Boolean class-inclusion, as we see in almost every text-book on logic, can be represented on the one hand by the houses in a town whose perimeter is fixed and does not touch any house and, on the other hand, by the houses in a county whose border is similarly fixed, provided that the county surrounds the town. It is then, of course, always possible to indicate the houses which lie in the county but not in the town. We might, however, assume that the town lies within the county, that about some houses we know that they lie in the town and therefore in the county, that we also know how to give further examples of such; but, while assuming all this, assume also that nevertheless we do not know any of the borders. We then cannot give any example of a house which lies in the county but not in the town. In making these assumptions we should not be guilty of any contradiction in terms. There is similarly nothing in the nature of ostensive rules which makes it self-contradictory to say that *some* inclusions between ostensive classes (and therefore between ostensive concepts) have no exemplifiable and thus no ostensive complements.

If the thesis that every inclusion has a complement is false for ostensive "classes" a further assertion must also be false, namely, that every inclusion has what we might call a "remainder". An inclusion of 'α' in 'β' has the remainder 'ρ' if, and only if, (1) 'α' is included in 'ρ', (2) 'α' consists of all things which belong both to 'β' and 'ρ' and of no other members, (3) the inclusions of 'α'

in 'β' and of 'α' in 'ρ' have complements. For example, the inclusion of 'the class of fathers' in 'the class of males' has as remainder 'the class of parents'. The thesis that every inclusion of one ostensive class in another has an ostensive remainder is false, since the third condition is, as we have seen, not necessarily fulfilled for ostensive classes.

The reasons why the complement-thesis is false for ostensive concepts follows from a consideration of ostensive concepts and their logical relations. That it is false has been known for a long time. W. E. Johnson's famous discussion of the relation of the determinates under a determinable to this determinable and to each other amounts to a denial of this dogma, which underlies a great deal of modern epistemology and philosophical logic.[1]

At the basis of Boolean algebra and the theory of sets lies a fundamental assumption which is embodied in Cantor's famous and often repeated definition of a set (or class) as "a collection into one whole of certain definite, well distinguished, objects of our intuition or our thought...". Whatever subsequent improvements on Cantor's theory have been made or suggested, the requirement that classes have definite borders and stand only in exact logical relations has always been observed. It should by now be quite clear that ostensive concepts do not fulfil this requirement.

In conclusion, I should like to consider the perfectly reasonable objection that we are never entitled to assert an inclusion or exclusion between purely ostensive concepts and that, for example, we cannot even assert that the purely ostensive derivative of 'red' is included in that of 'coloured', or that the purely ostensive derivatives of 'being a sound' and of 'being a colour' are exclusive of each other. My answer would be first that we can construct both a satisfactory system of ostensive concepts in which overlap is the only exact logical relation and one which contains in addition inclusion and exclusion.[2] I should point out secondly that in a sketch of the logic of ostensive concepts the main emphasis must be put on the much neglected, not to say entirely ignored, *inexact* logical relations.

[1] See Johnson, *Logic* (Cambridge, 1921), pt. I.
[2] The system mentioned in the footnote to p. 32 is of the latter type.

CHAPTER VI

A COMPARISON OF FULL AND PRIMITIVE LOGICAL RELATIONS BETWEEN OSTENSIVE CONCEPTS

WE have already noted that the primitive and the full logical relations between concepts do not necessarily coincide. In the present chapter I propose to compare the primitive with the full. Apart from being of interest in itself, this comparison will, I hope, prove relevant to the theory of conceptual levels and hierarchies to be developed in Part II. Together with what has already been said about the nature of ostensive concepts it should also help to throw light on some of the questions involved in disputes about the conventional or non-conventional character, and the analytic or synthetic character, of logical propositions.

The five possible primitive relations which we have seen to obtain between ostensive concepts (and between ostensive propositions) can be ordered thus—according to their degree of exclusiveness, namely: exclusion, exclusion-or-overlap, overlap, inclusion-or-overlap, inclusion. While still remembering that the full and the primitive relations between ostensive concepts need not necessarily coincide, we can go on further to say that the possible full relations between ostensive concepts are again: exclusion, exclusion-or-overlap, overlap, inclusion-or-overlap, inclusion. Whether we are referring to full or primitive relations will usually be clear from the context, and unless there is any doubt we need not always qualify the logical relation explicitly.

Beginning from the full logical relations between two ostensive concepts the transition to the primitive is merely a process of progressively disregarding all rules governing the use of conceptual signs except the ostensive. The converse transition from a primitive logical relation to a full consists in accepting further rules for the use of signs which so far have been used only as purely ostensive concepts.

Considering now the latter transition we should *prima facie* expect the making of it to have one or other of the following results: (1) The full relation is of the same kind as the primitive one; as we shall put it, the full relation coincides with or does not modify the primitive relation. (2) The full relation is more exclusive than the primitive. It increases, so to speak, the exclusiveness of the primitive relation. (3) The full relation is less exclusive than the primitive—or decreases its exclusiveness. (4) (*a*) The full relation is that of inclusion or that of overlap whereas the primitive is inclusion-or-overlap, or (*b*) the full relation is exclusion or overlap whereas the primitive relation is exclusion-or-overlap. In either of these cases we shall say that the full relation "sharpens" the primitive relation. (5) The full relation is inexact whereas the primitive is exact, when we shall put it that the full relation "blunts" the primitive relation.

It is easy to demonstrate by examples how the full relation sometimes does not modify the primitive. Thus 'green' is included in 'coloured' whether we are speaking of the full relation between the two or the primitive. An example of a pair of concepts where the full relation increases the exclusiveness of the primitive are 'being the frontal view of an elephant' and 'appearing to be the frontal view of an elephant'. For while the ostensive rules which govern these concepts differ only in their labels—while for both the "this and this and this" (the exemplifying set) and the "everything like it" (the comparing clause) are identical—their *full* relation is not mutual, but only unilateral, inclusion. While from the point of view of the ostensive rules alone every front view of an elephant is an appearance of such a view, and *vice versa*, this is no longer the case if we consider all the rules governing 'frontal view of an elephant': for, clearly, some *appearances* of frontal views of elephants do not belong to elephants at all. There is again an abundance of cases in which the full relation between two concepts sharpens their primitive relation. Thus while the primitive relation between 'raven' and 'black' is inclusion-or-overlap, the full relation is inclusion, 'raven' being included in 'black' *by definition*, as it is often put.

This leaves, as unexemplified possibilities, the full relation which blunts the primitive relation and the full relation which decreases the exclusiveness of the primitive relation without at the same time sharpening it. Nothing in what follows is based on the assumption that these possibilities cannot arise. A moment's reflection, however, shows that a full relation cannot decrease the exclusiveness of a primitive overlap. For if 'P' primitively overlaps with 'Q' their exemplifying sets overlap. Consequently a full relation of overlap-or-inclusion, or an inclusion of 'P' in 'Q', would be inconsistent with the overlap of their exemplifying sets.

A person who denies the *primitive* logical relation between two ostensive concepts, say 'P' and 'Q' (strictly speaking, a person who denies the applicability of this logical relation to 'P'and 'Q'), violates thereby the conjunction of the ostensive rules for 'P' and 'Q'. On the other hand, unless full and primitive relation coincide, a person who denies the *full* logical relation between 'P' and 'Q' does not thereby violate the conjunction of these ostensive rules; he violates some further rule, which since it supplements the conjunction, will be called a "supplementary rule for the use of ostensive concepts", or briefly "a supplementary rule". A proposition the denial of which would violate a supplementary rule will be called a "supplementary logical proposition".

For instance, a person who denies that every raven is black violates by this statement a supplementary rule which we might formulate by saying that 'raven and not-black' should not be applied to any basis. If anyone has accepted the ostensive rules for 'raven' and 'black' he is not logically committed to accept or not to accept the supplementary rule. By accepting it he superimposes, so to speak, the full on the primitive logical relation.

It is usual to regard primitive logical propositions as being dependent on reality in a way in which supplementary logical propositions are not. It appears from the preceding discussion that this account of the difference is not wholly unjustified. For, if we wish to state certain resemblances which we discover but do not create, we must accept ostensive rules, and it is only these rules, or rather conjunctions of these rules, which we violate by denying primitive logical propositions. On the other hand, even after having accepted ostensive rules we are still free to decide whether or not to accept supplementary ones, and on this decision depends the possibility of stating supplementary logical propositions.

What one might call the conventionalist attitude towards logical propositions, and in particular (since the inexact propositions are rarely, if ever, considered) towards entailments, may perhaps be expressed by the following two statements. First, that all logical propositions are conventions, that is, accepted rules which those who have accepted them could also have rejected. Secondly, that the appropriateness of all logical propositions depends entirely on our decisions.

The first of these statements is certainly false. Logical propositions, not being rules at all, cannot be accepted rules. The second is extremely vague. It can be taken in a sense in which it is certainly true. For we can conceivably decide to accept or not to accept any rule which we should satisfy by stating logical propositions. It is always logically possible that a rule should not have been accepted. If the statement means only this there can be no objection raised. It may mean, on the other hand, that not only can we choose to accept any logical rule: we can also make it *satisfiable*. On this interpretation the statement is false. For example, having accepted two ostensive rules governing two concepts whose exemplifying sets overlap we cannot make satisfiable the rule to the effect that the concepts stand in the relation of exclusion. This, to use the forceful language of some older philosophers, not even God can do.

This is the place for some remarks on the problem of synthetic *a priori* propositions. Kant, who introduced it into modern philosophy, has not sufficiently explained his key-terms "analytic", "synthetic" and "*a priori*" to prevent disagreement among his commentators, his followers and even his opponents. In more recent discussions these terms have been used in so many different senses that it is best to drop them altogether. While I propose to avoid their use, I nevertheless believe that important philosophical problems have been formulated, with the help of these terms, by Kant in particular. The distinctions drawn in the present and previous chapters are relevant to some of them, especially the distinctions between full and primitive logical propositions, between inclusions with and inclusions without ostensive complements, and lastly the trichotomy of propositions into rules, logical propositions and factual propositions.

Let us first consider a narrow interpretation of Kant's use of "analytic": A proposition is analytic if, and only if, it is an inclusion with a complement which belongs to the same kind of concept as do the antecedent and the consequent of the inclusion. If we accept this definition, then it follows from what has been said about the complement-thesis for ostensive concepts (Chapter v) that not all logical propositions are analytic.

One might justifiably object to this definition of "analytic propositions" that it ignores without good reason those logical relations which are not inclusions. In an attempt to widen the range of our definition one might make it cover not only inclusions for which the complement-thesis holds good, but also all supplementary logical propositions, that is, all propositions which, like, for example, '('P' entails 'Q' by definition)', cannot be denied without violating a supplementary rule. But we have seen that some primitive logical propositions, for example, 'Being green' entails 'Being coloured', do not belong to either category. Therefore not all logical propositions are analytic even in this wider sense of the term.

There are some who use the terms "logical" and "analytic" interchangeably, and no philosophical objection can be raised against this. The statement, however, that all logical propositions are analytic is then in no way surprising or helpful and, if implying a censure of Kant, quite unjustified.

When we note that the term "a priori" is used no less vaguely or less ambiguously than are "analytic" and its contradictory "synthetic", the so-called problem of synthetic a priori propositions is seen to be even more ambiguous. Kant defines "a priori knowledge" as knowledge which, translating his words literally, "is independent of experience and even all impressions of the senses". It is defensible to interpret the notion of independence, as it occurs here, as a logical relation between propositions, in the usual way—the sense being that a proposition 'p' is independent of 'q' if, and only if, 'p' neither entails 'q' nor entails 'not-q'.

If we accept this, we are led to view a proposition '*p*' as *a priori* if, and only if, for every empirical proposition '*q*', '*p*' neither entails '*q*' nor '*not-q*'. The crucial term of the definiens is, of course, "empirical proposition". Some philosophers (among them Hume) define this term in a way which makes it coextensive with a subspecies of ostensive propositions, for example, propositions describing uninterpreted immediate impressions. Others define the term in a wider sense which makes it coextensive with all ostensive and even all factual propositions, that is, all propositions which are neither logical propositions nor any sort of rules.[1]

Even if we understand by "empirical" simply "factual", it is clear that the class of *a priori* propositions is wider than that of logical propositions since it includes all rules. Kant's explicit definitions must not obscure from us the fact that, for him, the propositions of mathematics, those of what he called "pure natural science", and those of ethics, were all genuine instances of *a priori* propositions. We are not concerned here, however, with interpreting Kant or even with showing that merely to criticise the explicit definitions which he gives for the terms of his leading question (as to how synthetic *a priori* propositions are possible) is not sufficient to refute his philosophy. To give, as I have tried to do, good reasons for discarding the terms in which he formulates his main question and many of his answers, is not to refute his answers and is certainly not bringing a charge of meaninglessness against his questions.

By saying that all logical propositions are *a priori* some philosophers seem to imply that logical propositions relate not classes of actual objects but classes of possible objects. This doctrine presupposes a distinction between the actual and the possible among the objects to which a concept applies. It has been revived in different ways by some modern logicians. In ending this chapter I should like to show why I think that C. I. Lewis's distinction between what he calls the "comprehension" and the "denotation" of a concept is spurious.[2] I have chosen Lewis's

---

[1] A sense of "empirical" which is relevant to controversies concerning the logical status of laws of nature will be defined in Chapter XI.

[2] See *Analysis of Knowledge and Valuation* (La Salle, Ill., 1946), p. 39.

formulation of the distinction because it does not disguise his central point by a plethora of symbolic technicalities.

According to him we must distinguish, for example, between (*a*) the comprehension of 'man', to which belong all things possible or consistently thinkable to which the term would be applicable, and (*b*) the denotation, to which belong all actual things to which the term applies. Now, a concept cannot have a comprehension, for the simple reason that although one can think *of* that to which it is applicable, one cannot think *it* at all—certainly one cannot think it consistently or inconsistently. For, whatever else we mean by "consistent or inconsistent thinking", only sentences, propositions, predicates and concepts can be consistently or inconsistently thought. Nothing can be thought unless it may entail or be entailed; or, more generally, unless it may stand in logical relations.

Moreover, while no concept, ostensive or other, has a comprehension, non-ostensive concepts, for example, 'perfect triangle', have no denotation, since they are not applicable to actual objects. It would seem that historically the class of merely possible objects was first introduced to provide non-ostensive concepts with a reference—some kind of substitute for the actual objects to which they could not refer, the idea of an inapplicable concept seeming to have insuperable difficulties. We shall see later that the function of non-ostensive concepts can quite well be understood without postulating their applicability.

Lastly, ostensive concepts have not even a denotation. It is easy to show that those who speak of the denotation of a concept (certainly Lewis) are assuming that the logical relation between any two denotations is necessarily exact. Since, however, the logic of denotations is Boolean, and that of ostensive concepts non-Boolean, allowing as it does for inexact logical relations, the so-called denotation of an ostensive concept must be taken as at best but an idealisation of an ostensive concept.

That the distinction between comprehension and denotation fails will rule out a further theory which has proved, to some logicians, quite attractive. I refer to the view that the logical relations between concepts are always between their comprehensions, while the empirical or factual relations are between their denotations. On this theory entailments are explained as class inclusions between comprehensions; and formal implications as class-inclusions between denotations.

The distinction between the classes of things actual and things possible is made plausible by statements of which some are perfectly intelligible and grammatical. The impression, however, that they justify the distinction, and even require it, is mistaken. To dispel this impression it is sufficient to consider the following. First, 'All *conceivable* men are (must be) vertebrates'. Second, 'All *actual* men are featherless'. Third, 'The class of all conceivable includes the class of all actual men'. In the first of these—so runs the assumption—one comprehension is being said to be included in another. In the second one denotation is being said to be included in another. The third statement, unlike the others, is not one which would normally be made. It would, I think, be made only by someone under pressure to support a spurious distinction between a fictitious denotation and an equally fictitious comprehension of concepts.

The distinction we have rejected was in no way necessary to the intelligibility of the first two statements, which are perfectly in keeping with what has been said in the preceding section about ostensive concepts. That all conceivable men are (must be) vertebrates means that whenever the ostensive concept 'man' is applied in accordance with the ostensive and other rules for its use, the ostensive concept vertebrate would also be appropriately applied. In other words, the ostensive concept 'man' is included in the ostensive concept 'vertebrate'. The second statement—that all men are featherless—means that while the full logical relation between the two concepts is inclusion-or-overlap the exemplifying set of 'man' is included in the exemplifying set of 'featherless being'. It may, and often does, mean further that the relation of inclusion is expected to hold for any two exemplifying sets of 'man' and 'featherless being' however far we extend the original sets by incorporating new examples into them. Even the rather unnatural third statement can be regarded as compatible with the logic of ostensive concepts. That all the conceivable includes all the actual men may (somewhat charitably) be taken to mean that the ostensive concept 'man' is not given by its exemplifying set or any of the extensions thereof. This is, indeed, true of any ostensive concept. Any such concept is given by an exemplifying set and a comparing clause. These do not limit the possibility of extending the set in accordance with the ostensive rule in which they are the main factors.

CHAPTER VII

ON THE LOGICAL RELATIONS BETWEEN OSTENSIVE AND NON-OSTENSIVE CONCEPTS

FROM an early stage in our development all of us employ concepts of another sort than those whose use is governed by ostensive rules, and we certainly assert logical relations between such *non*-ostensive concepts. We do so whenever we state, for example, that a geometrical triangle is necessarily a plane figure, that is to say, that 'geometrical triangle' is included in 'plane figure'. Moreover, we often employ non-ostensive and ostensive concepts together in order the more efficiently to achieve the purposes for which the ostensive are used. To take an obvious example, the use of ostensive concepts jointly with the concepts of mathematics, which are always non-ostensive, has served technological progress to a degree incomparably higher than the unaided employment of ostensive concepts could have done.

To those who reflect, now, on the use of non-ostensive concepts the following questions are likely to occur. First, do we apply them? If so, to what do we apply them? Secondly, what is the nature of this "joint" use we make of non-ostensive with ostensive? In particular, how do ostensive concepts and the logical relations between them compare with non-ostensive and the logical relations between them? In the third place, what is the ontological status of non-ostensive concepts? It seems hardly too much to say that these questions or variants of them have occupied philosophers from the beginning of philosophical thinking.

We shall first attempt a preliminary—by no means exhaustive—classification of non-ostensive concepts. I shall then make some remarks on the first question, and try to show that to postulate bases to which non-ostensive concepts are "applicable", as well as to adopt some other devices for dealing with them, do little except postpone the problems about them, which they set out to solve. I shall then discuss in principle how ostensive concepts and the logical relations between them are related to the non-ostensive and logical relations between them. As to the question about the onto-logical status of non-ostensive concepts no solution will be offered; instead—what is perhaps more profitable—a discussion will be added later, on the logical nature of this question (Chapter XXII).

Now, if non-ostensive concepts—say mathematical ones—do have bases, they are certainly not given in the way in which those of ostensive concepts are given. It is tempting to say that while the bases of ostensive concepts are given in sensation, perception, memory or imagination, those of non-ostensive concepts are given in a peculiar way of their own. This puts the distinction conform-ably to tradition. It carries, however, a heavy burden of implicit commitment concerning the modes in which the bases of *ostensive* concepts are found, sensation, memory and the others. It will be necessary to discuss these later (Chapter XV).

If non-ostensive concepts have bases at all, they must be dif-ferent from ostensive ones. It is, of course, true that we often speak as if we did apply a non-ostensive concept and an ostensive one to one and the same basis, for instance, when we refer to what we see as *three apples*. Yet surely, the pair of concepts here, 'apple' and 'three', are not applied to the same basis. On this, at least, almost all philosophers—from Plato to Frege and Russell—would agree.

There are many kinds of non-ostensive concept. Integers, as they are used in the ordinary operations of arithmetic, represent probably the most common, and the one whose use is learned soonest after the use of ostensive concepts has been mastered. Another kind of non-ostensive concept is found in geometrical reasoning. Although many persons never learn (or need to learn) how to use them, some geometrical concepts are, as it were, specially near to ostensive ones—near enough to be learned with-out difficulty. This will be familiar to readers of Plato's *Meno*.

Yet another species of non-ostensive concept is used in the sciences. The unexemplifiable concepts of particles or fields, although non-ostensive, show more similarity to ostensive con-cepts than to the mathematical sort just mentioned. In a sense to be presently made clearer, many such scientific concepts of what we would call ideal constituents are only provisionally non-osten-sive, being in this point distinct from those of mathematics. An atomic nucleus might conceivably some day be pointed out, but 'perfect triangle' is non-ostensive in principle.

A further species of non-ostensive concept which is, at least *prima facie*, different from those so far alluded to, lies within the special beat of the philosopher, particularly if he concerns himself about what is commonly called theory of knowledge. To the stock-in-trade of this discipline belong such non-ostensive concepts as 'proposition', 'concept', 'judgment' and others.

The fact that non-ostensive concepts are never applicable to an ostensive basis still does not settle whether they actually have not got bases; or whether, perhaps, they have bases of some special kind. Philosophers of Platonic cast who assign bases *sui generis* to them either profess to be aware of these through some special kind of intuitive apprehension or they simply postulate them. Procedure of the one type or the other is in particular made use of in introducing professed solutions to the problem of how mathematical truths are related to experience.

A classical answer to this persistent question is, of course, that provided by Plato himself; and it is still often given. The conten-tion is that mathematics applies to empirical fact because its con-cepts are applicable to ideal mathematical particulars, *and* these are sufficiently similar to ostensive particulars to prevent serious inaccuracies in the application of mathematics. It is argued that, for example, the theorems about *perfect* could not be applied to *physical* circles, triangles, etc., unless the physical ones approximated to the perfect. Moreover, since we understand what is meant by this "approximation" we must in some way be apprehending the perfect figures themselves which are being approximated to. All such reasoning has at the utmost but a very limited usefulness.

First, the proposition that a certain basis *b* of, say, 'physical triangle' approximates to a (or the) perfect triangle entails, and is entailed by, the proposition that this basis is a physical triangle. In other words, 'approximating to a perfect triangle' and 'being a physical triangle' are logically equivalent ostensive concepts, applicable to ostensive bases.

So is it also, exactly, with the argument that if we understand the statement that a certain physical triangle t_1 approximates to a (or the) perfect triangle to a greater degree than another t_2, we must necessarily be apprehending a (or the) perfect triangle in some way. The concept 'approximating to a (or the) perfect triangle to a greater degree' entails and is entailed by 'being physically more triangular'. The latter concept is clearly ostensive, and so must also its equivalent be.

The alleged special apprehension of ideal particulars, therefore, or their postulation, although not necessarily harmful, throws but little light on the problem of how mathematics is applied to empirical fact. At best it amounts to the view that mathematical concepts and propositions are ostensive ones idealised; the nature of the idealisation is still left in the dark.

What has been said about postulating ideal mathematical particulars or appealing to a special apprehension in evidence of such, applies with slight modifications to philosophical theories which postulate ideal scientific objects or hypostatise propositions, or which appeal to some special faculty for apprehending these.

As against this, another theory has had some currency according to which the application of mathematics to empirical fact consists simply in drawing conclusions from ostensive definitions in some well-regulated manner. Its core has been aphoristically expressed in Peirce's saying that mathematics is the science of drawing necessary conclusions.[1] On this view to state a mathematical proposition is, indeed, never to apply a mathematical concept to a non-ostensive basis. Compared with the Platonic position, this is a strong point in the theory. Nevertheless, the theory fails. In many cases where one speaks of applying mathematics it is simply not true that one directly deduces ostensive propositions from ostensive propositions. Very frequently the procedure is first to replace ostensive propositions by non-ostensive, and only after this to proceed to calculation. The calculation over, the further step is taken of exchanging the resulting non-ostensive proposition with an ostensive one. Indeed, when I put an apple into my pocket and then another one, and after that assert that

---

[1] *The Philosophy of Peirce*, ed. Buchler (London, 1940), p. 141.

I have two apples in my pocket I have, among other things, twice exchanged the ostensive relation of 'putting together' with the non-ostensive relation of 'arithmetical addition'. Needless to say, what is done almost automatically in adding apples, demands, when first performed in a new field, great care and creative imagination.

The so-called application of mathematics to empirical fact, then, involves a double replacement, the twice interchanging of, in the case of the example just given, 'arithmetical addition' and the ostensive concept 'putting together'. Philosophers who have taken note of this, however, have, so far as I can judge, done hardly more than given it a name such as "correlating definition"[1] or "epistemic correlation".[2] Something more significant becomes possible as soon as we consider the replacement, fundamentally regarding it in the light of what has been said on the logic of ostensive concepts. If we are to understand the relation of mathematics to experience, we must first try by simple illustrations to become familiar with this interchange of ostensive with non-ostensive concepts, with which the whole issue is bound up.

Consider, then, first these ostensive concepts: 'visual circle', 'visual ellipse'. Assume—for we well may—that their exemplifying sets overlap. That is to say, that to some bases both the two concepts are applicable and that the concepts, therefore, stand in the relation of overlap.

Suppose now that for some sufficient reason it becomes desirable deliberately to ignore the overlapping cases; in other words, to say "not overlap but exclusion between 'visual circle' and 'visual ellipse'". Nothing is now to be both a visual circle and a visual ellipse. We are no longer so to use the terms. Indeed, we had better use new terms in order to mark the change. Let the new concepts then be called 'geometrical circle' and 'geometrical (non-circular) ellipse'. The new rules—the rules violated if we go on applying both concepts to any one (or more) basis whatsoever—are, of course, rules inconsistent with the conjunction of the original ostensive ones. The original rules clearly cannot consistently have

[1] *Zuordnungsdefinition*; for example, Reichenbach, *Wahrscheinlichkeitslehre* (Leiden, 1935).
[2] Northrop, *The Logic of the Sciences and the Humanities* (New York, 1948).

the new rules added to them. In a word, the new rules cannot *supplement* the ostensive rules; only take their place. It is to mark this replacement that it becomes advisable, as suggested, to change the terms; to say that whereas 'visual circle' and 'visual ellipse' overlap, the relation of exclusion holds between 'geometrical circle' and 'geometrical ellipse'.

The contrast between supplementing ostensive rules and replacing them by others should be obvious. Thus to revert to an old example, we could have supplementation of the rules governing 'raven' and 'black' by deciding that 'raven' by definition is to entail 'black'. Here the new definition decided on furnishes a rule which can supplement the already accepted ostensive rules according to which the concepts stand in the relation of inclusion-or-overlap. The new definition is quite compatible with the exemplifications and the comparing clauses of the ostensive rules which govern the use of 'black' and 'raven'. In other words, after accepting the supplementary rule that ravens are by definition black, we might convey the use of 'raven' and 'black' by saying as before, with appropriate gestures, that this and this and everything like it is to be called "black", that that and that and everything like it is to be called "raven"; *and add* without inconsistency that nothing is to be called "a not-black raven". It is quite otherwise if we try to keep to our overlapping exemplifications of 'visual circle' and 'visual ellipse' *and add* the rule to the effect that the conjunction of the two concepts is not applicable to any basis. This would be to give ourselves a contradictory set of rules to obey.

We can now intelligibly speak of two different ways in which the use of ostensive concepts is capable of being changed: By *supplementing* a conjunction of ostensive rules we make a transition from purely ostensive concepts to ostensive concepts which are governed by ostensive rules and others. By *replacing* an overlap by an inclusion or exclusion, as in our example, we make a transition from ostensive to non-ostensive concepts. Merely another way of putting the matter is to point out that the concept-concept relation which results from a replacement, unlike the concept-concept relation resulting from a supplementation, does not have a corresponding primitive concept-concept relation, and the related concepts, not being ostensive, have no purely ostensive derivatives.

In spite of its simplicity our illustration has shown in what consists the application to visual circles and ellipses, of the "geometry" of our geometrical circles and ellipses (which are still a long way off Euclidean circles and ellipses). It consists in the replacement of the overlap between ostensive by an exclusion between non-ostensive circles and ellipses. Our illustration, moreover, suggests that replacements of the sort occurring in it are essential, in the application of more complicated geometrical theories to ostensive fact. If mathematisation is idealisation, then one type at least of this idealisation consists in replacements of the kind described.

The replacing of the *overlap* between the *ostensive* concepts 'visual circle' and 'visual ellipse' by the *exclusion* between the *non*-ostensive concepts 'geometrical circle' and 'geometrical ellipse' might again seem to throw us back, for explanation, upon the notion of ideal particulars. In the act of replacement, it might be said, we have, knowingly or unknowingly, created two classes of such particulars, namely, ideal circles and ideal ellipses. In consequence, either the exclusion between the classes of ideal particulars resembles the overlap between the ostensive concepts *because* the ostensive bases resemble the ideal particulars or—as an alternative consequence—the overlap between the ostensive bases resembles the exclusion between the ideal particulars, although we cannot, as Plato supposed, compare ostensive bases and ideal particulars. It is, however, perfectly possible to discard ideal particulars. In making the replacement we have merely, I suggest, for our convenience, simplified an overlap between ostensive concepts into an exclusion between non-ostensive ones.

The main point of the preceding argument was to draw attention to the transition from the logical relations between ostensive to those between non-ostensive concepts, and to show that the so-called application of mathematics to empirical fact unavoidably involves such replacements. The argument is directed not so much against the postulation of ideal particulars as against the idea that postulation, here or anywhere else in philosophy, solves any problems.

Our next example is intended to show the first steps of a transition from ostensive rules and logical relations between ostensive concepts, to arithmetic. Ostensive *aggregates*—I refer here to ostensive units, couples, triples, etc.—are instances of ostensive concepts, namely, the concepts 'ostensive unit', 'ostensive couple', 'ostensive triple', ..., 'ostensive *n*-tuple'. Any of these concepts of an ostensive aggregate is an ostensive concept. Their use, like that of other ostensive concepts, is governed by ostensive (among other) rules. They must, therefore, be distinguished from such *non*-ostensive concepts as numbers or sets—as defined in various systems of class-algebra and set-theory.

Just as, for example, 'ostensive couple' and 'ostensive triple' are ostensive concepts, so 'ostensive putting together of an ostensive couple and an ostensive triple' is an ostensive concept. Often, *though by no means always*, when we (physically or "mentally") put an ostensive couple and an ostensive triple together, there emerges an ostensive quintuple. To express this more clearly, if somewhat clumsily, we might say that the ostensive concepts 'ostensive addition of an ostensive couple and an ostensive triple' and 'ostensive emergence of an ostensive quintuple' overlap.

It might for some sufficient reason become desirable to replace the overlap between the ostensive concepts by an inclusion. To do so would violate the ostensive rules for the two concepts. Therefore if we wish to accept the new rule we could accept it only for concepts which are non-ostensive and which would replace the ostensive ones. Its acceptance involves the transition from (*a*) the overlap between 'ostensive addition of an ostensive couple and an ostensive triple' and 'ostensive emergence of an ostensive quintuple' to (*b*) the inclusion between 'arithmetical addition of an arithmetical couple and an arithmetical triple' and 'arithmetical emergence of an arithmetical quintuple'. In the expressions between quotation marks here I have replaced ‹ostensive› by ‹arithmetical› in order to mark the replacement of the ostensive by non-ostensive concepts.

This, however, is only a beginning. After effecting the replacement we are still a very long way from arithmetic. The further steps, leading from a system of ostensive operations on ostensive aggregates to an axiomatic system of arithmetic, cannot be taken here. They would amount to a theory of the foundations of arithmetic, arithmetic being "founded"—not, as is usual, on some other system of non-ostensive concepts, but—on the logic of ostensive concepts. To prevent unnecessary misunderstanding I must emphasise again that what I have called "concepts of arithmetical aggregates", such as arithmetical couples, are not concepts of numbers.

Our examples have shown that some *non-ostensive* concepts stand in logical relations of exclusion or inclusion, which, as it were, simplify the logical relation of overlap between ostensive concepts. It is convenient to distinguish these non-ostensive concepts as *simplifying* concepts from others. The rudimentary geometrical and arithmetical concepts considered above, and clearly many other mathematical concepts, are simplifying concepts. A detailed investigation comparing systems of ostensive concepts with corresponding systems of simplifying concepts might easily fill a volume of its own.

From this necessarily brief discussion of simplifying concepts I turn to an even briefer treatment of another species of non-ostensive concepts. To it belong on the one hand concepts of ideal scientific objects such as atoms or atomic nuclei, on the other hand concepts used by the epistemologist and logician, for example, 'concept', 'proposition'. It will, I trust, not be necessary to explain at length that in order to understand the employment of these concepts the postulation of ideal bases is again of little service.

Let us call a concept 'P' "completable" or, more explicitly, "ostensively completable", if the following conditions are fulfilled: (1) 'P' is non-ostensive. (2) Although non-ostensive, it can be combined with ostensive concepts to form ostensive concepts after the manner in which ostensive concepts themselves are combinable with ostensive concepts to form ostensive concepts. (3) To the rules governing the use of 'P' an ostensive rule could conceivably be added without an inconsistency arising between this rule and the other rules governing the use of 'P'.—If we take 'atom' as not being governed by an ostensive rule then it is a good example of a completable concept. Although non-ostensive it can be combined with ostensive concepts, for example, to form the ostensive concept 'physical object consisting of atoms', which bilaterally includes 'physical object'. It is in principle possible to observe atoms directly and thus to add without inconsistency an ostensive rule to the rules for ‹atom› which hitherto have governed its use as a non-ostensive concept.

Different species of completable concepts can, though not always without some cross-classification, be distinguished according to the category to which the completed ostensive concepts belong. Thus 'atom' and other concepts used in natural science can be completed into ostensive concepts which belong to the categories 'physical object' or 'physical process'. The definition of "ideal-constituent concepts" as referring to completable non-ostensive concepts whose completions belong to either of these two categories will prove convenient. It will be somewhat sharpened by a discussion of ostensive and non-ostensive categories (in Chapter XVII).

The present account of ideal-constituent concepts, although it admits of much technical refinement, exhibits their difference from what we have been calling simplifying concepts. It also shows that the employment of ideal-constituent concepts in the context of scientific theories can be understood without postulating ideal bases or provisionally ideal bases. The postulation in itself, of course, need not necessarily lead to confusion, but as has been argued with regard to simplifying concepts, mere postulation will not solve the problems which occasioned it. At least part of what one wishes to know about the relation between our use of ostensive concepts and of ideal-constituent concepts has been embodied in the definition of the term "ideal-constituent concepts" which we have given.

In discussing conceptual thinking we use ostensive and non-ostensive concepts. An important ostensive concept is, for example, 'A person X applies a concept 'Y' to a basis b'. It is ostensive because we must in explaining its use give examples of people talking, writing or acting in other ways. I shall not attempt to give a precise definition of "ostensive epistemological concept" or even to give a list of the ostensive epistemological concepts used in the present inquiry. Given such a definition or list we could say with respect to it that a non-ostensive epistemological concept is a completable concept and that its completion is an ostensive epistemological concept. All non-ostensive concepts which are used in this present discussion of conceptual thinking can easily be completed to ostensive ones.

To sum up: We have distinguished between two main types of non-ostensive concepts, namely, simplifying and completable. The distinction has been drawn by considering their relations to ostensive concepts. These relations have been described without postulating ideal particulars. Questions of ontology have not been discussed and the consideration of the logical nature of these questions has been postponed.

CHAPTER VIII

PRIMITIVE LOGICAL RELATIONS OF HIGHER ORDER

IN previous chapters we have considered logical relations between such concepts as are not themselves logical relations. In this and the next chapter we shall be concerned with those which hold between logical relations themselves. In the present chapter I shall distinguish first between different "orders" of logical propositions and concepts. I shall then try to distinguish, within every order, logical propositions to which in a precise sense of the words every conceptual thinker is committed, and logical propositions to which not every conceptual thinker is committed. I shall then briefly discuss the system of primitive logic which is constituted by the former kind of propositions. By this discussion I hope to dispel such of the uneasiness about logical relations between logical relations as seems to be attributable to the natural tendency of logicians to attend to *one type* of such relations, and to extend the results of their inquiries more or less uncritically to other types. Lastly, I shall make some remarks on the so-called paradoxes of the system of strict implication and similar systems.

In defining "order" as applied to logical concepts and propositions, we start by considering those which are not logical or, as we may say, which are concepts and propositions of *order zero*. A concept is of order zero if by asserting or denying its incidence we do *not* assert or deny the incidence of a logical relation, that is, an inclusion, overlap-or-inclusion, overlap, overlap-or-exclusion or exclusion. A proposition is of order zero if by stating it one states the incidence of a concept of order zero. All ostensive concepts are examples of concepts of order zero and so are the non-ostensive concepts 'arithmetical couple', 'geometrical triangle', 'atom', 'concept'.

If by asserting or denying the incidence of a concept we are asserting or denying the incidence of a logical relation between concepts of order zero, or propositions of this order, then we shall call the concept "a logical concept of first order" and the corresponding proposition "a logical proposition of first order". Lastly, if to assert or to deny the incidence of a concept is to assert or to deny the incidence of a logical relation between concepts of order n or propositions of that order, then the concept will be called "a logical concept of order $n+1$"; and the proposition which is stated when the incidence of the concept is asserted will be called "a logical proposition of order $n+1$". The foregoing embodies a definition of order sufficiently complete for present purposes.

It does not assign an order to all logical propositions and concepts—only to those of order zero and to those whose antecedents and consequents are of the same order, that is, which are in this sense *homogeneous*. Our definition ascribes, for instance, no order to the proposition that '('p' and '('p' entails 'q')')' entails 'q'. There are a number of ways in which we could assign an order to this or any other heterogeneous logical proposition, while preserving the particular ordering of homogeneous propositions just described. I desist, however, from further descent into technicalities, since what remains to be said about homogeneous propositions can with slight modifications be extended to heterogeneous propositions, whatever additional principle of ordering we adopt for them.

We can now discuss the commitments of conceptual thinkers to logical propositions of any order. For that purpose we recall our definition of the appropriateness of propositions. A proposition is *appropriate*, we said (Chapter IV), if by stating it we should not violate the rules for the use of the concept which we apply in stating the proposition. We further recall the definition of "essential", when a concept (or a proposition) is said to be essential to a logical proposition. It is so essential if (*a*) the logical proposition is appropriate and (*b*) the replacement of the concept by its negation, wherever it occurs in the logical proposition, yields an inappropriate logical proposition (Chapter IV). Let us now say that by stating a logical proposition we are indicating the *logical content* of a concept, say 'P', if the following two conditions are fulfilled: (1) that to assert the logical proposition is to assert the incidence of a logical relation between 'P' and some other concept or concepts; (2) that all the members of the antecedent and the consequent of the logical proposition are essential to it. Sometimes, for brevity's sake, instead of saying, correctly, that someone indicates the logical content of a concept by stating a logical proposition, I shall say succinctly that the logical proposition indicates the logical content of the concept. The use of <logical content>, here, I intend to be wider than some other uses, at least thus far, that according to it not only entailments but also other kinds of logical relations indicate the logical content of concepts. It is, on the other hand, narrower than other uses of the term, in that the antecedents and consequents of those logical propositions which indicate the logical content of concepts have no inessential members.

Let us say a set of concepts or propositions *directly involves* (a) any logical proposition '*p*' which indicates the logical content of a member of the set and (b) any logical concept which is applied by stating '*p*'. If a concept or proposition, say '*P*', directly involves '*R*', which in turn directly involves '*S*', then we shall say that '*P*' *indirectly involves* '*S*'. We shall also say that '*P*' indirectly involves '*S*' if '*P*' is connected with '*S*' by any number of the described direct links between concepts. It is clear that if '*P*' directly involves a concept '*Q*' or a proposition '*r*', the involved concept or proposition is of the next higher order than the involving one.

For example, the zero-order concepts 'red' and 'round' directly involve the first-order logical proposition that 'red' overlaps with 'round' and indirectly the second-order logical proposition that '('red' overlaps with 'round')' excludes '('red' includes 'round')'.

I shall say that a person is *committed* to all of such logical concepts and propositions as are involved, directly or indirectly, by the concepts which he accepts. This definition of "commitment" allows us to replace some unnecessarily vague questions with reasonably precise ones. An example of the vague type of question is to ask which logical propositions are *valid* for every *rational being*. Instead, I propose to ask which are the logical propositions to which every conceptual thinker is committed. Whether or not this substitution satisfies everyone who is exercised about the original question, the substituted question seems at least important enough to claim an answer in its own right.

The only kind of proposition of first order to which *every* accepter of ostensive concepts—and therefore (according to our minimal definition of 'conceptual thinker' as 'accepter of ostensive concepts') every conceptual thinker—is committed, is the sort which we have so far called "*primitive* propositions relating ostensive concepts" (Chapter v). These logical propositions I shall from now on also call "primitive propositions of first order". All the primitive propositions of first order constitute, I shall say, the *primitive logic* of first order.

It is clear that no conceptual thinker is committed to the complete primitive logic of first order, but that every conceptual thinker is committed to a subsystem of it. Moreover, since we do not create the resemblances which we describe by applying purely ostensive concepts, different people cannot conceivably be committed to incompatible primitive propositions of first order. In other words, while different persons might be committed to different subsystems of the complete primitive logic of first order, no two persons can be committed to incompatible subsystems of it.

We now ascend to the second order of the logical hierarchy and ask which are the logical propositions of *second* order to which every conceptual thinker is committed. Before attempting an answer we note how incomparably poorer than the complete primitive logic of first order, is the complete primitive logic of second order, that is, the system of all primitive propositions of second order. The only concepts related by primitive propositions of second order are the five relations: 'inclusion', 'inclusion-or-overlap', 'overlap', 'exclusion-or-overlap', and 'exclusion'; and the only propositions related by primitive propositions of second order are propositions of first order which we state by applying one of these five relations to propositions and concepts of order zero.

While it is impossible to present the complete primitive logic of first order, either by means of a list of its propositions or by the construction of an axiomatic system, it should not be difficult (apart perhaps from some logical propositions whose primitive or non-primitive character may be doubtful) to present the complete primitive logic of second order as an axiomatic system. To undertake this task would transcend the scope of the present inquiry. I shall, therefore, limit myself to the formulation of some rather obvious guiding principles for the construction of such a system.

First, while there are five primitive relations of first order, there are only three of second order. These are the three exact relations —the inexact of inclusion-or-overlap and of exclusion-or-overlap being bound up with the special character of ostensive concepts. In naming the remaining three it may seem advisable to replace the terms "inclusion", "exclusion" and "overlap" by others which are not borrowed from the vocabulary of visual experience. I shall, therefore, speak of entailment, incompatibility and in-difference when referring to the primitive relations of second or higher order.

An example of a primitive entailment-proposition of second order is the proposition that '('pale green' is included in 'green')' and '('green' is included in 'coloured')' together entail '('pale green' is included in 'coloured')'. An example of a primitive incompatibility-proposition of second order would be the pro-position that '('green' is included in 'coloured')' is incompatible with '('green' excludes 'coloured')'. An example of a primitive indifference-proposition of the second order would be the pro-position that '('green' is included in 'coloured')' is indifferent to '('shrill' is included in 'noisy')'. In strictness we have to stipulate that the concepts of zero order used in our examples are all purely ostensive. Yet, as will appear, the omission of this condition would not affect the argument.

The second requirement is the obvious one that any primitive second-order relation between two concepts or propositions (of first order) is incompatible with any other between them. For example, entailment between two first-order propositions is in-compatible with indifference between them.

The third requirement follows from the fact that the conceptual thinker, *qua* accepter of ostensive concepts, is committed only to logical propositions which indicate the logical content of these concepts and of the relations between them. It is the requirement that no second-order proposition and none of its first-order com -

ponents contain inessential members. Among the admitted second-order propositions are: (1) the primitive principle of transitivity according to which '("('p' entails 'q')' and '('q' entails 'r')')' entails '('p' entails 'r')'; (2) the primitive principle of contraposition according to which '('p' entails 'q')' entails '('not-q' entails 'not-p')'; (3) the primitive principle of the antilogism according to which '('p and q' entails 'r')' entails '('p and not-r' entails 'not-q')'. Not admitted as primitive are all self-entailments such as '('p' entails 'q')' entails '('p' entails 'q')' and all entailments which although not self-entailments yet contain components with inessential members. I shall call the latter "excessive" entailments. An example would be the proposition that '(('p' entails 'q') and ('q' entails 'r'))' entails '('p' entails 'q')'.

While no conceptual thinker is committed to the complete system of the primitive logic of first order, every conceptual thinker who accepts ostensive concepts related by each of the five primitive relations is committed to the complete primitive logic of second order. For the primitive propositions of second order are the logical propositions which are involved by the five primitive logical relations of first order and the first-order propositions whose statement consists in the application of these relations. The great variety of first-order propositions is here of no consequence, since by stating the second-order propositions we suspend the concept-basis relations between the first-order concepts and their bases (Chapter IV).

It may seem that since the primitive logical propositions of second order directly involve primitive propositions of third order and indirectly involve primitive propositions of higher order without limit, we are exposed to the danger of an infinite regress or, at least, to unwelcome surprises at some stage of the dreary progression from order to order. That the fear of an infinite regress is unfounded can be seen by considering, for example, the second-order proposition that '('P' includes 'R')' is incompatible with '('P' excludes 'R')'. Since the second-order proposition suspends the concept-basis relations between 'includes' and 'P' and 'R' on the one hand and 'excludes' and 'P' and 'R' on the other, its appropriateness is not affected if we replace 'P' and 'R' by any concepts, among them primitive relations of any order. It follows that by being able to notice the appropriateness of the lower order propositions one is also able to notice the appropriateness of the higher order ones, and that it is *not* the case that in order to notice the appropriateness of a logical proposition we must first notice that of a higher one and so on *ad infinitum*.

The fear of unwelcome surprises is equally groundless. The primitive logic of second order, to put it briefly, relates the *five* first-order relations by three second-order ones, while the primitive logic of third order relates the *three* second-order relations of entailment, incompatibility and indifference. If third-order primitive logic is like second-order primitive logic except for (*a*) its order and (*b*) for relating only three and not five logical relations, then the primitive logic of fourth and any higher order differs from the primitive logic of third order only in the order of their propositions. Thus the structure of the whole of primitive logic is simple and easily grasped. With the exception of what is stated in the next section the necessity to ascend to an order higher than the second will not arise.

A system of primitive logic would exhibit only those logical propositions to which we stand committed by our accepting and applying ostensive concepts. It would, therefore, not do justice to the many other uses of concepts—ostensive and non-ostensive—in deductive inference and definition (Chapter XII). An advantage of the system, if it is an advantage, would be its freedom from the "paradoxes" which attach to the systems of "implication" and "strict implication".

Each of these concepts has had its rules embodied in some algebra of which it has been assumed at one time or another that all its theorems of a certain form could be interpreted as in an obvious way appropriate entailments. Thus Russell at one time held that every theorem of the form "$((\ldots) \supset (\ldots))$" in *Principia Mathematica* could be interpreted as an appropriate entailment. A similar view has been held by C. I. Lewis concerning every theorem of the form "$((\ldots) \prec (\ldots))$" in the calculus of Strict Implication. Both these systems, and other systems of implication, contain paradoxical theorems, that is, theorems of which the following two statements are true: (1) their interpretation as appropriate entailments confronts us with the alternative that either the rules governing the use of the implication-relation differ from those governing the use of 'entails', or else the rules for the use of the latter concept are different from what they were supposed to be before the derivation of the theorem; (2) no good reason is known why one of these alternatives should be preferred to the other. The second statement may only hold temporarily, the solution of the paradox consisting in giving the good reason which was hitherto lacking. It will be sufficient to consider the following two paradoxes, namely, that an internally inconsistent conjunction *implies* every proposition and that an exclusive alternation *is implied* by every proposition.

We note first of all that there are three main types of excessive entailments. First, excessive entailments with self-entailments as their cores. These are (*a*) any entailment whose antecedent is a conjunction and whose consequent is a member of the conjunction, e.g. '('*p* and *q*' entails '*p*')', (*b*) any entailment which, by applying the principles of antilogism and of contraposition any number of times and in any order, can be shown to entail and to be entailed by a proposition of type (*a*). An example is '('not-*p*' entails 'not-*p* or not-*q*')'.

Secondly, excessive entailments with primitive entailments as their cores. These are: (*a*) any entailment whose antecedent is a conjunction and whose consequent is a member of the conjunction to which another of its members stands in a primitive entailment relation. An example would be '('blue and round' entails 'coloured')'; (*b*) any entailment which, by applying the principles of antilogism and of contraposition any number of times and in any order, can be shown to entail and to be entailed by a proposition of type (*a*).

Thirdly, excessive entailments with both primitive and self-entailments as their cores. An example of this rather pathological type, which we mention only for the sake of completeness, is '('blue and round' entails 'coloured or round')', which is logically equivalent to '('blue and round and not-coloured' entails 'round')' on the one hand and to '('blue and round and not-round' entails

NON-PRIMITIVE LOGICAL RELATIONS OF HIGHER ORDER AND THE SO-CALLED "LAWS OF THOUGHT"

EVERY conceptual thinker is committed to some logical propositions of first order; and if he accepts ostensive concepts standing in each of the five primitive relations, he is committed to the complete primitive logic of higher order. There is a very great variety of further logical propositions to which a person who has accepted ostensive rules may or may not commit himself. He does so by accepting further rules in addition to the ostensive ones.

In the present chapter I shall first discuss in a general way the different kinds of non-primitive propositions of higher order. I shall then make use of the distinctions (*a*) between logical propositions belonging to different orders and (*b*) between primitive propositions and non-primitive, in order to throw some light on what is meant by the so-called "principles of contradiction and excluded middle" and the so-called "laws of thought" in general.

It has been already pointed out concerning non-primitive propositions of first order that they may indicate the logical content of ostensive, though not purely ostensive, concepts; an example of this was the proposition 'raven' is (by definition) included in 'black'. Or they may indicate the logical content of simplifying concepts as in the statement 'geometrical circle' excludes 'geometrical ellipse'. Or again they may indicate the logical content of completable concepts as does 'being an atom' entails 'not being at rest'. The object, in this discussion, was, or was partly, to show how a person, having accepted, so far, only ostensive rules, commits himself further. We saw that he commits himself to the first of these non-primitive propositions by accepting, in addition to the ostensive rules he already accepts, a rule which we called a "supplementary" rule. To the second he commits himself by accepting, in addition to his present commitments, the obligation to respect also a rule which we described as permitting the replacement of an overlap between ostensive concepts by an exclusion between non-ostensive ones. His commitment to the third of these non-primitive propositions occurs upon his decision to add to those he already recognises, certain further rules providing for the possibility of combining the completable concept 'atom' with ostensive concepts to form ostensive concepts. These summary illustrations are of course not exhaustive of the subject. But they do show roughly how a person who is as yet committed only to primitive propositions may find himself to have enlarged his commitments to the point of accepting non-primitive propositions of first order.

One is naturally led, here, to ask the general question how a person who has hitherto been committed only to primitive logical propositions can commit himself to *non*-primitive logical propositions of *any* order. It is sufficient to consider logical propositions of the first order and the second, since no new features emerge from considering propositions of higher order. The following possibilities need consideration.

First, where a conceptual thinker, without accepting supplementary rules *governing the logical relations*, is yet committed to non-primitive second-order propositions. Consider, for example, the second-order proposition that '('being a raven' excludes 'being white')' is incompatible with '('being a raven' is included in 'being white')'. Here the concepts 'being a raven' and 'being white' are not purely ostensive, that is, they are not governed by ostensive rules only. Their primitive logical relation is exclusion-or-overlap, upon which the full relation of exclusion is superimposed as a result of accepting the supplementary rule to the effect that ravens are by definition not white. Since the second-order proposition relates two first-order propositions which are not primitive, it is itself not primitive.

What we must remember, however, is that even a person who accepts only purely ostensive concepts, and who is thus committed only to primitive logic, can be committed to a second-order proposition having the same structure as our example. For instance, even if he has accepted *only* the ostensive rules for 'being a sound' and 'being square', then he would be committed to the primitive proposition of first order that 'being a sound' excludes 'being square' and consequently to the primitive proposition of second order that '('being a sound' excludes 'being square')' is incompatible with '('being a sound' is included in 'being square')'. This proposition is essentially similar to our example, differing only in that it contains purely ostensive concepts where the latter contains concepts which are not purely ostensive. No supplementary rule governing 'excludes' and 'includes' need be accepted in order to make our non-primitive second-order proposition appropriate. It might, therefore, be argued with good reason that the term "primitive proposition of second order" could well be extended to cover all second-order propositions which share the same structure with such primitive second-order propositions as contain only purely ostensive concepts.

Secondly, consider the case where a conceptual thinker finds his logical commitments enlarged by his having accepted new supplementary rules governing the use of the logical relations. Being supplementary these rules are not incompatible with those governing the logical relations between purely ostensive concepts. Most formalisations of logic contain theorems which represent logical propositions as conforming to supplementary rules. The acceptance of these rules often means that greater efficiency in handling a calculus is bought at the price of so-called "paradoxes". For example, by accepting a suitable rule governing 'entails' we may commit ourselves to the non-primitive second-order proposition that for any three concepts 'P', 'Q', 'R'—'('P' entails 'Q')' entails '('P and R' entails 'Q')', and in this manner commit ourselves to the paradox that '('being green' entails 'being coloured')' entails '('being green and not green' entails 'being coloured')'.

Consider, lastly, the pathological case in which a person accepts a rule governing the use of a logical relation and commits himself thereby to propositions incompatible with second-order propositions of primitive logic. For example, he may accept the rule that for concepts of a certain type the entailment-relation is intransitive, that is, that for a certain type of 'P' 'Q' and 'R'—'('P' entails 'Q')'

and '('Q' entails 'R')', does not entail '('P' entails 'R')'. Such a rule is, of course, incompatible with the primitive rule which would be satisfied by stating the transitivity of 'entails'. It cannot, therefore, be regarded as a supplementary rule which can be *added* to the rules which govern the use of 'entails'. It *replaces* them. The situation is similar to that in which a rule which governs the use of overlapping ostensive concepts is replaced by one governing the use of non-ostensive concepts standing in the logical relation of exclusion or inclusion. However, the concept which replaces 'entails' is such that the statement or denial of its incidence is no longer the statement or denial of one or more of the five logical relations. It is therefore a concept of order zero, and any proposition which we state by applying it is a zero-order, or factual, proposition.

In contrast with the clearness of the distinction between primitive and non-primitive propositions of *first* order, what I have said about those of *higher* order leaves room for some of which it would be doubtful whether they are primitive or not. Such border-line cases, however, do not affect the usefulness of a distinction whose importance rests on the clearly distinguishable cases. A clear case of a primitive proposition of second order is, for example, the proposition that '('('P' includes 'Q')' and '('Q' includes 'R')')' entails '('P' includes 'R')'; or '('('P' includes 'Q')' is incompatible with '('P' excludes 'Q')')'. A clear case of a non-primitive proposition of second order is '('('P' entails 'Q')' entails '('P and not-P' entails 'Q')')'. It is possible that the description here offered of the logical hierarchy of primitive and non-primitive propositions may be found pedantic or again it may seem not pedantic enough; at least, I trust, it has shown and illustrated by examples that the conceptual thinker, that is, the accepter of ostensive rules, is *because of this acceptance* committed to some logical propositions but not necessarily to others.

With this in mind we now turn to a discussion of what have been called the "laws of thought". We may begin with the familiar <No proposition can conceivably be true and false at the same time>. In all its various uses this sentence has been given the name of "the principle of contradiction".

First, we note that when people speak of this principle they often refer to non-primitive entailments of first order, for example, to the proposition that '('p' is true)' is incompatible with '('p' is false)' where the words <true> and <false> are used as non-ostensive concepts of order zero. Many philosophers, especially whose who hold a correspondence theory of truth, use <true> in this way; for to define 'truth' as a relation between facts and propositions is to define a non-ostensive concept of order zero.

Now, if by asserting the so-called "law of contradiction" one is asserting a non-primitive proposition of first order which relates non-ostensive concepts, then one is not committed to it by the mere circumstance that one accepts ostensive rules. Indeed, we need not go far to find philosophers who by implication disclaim this commitment most vigorously. For no philosopher who denies that <true> is used as a concept, if he lives up to his doctrine, is committed to any non-primitive propositions which indicate the logical content of a concept of truth.

When people say that no proposition can conceivably be true and false at the same time they often refer secondly to self-entailments. For to say that 'p' cannot conceivably be true and false at the same time is often only a way of saying that 'p' entails itself. No self-entailment indicates the logical content of any concept and in particular not of a concept of zero order.

Thirdly, when people utter the sentence we are discussing, they may be using <true> as one of a number of concepts of *first* order. I shall discuss this use after considering the so-called "law of excluded middle".

The interpretations of the "law of contradiction" which we have considered do not by any means exhaust all that are possible. But they are enough to show how unprofitable discussion about whether the principle of contradiction is "valid for everybody" is likely to be, when it only adds the ambiguity of "principle of contradiction" to the vagueness of "valid for everybody".

The "law of excluded middle" has, I believe, on the whole been much more actively discussed than the "law of contradiction", although already Aristotle (in the fourth book of the *Metaphysics*) finds it necessary to argue against those who pretend not to accept the latter and demand that it be proved.

We note here first that by the name "the law of excluded middle" people again refer frequently to non-primitive entailments of first order, for example, to the conjunction of the proposition that '('p' is true)' entails '('p' is not false)' with the proposition that '('p' is not true)' entails '('p' is false)'. This conjunction takes care of the exclusive and exhaustive character of 'true or false'. It excludes a third truth-value, say 'indeterminate'. Its two members are non-primitive logical propositions which indicate the logical content of non-ostensive concepts. These non-primitive propositions may be rejected not only by those who do not use a concept of 'truth' of zero order, but even by those who do use such a concept, because, for example, they use more than two truth-values. Secondly, when people say that every proposition is necessarily either true or false they may again simply refer to self-entailments. A third possible use of the phrase as indicating the logical content of first-order concepts will be discussed presently.

In the usual interpretations of the propositional calculus, and in two-valued truth-functional logic in general, certain formulae, for example, "$\vdash p \vee \sim p$", are interpreted as the so-called "law of excluded middle". This interpretation amounts to the statement of a non-primitive logical proposition which indicates the logical content of a non-ostensive concept 'truth'. It is frequently pointed out that *we are not bound* to a two-valued logic, and in particular to its central principle of the excluded middle, but are on the contrary free to choose, and may choose a three-or-more-valued logic. This is certainly so if (1) *we*, whoever else we may be, are at least persons who accept some ostensive rules, and if (2) "not bound to" means what is meant by "not committed to" in the sense of the term used above. It is, however, wrong to assume, as is sometimes done, that our commitment to *all* logical propositions is of the same tenuous character as our commitment, if we are so committed, to two-valued logic. For *we* cannot, without ceasing to be accepters of ostensive rules, reject our commitments to (a) *all* primitive propositions of first order and (b) to any primitive proposition of second order.

If correspondence theories of truth employ truth-concepts of order zero and defend their employment, then many so-called "coherence theories of truth" seem to regard the concept of truth as a logical concept of first order. Truth according to them is not a property of propositions or a relation between propositions and facts but a logical relation between propositions that constitute a system. What exactly in these theories is meant by "truth" and "coherence" is often difficult to discover. Yet it seems that according to some of them to state that 'p' is true is to state, among other things, that 'p' is entailed by some internally consistent conjunction.[1]

To show that concepts of truth can be defined as concepts of first order is of interest, not only because of their use in coherence theories, but also for other reasons. We can, in particular, interpret in terms of them some otherwise puzzling "laws of thought" and show that *some* apparently serious controversies about the nature of logic are merely verbal disagreements. Instead of speaking of concepts of truth of first order I shall—I think without violating philosophical usage—use the term "concepts of correctness".

In defining some of these it is convenient to introduce a few abbreviations. Instead of '('p' is incorrect)' I shall write 'Np'; instead of 'It is incorrect that 'p' is incorrect' I shall write 'NNp', etc. Instead of writing m 'N' signs in front of 'p' I shall write '$N_m p$'. I shall write '$N_0 p$' instead of '('p' is correct)'. Lastly, I may write 'N_m' for '$N_m N_0$' or '$N_0 N_m$'. ("N" might also be read as "Non".)

I shall be concerned with interpretations of the following "skeleton" expressions:

(1) '$N_m p$' is incompatible with '$N_{m+1} p$'.

(2) '$N_m p$' entails and is entailed by 'not $N_{m+1} p$'.

(3) '$N_m p$' entails and is entailed by '$N_{m+2} p$'.

These three expressions are skeletons of appropriate logical propositions of second order in the sense that we can by suitable definitions of '$N_0 p$', 'Np', etc., turn them into such propositions. To state these second-order propositions might then be regarded as formulating a "law of contradiction", a "law of excluded middle", and a "law of double negation".

---

[1] For a discussion of coherence, and other theories of truth, see Chapter XXIII.

As a preliminary to different definitions of '$N_m p$' (for $m = 0, 1, ...$), we assume that an otherwise unspecified conjunction 'c' of propositions, say, of axioms, of some deductive theory, is internally consistent so that '('c' entails 'p')' is incompatible with '('c' entails 'not-p')'. If 'c' and 'p' are ostensive they are certainly internally consistent.

Our first definition of '$N_m p$' for $m = 0, 1, 2, ...$ consists in deciding that '$N_{2m} p$' is to be interchangeable with 'not ('c' entails 'not-p')' and that '$N_{2m+1} p$' is to be interchangeable with '('c' entails 'not-p')'. By this definition we turn the first skeleton into a law of contradiction, the second into a law of excluded middle and the third into a law of double negation.

Next we define '$N_m p$' by deciding on the interchangeability of '$N_{2m} p$' with '('c' entails 'p')' and of '$N_{2m+1} p$' with 'not ('c' entails 'p')'. Although the concepts of correctness thus defined differ from the preceding ones we again, by substituting them into the skeletons, turn the latter into appropriate logical propositions of second order, whose statement is a formulation of the three laws of thought for a concept of correctness.

One often finds it stated or implied that logic is not concerned with the truth and falsehood of propositions but with their correctness, and this correctness is explained sometimes as consistency with, at other times as deducibility from, other propositions. Our first definition of '$N_m p$' corresponds to the former view of logical correctness, our second to the latter.

Our third definition of '$N_m p$' is intended to show that a law of excluded middle need not be characteristic of every concept of correctness. We may decide that '$N_{2m} p$' be interchangeable with '('c' entails 'p')' and '$N_{2m+1} p$' with '('c' entails 'not-p')'. By substitution of these definientia in (1), (2) and (3) the first and third skeletons become appropriate logical propositions whose statements are formulations of a law of contradiction and of double negation, while the remaining skeleton becomes the proposition that '('c' entails 'p')' entails *and is entailed by* 'not ('c' entails 'not-p')'. The second of these entailments is clearly inappropriate. For instance, the proposition that ('the sun shines' does not entail 'logic is not the whole of philosophy') does not entail the proposition that ('the sun shines' entails 'logic is the whole of philosophy'). In other words, the last defined concept is *not* characterised by an appropriate second-order proposition whose statement would be a formulation of a law of excluded middle.

Lastly, we define '$N_m p$' by deciding on the interchangeability of '$N_0 p$' with '('c' entails 'p')' and otherwise on the interchangeability of '$N_{2m} p$' with 'not ('c' entails 'not p')' and of '$N_{2m+1} p$' with '('c' entails 'not-p')'. It is characteristic of these concepts that substitution of the definientia into the first skeleton leads for any value of m to an appropriate logical proposition, while substitution into the second and third skeleton leads to appropriate logical propositions for some values of m only. This may be expressed briefly, though somewhat imprecisely, by saying that for the concepts of correctness just defined the laws of excluded middle and of double negation are not generally valid. It is noteworthy that *some* of the laws of thought resulting from substituting (for different values of m) the definientia of our last definition in our three skeletons, remind us of logical principles which have been put forward by intuitionist logicians as being on the one hand inconsistent with traditional logic and the logic of *Principia Mathematica*, and yet, on the other hand, self-evident on reflection. While appropriate logical propositions are probably as self-evident as can reasonably be expected, it is unlikely that any intuitionist would accept the interpretation of his apparently unorthodox principles in terms of appropriate logical propositions of second order.

CHAPTER X

LOGICALLY NECESSARY AND GENERAL
PROPOSITIONS

A LEADING distinction in the preceding has been the distinction between two logics, the logic of ostensive concepts and the Boolean logic, the former with its exact *and* inexact relations, the latter with its principle of sharply delimited classes, confining itself to the exact relations only, that is, those of inclusion, exclusion and overlap. Clarity about this distinction requires that we make—apart from more radical changes in our views—some minor adjustments in our definitions. Some of this tidying up will be undertaken in the present chapter. It will mainly be concerned with the notions of logically necessary and general propositions.

A source of some of the confusion is the issue as to whether logical propositions are logically necessary. We recall that by a "logical proposition" we understand any proposition in which one asserts or denies the incidence of a logical relation, for example, '('p' entails 'q')'. Such a logical proposition must in particular not be confused with a factual proposition (a proposition of order zero) and especially not with the particular factual proposition that somebody is committed to it. It must further not be confused with either the rule which we should be satisfying by stating it, or any command, recommendation or other manner of imposing or trying to impose such a rule. The distinction between logical propositions, factual propositions and rules has been emphasised in the Introduction, so that whoever uses, for example, "entailment-proposition" as referring to rules or factual propositions should find it easy to distinguish his use of the term from the use here being made of it.

Once we accept the distinction between logical propositions, factual propositions and rules it would seem natural to regard all appropriate logical propositions as *logically necessary*. Our decision to do so is indeed of little importance until accompanied by certain further definitions. Until then little else depends on it. Yet it is interesting to note that even philosophers who distinguish between logical propositions on the one hand and rules and factual propositions on the other, often still do not regard logical propositions as logically necessary. Here they could appeal, in defence, to the authority of G. E. Moore.

In a famous paper on 'External and Internal Relations',[1] he introduced "entails" as a technical term into philosophy. Now there is no doubt that in the paper quoted Moore holds that an appropriate entailment, say '('p' entails 'q')', is not logically necessary. It is merely true. He holds, moreover, that if, but only if, '('p' entails 'q')' is true, can we say that '(not-p or q)' is logically necessary. Yet although Moore coined the technical term we may reasonably object to his proposed use of it, because he links his proposal clearly with what he believes to be a report on the use of "is deducible", "follows necessarily from" and their cognates. Indeed, he declares that "entails" is used as the converse of "is deducible from", whose use has a long tradition behind it, both within logic and outside.

Now, surely a person who correctly stated about the conclusion of a deductive argument that it "followed" from its premisses, would be said to state a logically necessary proposition. If, then, "entails" be the converse of "is deducible from", we must surely equally say of any person who states that the premisses of a certain deductive argument entail its conclusion, that he is stating a logically necessary proposition and not a merely true one. Moore has not, I think, either shown that this is out of line with traditional usage, or given any good reason for changing it.

As entailments are logically necessary, so also must exclusions be, since every exclusion is logically equivalent to an entailment. Moreover, if to assert the incidence of an entailment and an exclusion-relation be to assert a logically necessary proposition, we can hardly withhold the title of "logically necessary propositions" from those to state which is to state the incidence of any of the other three logical relations, that is, an overlap, an inclusion-or-overlap and an exclusion-or-overlap.

[1] In *Proceedings of the Aristotelian Society*, vol. 20 (1919–20).

In proposing that appropriate entailments be regarded as logically necessary and not merely as true, I do not wish to deny that, for example, '('p' entails 'q')', if appropriate, entails, and is entailed by, the proposition that 'not-p or q' is logically necessary. In other words, I do consider it natural to call an appropriate alternation logically necessary if its appropriateness is entailed by that of an appropriate entailment.

Lastly, it is generally agreed that a conjunction of propositions is logically necessary if, and only if, all its member-propositions are logically necessary, and that an alternation of propositions is logically necessary if, and only if, at least one of its members is logically necessary. If the only compound propositions with which we are concerned be those compounded by means of 'and', 'or', 'not', it could then be easily shown (by the method used in the reduction of compound propositions of the propositional calculus to normal forms) that every compound proposition is logically equivalent to a conjunction of alternations or an alternation of conjunctions.

The present would appear to be the place to propose the following definition of "logically necessary proposition". By this term, then, I shall refer (1) to any appropriate logical proposition of whatever kind or order whose assertion is the assertion of the incidence of one of the five logical relations; (2) to any appropriate alternation the appropriateness of which is entailed by that of an appropriate entailment; (3) to any conjunction all of whose members are, and to any alternation one, at least, of whose members is, logically necessary; and (4) to any proposition which is logically equivalent to a logically necessary proposition. Although I have tried to show that this definition is largely a report on the use of "logically necessary" and its cognates by philosophers, I am fully content to have it regarded as a proposal, and as placing on record my own intended use.

One sometimes calls a proposition "logically necessary" if one wishes to indicate that it follows logically from other propositions which are clear from the context. This use of the term is elliptical, and the complete expression, by which we should replace the elliptical one in the case of any misunderstanding, would clearly be covered by our definition.

To adjust the use of "logically necessary proposition" to the logic of ostensive concepts occasions little difficulty. It is not quite so easy to effect a similar adjustment for the notion of a general proposition. The reason lies in the divergence between two ways of characterising general propositions: on the one hand by purely linguistic criteria, and on the other by criteria which are at least intended to be unaffected by the peculiarities of any particular, natural language. I shall indicate the difference by speaking of linguistic or grammatical definitions as opposed to philosophical or logical ones.

According to the usual *grammatical* definition, a proposition is general if the signs used contain the word "all" ("every", "some", "no", etc.). This definition, in many ways unobjectionable, has certain disadvantages. It is, as one might say, too provincial. It takes but one language into account—or one family of languages. Also it admits of unwelcome ambiguities, since we often cannot, except by decree, decide whether a certain rule governing the use of the relevant words does or does not belong to the English language. It further fails to avoid possible and inconvenient surprises, since the English language is changing. To overcome these disadvantages we must either construct an artificial language, which can be precise and unchanging, or we must look for some clear "philosophical" criteria of generality.

According to the usual *philosophical* definition of generality a proposition is general if in asserting it we state an inclusion, an exclusion, or an overlap, between classes or concepts.[1] In view of the possibility of inexact relationships between ostensive concepts, I propose to modify this definition as follows: A proposition is general if in asserting it we state a logical or concept-concept relation between two concepts, that is, an inclusion, overlap, exclusion, inclusion-or-overlap, exclusion-or-overlap. This philosophical definition is obviously not coextensive with the grammatical. Some propositions grammatically general are clearly also philosophically general, but others clearly are not; and there are doubtful cases.

Those logically necessary propositions by means of which we

---

[1] See, for example, Stebbing, *A Modern Introduction to Logic* (London, 1942), p. 43.

assert concept-concept relations are by our definition general. For example, in asserting that 'being green' entails 'being extended' we assert a philosophically general proposition, which in English is frequently expressed by saying that all green things are (necessarily) extended. There are, however, logically necessary propositions which are neither philosophically nor grammatically general, e.g. self-entailments such as '('p' entails 'p')' and excessive entailments such as '('p and q' entails 'p')' where 'p' and 'q' are particular propositions.

Among the grammatically general propositions which are not also philosophically general there are certain types of conjunction expressed by means of "all", and certain alternations expressed by means of "some" or "there exists". For example, assuming that a and b are the only people in this room, the proposition that all the people in this room are tall entails, and is entailed by, the proposition that a is tall and b is tall. The only peculiarity of this proposition is that the concept 'tall' is being applied twice. The phrase ‹all the people in this room› is used to collect a number of separately identifiable bases for the application of one and the same (non-logical) concept to them. To distinguish such conjunctions from those in which different concepts are applied we might call them "collective". In an analogous way we might speak of collective alternations, which are of course negations of collective conjunctions.[1] As long as the number of collected bases is finite no problem arises. However, once we suppose that their number is, or is possibly, "infinite", matters are far from clear.

That the rules governing "all" and "some", in statements about an infinite number of "objects", are different from the rules governing these words in statements about finite collections, is generally recognised. At best the use of the finite "some" and "all" can be used as an "heuristic analogy" in looking for suitable rules governing the infinite or possibly infinite "some" and "all".[2] The concept, or rather the many different concepts, for which

---

[1] All this has often been noted, for example by Bosanquet, who speaks of collective judgments (*Logic* (Oxford, 1888), vol. I, p. 162).

[2] See Hilbert and Bernays, *Grundlagen der Mathematik* (Berlin, 1934), vol. I, p. 99.

‹infinite in number› is being used, is a non-ostensive concept of great complexity. This becomes obvious when we remember (Chapter VII) that even the concepts of finite numbers are idealisations of ostensive concepts. Moreover, while, for example, the concept 'arithmetical couple' corresponds in a clear way to the ostensive concept 'ostensive couple', there is no ostensive concept which in an analogous way corresponds to 'infinite in number'. We should therefore be rather naïve if we believed that in translating grammatically general propositions into possibly infinite, collective conjunctions, we have "analysed" or exhibited the logical structure of general propositions.

A similar difficulty attaches to Russellian formal implications and their negations, that is, to the interpretation of formulae such as "$(x)(\phi(x)\supset\psi(x))$" and "$(\exists x)\sim(\phi(x)\supset\psi(x))$", where we assume that the compound concept '$\phi(x)\supset\psi(x)$' is of order zero, that is to say, non-logical. Is the formal implication to be interpreted as asserting a logical relation between '$\phi(x)$' and '$\psi(x)$' or is it to be interpreted as a factual proposition? No clear answer can be given. On the one hand we might argue that since every proposition in which '$\phi(x)\supset\psi(x)$' is applied to a basis is factual, any conjunction of such propositions, even of "infinitely many", must again be factual. This view is implied by those philosophers who hold that empirical laws of nature are formal implications and at the same time factual propositions. On the other hand, we might argue that the transition from a finite, collective proposition to an infinite one implies that one is no longer asserting a factual proposition but a logical relation between '$\phi(x)$' and '$\psi(x)$'. This view may seem at times to be implied by Russell himself.[1]

Empirical laws of nature are another type of grammatically general propositions of which it is doubtful whether or not they are general in the sense in which to assert them is to state logical relations between concepts. Both these views have been frequently stated and the answer to this problem is by no means obvious. It demands that attention be given to the inexact relations between ostensive concepts and will be reserved for the next chapter.

---

[1] See, for example, *Introduction to Mathematical Philosophy* (London, 1919), p. 165.

The fact that the same combination of words may be used for propositions of different type and order may easily lead to confusion. For example, ‹all P's are Q's› may be used both for the first-order or logical proposition that 'being a P' entails 'being a Q' and also for the zero-order or factual proposition that a finite number of bases identified by means of 'P' are Q's. Now the negation of the logical proposition is the proposition that 'being a P' does not entail 'being a Q'; while the negation of the factual proposition is that there exists a P (that there is an identifiable instance of P) which is not a Q. The two negations do not entail each other. Indeed, having proved that 'being a unicorn' does not entail 'having two horns', we cannot infer from this proposition that there exists a unicorn which has not got two horns. Again, to take a more serious example, having proved that 'being a number with the property P' does not entail 'having the property Q', we cannot infer from this that there exists a number with the property P but without the property Q.

Apart from possible technical advantages, nothing seems to be gained by regarding all general propositions, factual and logical alike, as formal implications and their negations as "existential" propositions of the form "$(\exists x) \sim (\phi(x) \supset \psi(x))$". On the contrary, the formula only confers the dignity of apparent mathematical precision upon our failure to distinguish between factual and logical propositions.[1]

Indeed the phrase "there exists", and the symbol "$(\exists x)$", obscure not only the difference between logical and factual propositions but other differences as well. Thus we have seen that ostensive concepts are applicable, in a sense in which non-ostensive concepts are not. To state that a number *exists* is quite different from saying that a green patch or a house *exists*. Since this and similar differences will be shown to be of philosophical importance (Chapters XXI, XXII), the indiscriminate use of "$(\exists x)$" can be even more confusing than we have yet had occasion to show.

---

[1] Contemporary mathematical logicians are aware of, and concerned with, the problems involved in quantification with respect to an "infinite range of individuals".

CHAPTER XI

ON EMPIRICAL LAWS OF NATURE

LAWS of nature in a wide sense of the term are grammatically general propositions, to which observation and experiment are relevant and which can be used for successful prediction. This rather vague definition covers propositions of many different types, among them a certain kind of entailment (Chapter XXVI) and a certain kind of rule (Chapter XXX). In practice it is often difficult to decide whether a sentence is being used for a law of nature of one type or of another, and the difficulty is increased by the fact that the same sentence is often used for laws of different type.

The present chapter will be concerned chiefly with one species of laws of nature, a species which, for want of a better term, I shall call "empirical" laws.[1] Ever since Hume's examination of the idea of necessary causal connection, the logical status of empirical laws of nature has been a central problem for epistemology. The main advance made in recent discussions towards its solution has consisted in formulating more clearly than had hitherto been done the conditions which a solution would have to fulfil. The main obstacle to our reaching clarity about empirical laws of nature has been the persistent failure to do justice at once to their empirical and their hypothetical character. One reason for this in turn lies, as I hope to show, in the indifference of logicians to the logic of ostensive concepts, especially to the possibility of inexact logical relations.

The argument will proceed as follows. After a few terminological preliminaries are settled, empirical laws will be characterised by certain requirements which they must fulfil, although it will at first sight be difficult to see how these can be fulfilled by any proposition. Next, two mutually exclusive attempts at overcoming this difficulty will be examined. Finally, a solution of the problem will be proposed.

---

[1] Duhem, in *La Théorie physique: son objet—sa structure* (Paris, 1914), speaks of "experimental" laws.

In stating an empirical law of nature we may make use of grammatically-universal sentences, such as ‹All bodies deprived of support fall downwards›. We may however also use sentences of other grammatical types and, in particular, grammatically-conditional sentences, such as ‹if a piece of iron has been magnetised then it attracts iron filings›.

I shall say of any grammatically-conditional sentence which is used for a proposition that its "if" part is used for the protasis and its "then" part for the apodosis of the proposition. Thus empirical laws of nature, though of course also propositions of other kinds, must have a protasis and an apodosis. There are, however, other conditions whose simultaneous fulfilment is required only of empirical laws of nature. These are the following:

First, to state an empirical law is to state a relation between two concepts. It is not, or at least not only, to apply two concepts to the same basis (or bases). When, for example, I assert of the basis which I identify by means of the phrase ‹my pen› that it is black and smooth, or when I assert that deprived of support it is falling downwards, I am asserting not an empirical law of nature, but a mere coincidence. It has been clearly seen and said by Hume and earlier thinkers, that to state an empirical law of nature is more than to state a coincidence, even if the number of cases in which the coincidence has been observed is very great.

A second condition required of an empirical law of nature is that its protasis and apodosis be ostensive concepts. Thus among the rules for the concept 'deprived of support' there is an ostensive rule by whose statement one exemplifies the concept; and the same is true of 'falling downwards', of 'magnetised piece of iron' and, in general, of the protasis and the apodosis of any empirical law of nature. We can, of course, define most ostensive concepts without stating ostensive rules. If, however, we persist in tracing the genealogy of the definientia of any ostensive concept all the way home, so to speak, we must finally arrive at a definiens whose use cannot be explained without the formulation of an ostensive rule. This second requirement is admitted in effect by everybody who holds that an empirical law of nature relates concepts whose instances are events, things, impressions, sense-data or observable entities.

Our third requirement is that every empirical law of nature be a hypothetical proposition (I am using the term "hypothetical proposition" in the sense in which some writers speak of counterfactual or contrafactual, hypothetical or conditional propositions). Hypothetical propositions are either general or applied. The protasis and apodosis of a general hypothetical proposition are concepts; the protasis and apodosis of an applied hypothetical proposition are propositions. To state that if anything is a body deprived of support it falls downwards, is to state a general hypothetical proposition because ‹anything› and ‹it› are not used to refer to particular bases.

On the other hand, the proposition that if my pen is deprived of support it falls downwards, is an applied hypothetical proposition. It is, moreover, an application, though not the only one, of the preceding general hypothetical proposition. The transition from such a general hypothetical proposition to one of its applications is obvious enough. The main step consists in applying the concept of the protasis and apodosis to a particular basis. In our example this step finds expression in the replacement of ‹anything› by ‹my pen›.

An applied hypothetical proposition is fulfilled, if its protasis is theoretically appropriate. If its protasis is theoretically inappropriate it is unfulfilled. If a general hypothetical proposition is theoretically appropriate all its applications are necessarily also appropriate, whether they are fulfilled or not. The appropriateness or otherwise of any applied hypothetical proposition is not logically dependent on its being fulfilled or unfulfilled.

The above characterisation of hypothetical propositions agrees on the whole with the usual account of them. It is distinctive only in that it avoids all use of the notions of truth or falsehood, and uses instead theoretical appropriateness or inappropriateness. The reason for this choice of terms is the ambiguity of the terms "true" and "false" (see Chapter XXIII).

Not only empirical laws of nature, but other propositions, for example entailments and disposition-statements of various kinds (Chapter XIX), are hypothetical. On the other hand grammatically-conditional sentences can be used for propositions which are not hypothetical. Examples are those Russellian and similar formal implications which are factual propositions, that is, propositions of order zero. (Whether or not '$(x)(\phi(x) \supset \psi(x))$' is true '$\phi(a) \supset \psi(a)$' must be true if '$\phi(a)$' is false. In other words the inappropriateness of '$\phi(a)$' entails the appropriateness of '$\phi(a) \supset \psi(a)$'.)

As a fourth requirement empirical laws of nature must be empirical in a sense which implies more than merely that experiment and observation must be in some way relevant to them. In defining "empirical proposition" more precisely, I am trying to do justice to Kant's use of "not transcending possible experience" and to similar notions whose meaning can be better gleaned from their authors' use than from the explicit definitions given. The following characterisation of empirical propositions resembles Popper's characterisation of falsifiable propositions.[1]

We are led to a definition of empirical propositions by considering the role of experiment and observation in empirical inquiries. The simplest propositions describing experiments and observations are ostensive propositions, that is, propositions by whose statement we apply ostensive concepts. Yet ostensive propositions are not sufficient for this purpose. It is often necessary to describe experiments and observations by the negation of ostensive propositions, and by conjunctions of propositions the members of which conjunctions are themselves ostensive propositions or negations of such propositions. Not all such conjunctions, only those which are not internally inconsistent, can conceivably describe experiments or observations.

Of ostensive propositions, of their negations, and of internally consistent conjunctions of such propositions, we might say that they "describe possible experience". Empirical laws of nature do not describe possible experience, but neither do they "transcend" it. A more precise way of putting this is to say that an empirical law of nature must be incompatible with some proposition of the preceding type.

In accordance with these considerations I shall say that a proposition is empirical if, and only if, it is an ostensive proposition or the negation of an ostensive proposition, or a conjunction whose

[1] *Logik der Forschung* (Vienna, 1935).

members are ostensive propositions or negations of ostensive propositions, or lastly a proposition which is incompatible with a proposition of any of these types.

The empirical law of nature that all bodies deprived of support fall downwards is an empirical proposition, because it is incompatible, for example, with the internally consistent conjunction that my pen is deprived of support and does not fall downwards. It does not matter that this conjunction of an ostensive and a negated ostensive proposition happens to be theoretically inappropriate. The formal implication '(x) (x is a body deprived of support $\supset x$ falls downwards)' is likewise empirical. It is, of course, not also hypothetical in the sense defined above.

Fifthly, an empirical law of nature must entitle us to infer from unobserved instances of its protasis unobserved instances of its apodosis. One might even characterise the nature of these inferences further, by adding that the protasis of an empirical law of nature does not entail its apodosis. Since, however, as I hope to show, an empirical law of nature neither is nor entails an entailment-proposition, there is no need to insist on this qualification.

By saying that an empirical law of nature entitles us to make inferences from unobserved instances of its protasis to unobserved instances of its apodosis, it is implied that such a law is more than a concise report of past observations, and in particular that in addition it is a means of prediction. The empirical law of nature, for example, that if anything is a body deprived of support it will fall downwards, can be used to predict the behaviour of any body which is ever deprived of support.

We turn now to the question how these requirements can be satisfied. Apart from theories which reach their answer by postulating propositions *sui generis*, I know of no account of empirical laws of nature which satisfies all the requirements just stipulated. Of these latter accounts I shall briefly examine only what I shall call the "logical" and the "factual" theories, my reason being that they present us with an apparent dilemma whose solution, as I venture to think, leads to the solution of the problem. The dilemma in question might be expressed by saying that although the requirements of the hypothetical and the empirical character in an empirical law of nature cannot be shown to be incompatible requirements, it nevertheless seems *prima facie* as if no empirical proposition could be hypothetical and no hypothetical proposition empirical.

On the logical theory, to state an empirical law of nature is to state a logically necessary proposition, more precisely an entailment. This theory fails to rise to the empirical character in empirical laws of nature. A defender would therefore have to dispute the requirement, and argue that empirical laws of nature only seem empirical. He would consequently have to explain why empirical laws of nature do, in fact, so seem.

This he might seek to show by comparing an observer or experimenter with a child who "sees" that 1 and 1 must equal 2—that that is, as we would say, a logically necessary proposition—but who in order to discover that $15 + 3$ makes 18 has to resort to counting, or who again sees that $1 + 1$ cannot equal 3—that this is a logically impossible proposition—but yet has to count apples to discover that $15 + 3$ does not make 19. Just as the difficulties of dealing with the larger amounts, where the necessity of the result ceases to be "seen", do not make the statement of a difficult sum any less a necessary statement, so, a defender of the logical theory might argue, the scientist's inability to "see" any necessary truth or falsehood in a law of nature, and his need to have recourse to experiment, does not imply that the law itself is really empirical.

He might further hold that while true empirical laws are entailments, and thus logically necessary, false empirical laws are false empirical propositions. This view implies that we sometimes not only do not know whether or not a logical proposition, *i.e.* a proposition of first order, is logically necessary, but also whether a proposition is logical or empirical. The first of these kinds of ignorance is quite possible. An example might be our not knowing whether or not Fermat's last theorem is entailed by the postulates of a system of arithmetic. I do not think that our ignorance is ever of the second kind. But if we sometimes do not know whether a proposition is logical or empirical, we must necessarily also doubt its empirical falsifiability, and *a fortiori* every claim that it has been falsified.

It must be insisted, in view of these contentions, that to show, however plausibly, that some apparently empirical propositions might after all be heavily disguised entailments, is not to prove that empirical laws are entailments. Similarly a valid argument to the effect that alternative accounts of empirical laws are faulty does not prove the logical theory, unless it and its alternatives are shown to exhaust all the possibilities.

The factual theory is an important though by no means the only alternative to the logical theory. According to this every empirical law is a Russellian or similar formal implication, of order zero. Since such formal implications are not hypothetical, because necessarily appropriate if unfulfilled, the advocates of the factual theory have to dispute the requirement that empirical laws must be hypothetical. It must consequently be explained why they seem hypothetical. This might be done by a distinction between empirical propositions which are apparently, and empirical propositions which are not even apparently, hypothetical, on lines which are familiar from "attitude" theories in ethics.

Logical and factual theories about empirical laws of nature seem to have the following two assumptions in common. They imply firstly that to state an empirical law is to state either a logically necessary or else an empirical proposition: they do not contemplate the possibility of, for instance, the conjunction of a logically necessary and an empirical proposition, or again the possibility of a rule. They secondly imply that empirical laws are propositions by whose statement one asserts an inclusion or an exclusion. According to the logical theory the inclusion is schematically characterised as '('P' entails 'Q')', the exclusion by '('P' entails 'not-Q')'. According to the factual theory the schematic representation of the inclusion is '$((x).P(x) \supset Q(x))$', of the exclusion '$((x).P(x) \supset \text{not-}Q(x))$'.

Once these assumptions are explicitly stated, it becomes apparent that they lack cogency. The first is clearly not implied by our requirements. It has in fact been rejected by philosophers who hold that empirical laws of nature are disguised rules. This suggestion, however, explains neither the hypothetical nor the empirical character of empirical laws and there is no need to consider it further.

The second assumption, namely that in stating an empirical law of nature one is stating a relation of inclusion or exclusion between its protasis and its apodosis, rests on the more general assumption that two concepts or classes *can only stand* in the relation of inclusion or exclusion, or overlap. To state an empirical law is not to state an overlap. For example if 'body deprived of support' and 'body falling downwards' overlapped, then the proposition that all bodies deprived of support fall downwards would not be an empirical law. By ruling out the possibility of overlap between protasis and apodosis we are, it is inferred, left with only the possibilities of inclusion or exclusion. This, however, was seen to be a mistake (Chapters V, VI) since it leaves out of account the possibility of the inexact logical relations, of inclusion-or-overlap and exclusion-or-overlap, between ostensive concepts. The apparent dilemma between the logical and the factual accounts of empirical laws, and with it the problem of their logical status, would seem to become soluble, if we reject the groundless assumptions shared by the two accounts. Let us try this approach.

To use, for stating an empirical law, a grammatically-conditional sentence such as ‹if anything is a *P* then it is a *Q*› (or ‹if anything is a *P* then it is not a *Q*›), is to state, as the empirical law, a conjunction of two propositions. The first of them is a logical proposition, and it is that the ostensive concepts for which ‹*P*› and ‹*Q*› are used stand in the relation of inclusion-or-overlap (or exclusion-or-overlap). The second proposition is factual; to state it is to state that anything and everything is in fact either not a *P* or else a *Q* (either not a *P* or else not a *Q*). The second proposition might be expressed in formalised language as a Russellian or similar formal implication. It is in any case a factual proposition, that is, a proposition of order zero.

We may, for example, use ‹if anything is a magnetised piece of iron then it attracts iron filings› or ‹if anything is a swan then it is not black› for empirical laws, that is, for conjunctions of the type just described schematically. Thus in stating the first empirical law, one states that the ostensive concepts, for which ‹attract iron filings› and ‹magnetised piece of iron› are being used, stand in the logical relation of inclusion-or-overlap, and that as a matter of fact anything and everything either is not an instance of the latter concept or is an instance of the former. The logical proposition which is the first member of this conjunction, and the factual proposition which is its second member, are logically independent. In stating that the logical relation of inclusion-or-overlap holds between two ostensive concepts we do not imply either that, in the universe, every instance of the first concept is in fact also an instance of the second, or that this is not so. We do not even imply that every instance of the first concept which is, ever has been, or ever will be observed, is also an instance of the second concept, nor do we imply that this is not so.

I believe that this account will be found to satisfy all the five requirements. Of the first and the second we may obviously say so. An empirical law is, further, a general hypothetical proposition in the sense in which the appropriateness of such a proposition entails the appropriateness of any of its applications, and in which no application which is unfulfilled is therefore necessarily appropriate. As an example consider the conjunction: 'falling downwards' includes-or-overlaps with 'being a body deprived of support' and anything and everything is in fact either not a body deprived of support or is falling downwards. The appropriateness of this proposition entails the appropriateness of any of its applications, for example the appropriateness of the conjunction: 'falling downwards' includes-or-overlaps with 'being a body deprived of support' and my pen is either not a body deprived of support or is falling downwards. If this application is unfulfilled because my pen is not deprived of support, then the second member of the conjunction is necessarily appropriate, but not also its first member, and therefore not the whole conjunction. Thus according to the suggested account of empirical laws, an unfulfilled application of an empirical law is not necessarily appropriate.

The second member of the conjunction: that 'falling downwards' includes-or-overlaps with 'being a body deprived of support' and that anything and everything is as a matter of fact either not a body deprived of support or is falling downwards, is incompatible with the factual proposition that my pen is a body deprived of support and is yet not falling downwards. Since the second member of the conjunction is incompatible with this proposition, the whole conjunction, that is, the empirical law, is incompatible with it. Since, moreover, the proposition with which the empirical law is incompatible is an internally consistent conjunction of an ostensive and the negation of another ostensive proposition, the empirical law is, in accordance with our fourth requirement, empirical.

Lastly, the fifth requirement is satisfied. According to it an empirical law entitles us to make inferences from unobserved instances of its protasis to unobserved instances of its apodosis. While the logical member of any conjunction which is an empirical law does not entitle us to such an inference, the factual proposition which is its other member gives us this right. The whole conjunction thus fulfils the fifth requirement.

If in the above account we substitute any exact logical relation for the inexact one in the first member of the empirical law, then its second member becomes either superfluous or incompatible with its first member. In order to test this let us, for example, assume that we are using the sentence ‹if anything is a swan it is white› for an empirical law, that is, for the conjunctive proposition that ‘white’ includes-or-overlaps with ‘swan’, and that everything is as a matter of fact either not a swan or white. If we replace the inclusion-or-overlap by the entailment that ‘being a swan’ entails ‘being white’ then the second member of the conjunction (and the same will hold for any of its applications) becomes a logically necessary proposition which is entailed by the first member. If we replace the inclusion-or-overlap by an overlap between ‘swan’ and ‘white’ then the first member of the conjunction would entail that some particular swans are in fact not white, which is incompatible with the factual proposition forming the second member of the conjunction. Lastly, if we replace the inclusion-or-overlap between ‘white’ and ‘swan’ by the entailment that ‘being a swan’ entails ‘not being white’, then the first and second members of the conjunction become incompatible with each other.

Since empirical laws for which mathematical expressions are customarily used have so far not been discussed explicitly, it seems advisable to show their place in the proposed account. This can be done by means of an example from elementary physics. The formula "$s = \frac{1}{2}.g.t^2$" is frequently used for a quantitative empirical law of free fall. In the formula "s" stands for the numerical result of measuring by means of a measuring rod or other instrument, within a certain margin of exactness, the distance travelled by a freely falling body; "t" stands for the result of measuring by means of a stop-watch or other instrument, again within a certain margin of exactness, the time taken by the body's journey; "g" stands for the acceleration due to gravity, whose numerical value is given within certain limits. It is convenient to say that "$\frac{1}{2}.g.t^2$" stands for the modified result of measuring the time taken by the journey. The modification, of course, consists in squaring t and multiplying the result by $\frac{1}{2}g$.

The whole formula is thus used for the empirical law that if a distance measurement associated with a falling body has a certain numerical value, then and only then does the modified time measurement associated with the body have this value. Since the concepts of its protasis and apodosis, for which we also use "s" and "$\frac{1}{2}.g.t^2$", are ostensive, this quantitative law is clearly covered by the general account of empirical laws. The meaning of "physical measurement" cannot indeed be explained without recourse at some stage to exemplification.

When using the formula "$s = \frac{1}{2}.g.t^2$" in calculations we idealise the ostensive concepts of the quantitative law, in particular by assuming an exact correspondence between the results of measurements of time and distance on the one hand, and members of the series of real numbers on the other. The nature of such idealisations was considered earlier in Chapter VII.

The above account of empirical laws is relevant to a number of further philosophical questions. Its bearing on the problem of causality and on the definition of general propositions will have to be dealt with in a few words. If, as is often done, the words ‹cause and effect› are used only in the sense in which we have used "protasis and apodosis of a hypothesis", then the philosophical problems of causal propositions and of empirical laws will be identical. Yet one often speaks of causal propositions in an altogether different sense, for example when one asks whether only external events or also impressions can be causally related.

CHAPTER XII

LOGICAL PROPOSITIONS IN DEDUCTIVE AND REGRESSIVE REASONING AND IN DEFINITION

IT is not as a rule for their own sake that we state or consider logical propositions—in particular entailments—but in order to promote efficiency in our use of factual propositions. When we try to discover by deductive or regressive reasoning to what logical propositions we do, or in certain circumstances would, stand committed; when we seek to exhibit the logical content and the internal consistency of concepts; it is mostly with this purpose in mind. Our theme in the present chapter, then, will be the place of logical propositions in the activities of deductive and regressive reasoning and of definition.

Of deductive reasoning it is often said that it is not concerned with establishing its premises. Not only our establishing the truth of 'p', but even our noticing that 'p' entails 'q', are regarded as merely preliminary to the actual deduction of 'q'. Since, however, to notice that 'q' is entailed by 'p' is to notice that on the assumption of the truth of 'p' one is *entitled* to deduce 'q' from it, it is difficult to see what is left to the actual deduction; apart perhaps from the formal declaration that one has not only noticed one's right to the conclusion, but actually drawn it. 148439

But if we look at syllogistic and mathematical reasoning, which are the most obvious examples of deduction, it becomes clear that they do not, or do not solely, consist in such formal declarations. Deductive reasoning does not *presuppose* that one has noticed an entailment between the premises and the conclusion. It aims at occasioning us to *notice* such an entailment (or a negation of it) and, if successful, it ends there. In unsuccessful deductive reasoning we *fail* to notice that the premises entail or do not entail the conclusion.

It seems to me that one can give a fairly adequate description of deductive reasoning by saying that it is exemplified by syllogistic and mathematical reasoning; and that it is a more or less well-regulated activity by which one aims at bringing entailments or their negations to one's notice. If our deductive reasoning is successful then the logical propositions noticed are answers to the question what concepts or propositions are entailed by our premisses, or to the question whether or not the premisses entail a specified concept or proposition.

Deductive reasoning cannot always be distinguished clearly from other kinds of conceptual thinking. Thus it would often be hard to decide whether one has brought an entailment to one's notice in a more or less systematic activity or whether one has just noticed it —effortlessly. Phrases such as "obviously" or "follows immediately" often mark cases where there is this sort of doubt. Moreover, deductive reasoning and calculation are often difficult to distinguish, meaning here, by calculation, the regulated manipulation of uninterpreted marks. Such calculation may be a stage in deductive reasoning or again it may not. Lastly, it may be doubted whether a regulated activity aimed at bringing entailments or their negations to one's notice is sufficiently well-regulated to deserve the name of "deductive reasoning".

Primitive entailments and other non-excessive entailments have certainly a place in deductive reasoning. But whether excessive entailments such as '('p and q' entails 'p')', self-entailments such as '('p' entails 'p')' and entailments with internally inconsistent antecedents ever enter deductive reasoning at all might be doubted.[1] Yet in some instances of deductive reasoning we bring certain entailments to our notice, and only then do we observe that they belong to one of these dubious kinds. In particular, in so-called reductions *ad absurdum* we often notice the inconsistency of our premisses only after having brought to our notice entailments with inconsistent antecedents. For example, we may first bring '('p and q' entails 'r')' and '('p and q' entails 'not-r')' to our notice, and only then see that 'p and q' is internally inconsistent.

From deductive reasoning we can distinguish regressive reasoning, though not always sharply. I have discussed the regressive or "critical" method of reasoning and its relevance to the present

[1] See, e.g., E. J. Nelson, 'Intensional Relations', *Mind*, vol. 39 (1930).

inquiry (Chapter I). Regressive reasoning is like deductive in that it often aims at bringing entailments or their negations to one's notice. Yet while in deductive reasoning the rules which must be satisfied by our logical propositions are explicitly accepted, in regressive reasoning the question of their acceptance must itself be decided. As has been pointed out earlier, recording the actual use of words is an important aid to regressive reasoning, but must not be confused with it. For just as the actual behaviour of people might violate the law of the land in spite of their best intentions to obey it, so might a perfectly correct record of the use of words be at the same time a record of the violation of implicitly accepted rules. The logical propositions which we try to bring to our notice by regressive reasoning may be of any kind.

Deductive and regressive reasoning aim at, and if successful end with, bringing logical propositions to our notice. The activities of definition, in many senses of the term, consist in stating logical propositions.

There is little doubt that in stating so-called "implicit definitions" one is stating entailments. Implicit definitions of predicates are usually characterised as conveying partial information about the content of the implicitly defined predicate, and as not indicating to which objects the predicate is applicable. We have seen that all non-excessive entailments fulfil these conditions. It is usual to regard the axioms which implicitly define geometrical and other non-ostensive mathematical concepts as typical examples of such implicit definitions. To state them is to state non-excessive entailments relating certain non-ostensive concepts, or it is, as we have said, to indicate the logical content of these concepts.

To "interpret" a system of implicit definitions is either to indicate ostensive rules which govern the use of the implicitly defined concepts; or, where this cannot be done without inconsistency, it is to indicate the relation between the implicitly defined non-ostensive concepts and some ostensive concepts, for example by showing that the former simplify the latter or that they can be combined with them to form ostensive concepts. In general, what has been said about entailments by the statement of which one indicates the logical content of concepts, about their different types, and about the applicability of the related concepts, is relevant to the question of the nature and "interpretation" of implicit definitions.

To define a predicate *implicitly* is not to state a rule to the effect that certain words or other signs can be used interchangeably as the same concept. To define a predicate *explicitly* is always to state such an interchangeability-rule. This is generally agreed. Whether, however, by stating an explicit definition one is, apart from stating an interchangeability-rule, also stating a logical proposition and, if so, what kind of logical proposition, is a matter of some dispute. While the controversy in itself is mainly verbal, it is yet connected with more important questions about the relation between interchangeability-rules and logical propositions, especially logical propositions whose statement is the statement of an internal consistency or inconsistency.

As an illustration, consider the well-worn explicit definition in which the definiendum is the predicate "father" and the definiens the predicate "male parent". To give this definition is, according to some logicians,[1] merely to state a rule to the effect that the word ‹father› can be used interchangeably with the phrase ‹male parent›. Whether the interchangeability-rule is stated as a record of past usage by some people, or as a proposal of future usage, is of no importance in the present context. According to other logicians,[2] the definitions consist not only in stating the interchangeability-rule but in stating also the internal *consistency* of the concept for which the interchangeable phrases can both be used. Instead of deciding the verbal dispute by appealing to "common usage", which here as in most disputes between logicians seems neutral, I shall distinguish between two types of explicit definition, namely, interchangeability-definitions and consistency-definitions. Only the latter state an interchangeability-rule *and* an internal consistency.

In discussing propositions to the effect that a concept or predicate is internally consistent or inconsistent, I shall assume that the concept in question is compound. For not only are the definientia

---

[1] For example, *Principia Mathematica*, vol. I, p. 11.
[2] For example, Poincaré, *Science et méthode* (Paris, 1920), p. 162.

of explicit consistency-definitions usually compound, but the question of the consistency of simple ostensive and some non-ostensive concepts has already been discussed (in Chapter v). Instead of considering all the kinds of compound concepts, I shall, moreover, consider only conjunctions, thereby avoiding unnecessary complications of a purely technical nature. Lastly, I shall, for the same reason, limit myself to statements of the internal consistency or inconsistency of conjunctions with three members only, say 'P', 'Q' and 'R'. I shall thus ask what logical proposition we are asserting in asserting that 'P and Q and R' is an internally consistent or inconsistent statement.

In saying that 'P and Q and R' is internally inconsistent we might *first* of all mean that ('P' entails 'not-Q') or ('P' entails 'not-R') or ('Q' entails 'not-R') or ('P and Q' entails 'not-R'). Instead of this alternation we could have chosen any other which was formed, like this one, in the following manner: Take the conjunction whose inconsistency is asserted and every subconjunction of it, and divide each of them into two subconjunctions. From each of these pairs form an entailment, of which one member of the pair is the antecedent and the negated other member the consequent. Lastly, form the alternation of all these entailments.

Our first definition of inconsistency (and consistency) is fundamental, in the sense that we can use it even if we are committed only to primitive logical propositions. Using this definition we can assert the inconsistency of conjunctions without asserting entailments with inconsistent antecedents, and indeed without asserting any excessive entailments whatever. For example, to assert the inconsistency of "green and blue and red" according to our definition, is to assert the alternation '(('green' entails 'not-blue') or ('green' entails 'not-red') or ('blue' entails 'not-red') or ('green and red' entails 'not-blue'))'. The last member of this alternation is excessive and has an internally inconsistent antecedent. However, to assert an alternation is not to assert all its members.

In saying that 'P and Q and R' is internally inconsistent we might *secondly* mean that 'P and Q' entails 'not-R'. Instead of this entailment we could have chosen any entailment which, like this one, is formed in the following manner: Take the conjunction whose internal inconsistency is asserted and divide it into two subconjunctions. To assert the internal inconsistency of the conjunction is to assert that one of the subconjunctions entails the negation of the other. If we do not admit either excessive entailments, or entailments whose antecedents are inconsistent conjunctions, or whose consequents are exclusive alternations, we could not, using the second definition, assert the inconsistency of some conjunctions. For to assert, for example, the inconsistency of 'green and blue and red' would be to assert that 'green and blue' entails 'not-red', that is, an entailment which is excessive and whose antecedent is inconsistent.

The definientia of the first and the second definition of "('P and Q and R') is internally inconsistent" do not generally entail each other. Whether or not they are logically equivalent depends on one's non-primitive commitments of second order (see Chapter IX). If we accept, after the fashion of the system of strict implication, the unrestricted principles of contraposition and antilogism, and what we might call the principle of excessive entailments according to which, for example, '('P' entails 'Q')' entails '('P and R' entails 'Q')', then the definientia would entail each other. In a system in which excessive entailments are not admitted the definientia would not be logically equivalent. That the second definition is less cumbersome than the first must not blind us to the wider applicability of the more cumbersome definition.

If we admit excessive entailments, but not also entailments with internally inconsistent antecedents, then we can define the internal inconsistency of 'P and Q and R' in yet a further way. In such a system the proposition '('P and Q and R' entails 'P')' would be appropriate if, and only if, 'P and Q and R' is internally consistent. By saying that 'P and Q and R' is internally consistent we might then *thirdly* mean that 'P and Q and R' entails 'P'. Instead, we could have chosen any entailment whose antecedent is 'P and Q and R' and whose consequent is either a member of the antecedent or any conjunction of its members. In particular, we could have chosen the entailment by the assertion of which we assert that 'P and Q and R' entails (and is entailed by) itself. The system in which the third definition could be employed does not seem to me in any way far-fetched. I believe, on the contrary, that many people, among them some logicians, would describe their use of "entails" or its cognates in a way which implies the admittance of excessive entailments, but not also of entailments with inconsistent antecedents. The fact that all or some of the latter are widely regarded as paradoxical lends some support to this view.

To give what we have called a "consistency-definition', as opposed to a mere interchangeability-definition of a predicate, is thus (1) to state a rule to the effect that two signs can be used interchangeably as the same concept and (2) to state a logical proposition as described in one of our three definitions of consistency. Other definitions of consistency are, of course, possible. However, according to all of them, to assert the internal consistency of a conjunction would be to assert either a simple logical proposition or a compound proposition each of whose components is a logical proposition.

Since to assert the internal consistency of a conjunction is to assert a logical proposition, the proposition by the assertion of which we state the consistency of, for example, "male parent", neither entails nor is entailed by the interchangeability-rule for "male parent" and "father". For rules do not entail, and are not entailed by, logical propositions. The rule to the effect that the words ⟨father⟩ and ⟨male parent⟩ can be used interchangeably has just as little to do with their use as an internally consistent concept, as the rule for the interchangeability of ⟨oh⟩ and ⟨ah⟩ has with their use as an expression of pain.

If an interchangeability-rule does not entail any logical proposition, then it does not, of course, entail any bilateral entailment. This is particularly obvious if we adopt the third definition of consistency—on the assumption, of course, that we admit excessive entailments while not also admitting entailments with inconsistent antecedents. For while we can then accept, for instance, an interchangeability-rule to the effect that "square circle" and "squircle" can be used interchangeably, our acceptance of this rule does not render appropriate the inappropriate entailment-propositions '("squircle" entails and is entailed by "square circle")' or '('square circle' entails 'square circle')'. In a system in which entailments with inconsistent antecedents are inappropriate, their inappropriateness remains unaffected by the acceptance of any interchangeability-rule whatsoever.

A confusion between interchangeability-rules and bilateral entailments may lend plausibility to the following account of the nature of entailments, an account which is, I believe, implicit in the writings of some contemporary philosophers of language. To avoid a lengthy exegesis of their writings, I shall criticise this theory as one which is made attractive by its simplicity apart from the question of whether or not it has been held by anybody. It is based on the following two assumptions.

First, that every appropriate entailment is entailed by some appropriate bilateral entailment. In other words, to every appropriate entailment say '('P' entails 'Q')' there exists a "remainder" 'X' different from 'P', such that 'P' entails 'Q and X' and 'Q and X' entails 'P'. This assumption, which is very often made and is incorporated in all the usual interpretations of the propositional calculus and Boolean algebra, has been discussed at some length under the name of the "complement-thesis" (in Chapter v). Then we found it to be false for ostensive concepts.

The second assumption is that every bilateral entailment is entailed by an interchangeability-rule. Now if the first assumption were correct this would mean that *every* entailment is entailed by an interchangeability-rule, that is, by a rule the acceptance and satisfiability of which depends wholly on our choice. Even if, as we must, we drop the first assumption, we might still hold that every entailment which had a remainder is entailed by an interchangeability-rule. However, even this modest statement is false, for as we have seen not even self-entailments are entailed by interchangeability-rules.

From the logical independence of interchangeability-rules and logical propositions it also follows that bilateral entailments do not entail interchangeability-rules. For instance, '("coloured" entails and is entailed by "extended")' does not entail the rule to the effect that "coloured" and "extended" can be used interchangeably or that they are synonymous. Indeed, most people who are committed to the bilateral entailment between "coloured" and "extended" reject the interchangeability-rule without inconsistency.

To sum up: Our discussion has shown that every kind of logical proposition treated in the preceding chapters is employed either in each of the activities of deductive reasoning, regressive reasoning and definition, or at least in some of them. This applies in particular to the *prima-facie* useless self-entailments and excessive entailments, with or without internally inconsistent antecedents. Indeed, once the conceptual thinker, that is, the accepter of ostensive concepts, ventures beyond the narrow confines of their acceptance and application, he must commit himself to logical propositions which, though compatible with primitive logic, no longer belong to it.

CHAPTER XIII

VALIDITY AND LOGICAL FORM

ALTHOUGH the topics which have been discussed so far belong to logic, no mention has been made of what may well appear as the central problem of the subject: namely, the problem of the relation between validity and logical form. In the present chapter I hope to show that, and why, this omission was not really serious. For this purpose I shall first of all try to clarify the two notions, and then I shall ask whether a proposition's form can ever be on the one hand a natural sign or on the other a sufficient reason for its validity. To both these questions the answer will be in the negative.

The terms "validity" and "logical form" are used in so many different, and often vague, ways that the definitions which I shall propose are hardly likely to find universal acceptance. I nevertheless believe that, so far as the problem of the relation of validity to logical form is concerned, the definitions I am to propose are relevant, and not a means merely of replacing one problem by another.

What is often meant by "valid logical proposition" can be expressed in terms of the notion—introduced earlier—of theoretical appropriateness. We recall it by means of an example. To state that the logical proposition '('round' overlaps with 'green')' is appropriate, is (according to Chapter IV above) to state that an accepter of the rules governing the use of 'round' and 'green' would not, by stating the logical proposition, violate the conjunction of these rules. And we recall (from Chapter III) that in stating about any activity that it does not violate a certain rule, one is stating a logical proposition. For the proposition that an activity does not violate a rule entails and is entailed by the proposition that the indicative of the rule and the proposition describing the activity are compatible.

In order to define the notion of an appropriate logical proposition more generally, and perhaps more clearly, let us use the following abbreviations. Let us write '$l('P_1' \dots 'P_n')$' or briefly 'l' for a logical proposition which relates the concepts 'P_1' ... 'P_n'; let us write '$r('P_1' ... 'P_n')$' or briefly 'r' for the conjunction of rules governing the use of these concepts and (as in Chapter III) '$i(r)$' for the indicative of 'r'. Lastly, let us write 's' for the proposition that an accepter of 'r' states 'l'. Using these abbreviations we can say that 'l' is appropriate if, and only if, an accepter of 'r' would by stating 'l' not violate 'r', in other words if, and only if, '$i(r)$' does not entail 'not-s', that is, is compatible with 's'. In stating that 'l' is appropriate one is thus clearly stating a logical proposition. This latter proposition—the proposition '('l' is appropriate)'—unlike 'l' itself, which may or may not be a compatibility-proposition and may or may not be of first order, is always a compatibility-proposition of first order. That it is a compatibility-proposition is obvious; and that it is of first order is clear if we consider that every indicative of a rule and every proposition entailed by it describes human activities and is thus of order zero. Consequently to state 'l' is not to state the same proposition as to state that 'l' is appropriate.

It is, of course, true that "valid logical proposition" is often used in senses to which an explicit definition in terms of appropriateness would not do justice. Thus the word ‹valid› is often used to mark the acceptance or the recommendation of a rule. The person who says that '('raven' entails 'black')' is "valid" may merely wish to record his or other people's acceptance of a rule 'r('raven', 'black')' or merely recommend it for acceptance. The person who says that '('('P' entails 'Q')' entails '('P and R' entails 'Q')')' is "valid" may similarly only wish to record or propose the acceptance of a rule 'r('entails')' and thus to record or propose a commitment to a non-primitive logical proposition of second order. In other senses of the term, valid and invalid propositions are often contrasted with true and false propositions. This use is often vague. In particular, it is often not clear how far truth and validity on the one hand, and falsehood and invalidity on the other, are species of the same genus. Moreover, any vagueness of the terms "true" and "false" affects the terms "validity" and "invalidity" defined in terms of the former. (For a discussion of various concepts and theories of truth see Chapter XXIII.)

I now turn to the notion of logical form. Generally speaking to describe the logical form of a proposition is to describe those of its features which are considered relevant to the purposes of logical inquiry. In describing propositions, for example, in terms of concepts and bases of various types, one is describing their logical form. Other ways of describing propositions can with equal right be called "formal".

Since written signs and sequences of signs are frequently used as propositions, it is possible and usual to describe the form of a proposition by emphasising or modifying certain features of a sign or a combination of signs used as a proposition. We exhibit, for example, the form of 'all men are bipeds', by turning the phrase ⟨all men are bipeds⟩, which is used as this proposition, into the formula ⟨all X's are Y's⟩.

Clearly, some formulae are better suited than others to exhibit features which we desire to emphasise in propositions. If we assume, for instance, that for some reason or other the distinction between propositions of order zero, propositions of order one, and mixed propositions is important, then the formula ⟨all X's are Y's⟩ derived, for example, from the phrase ⟨all men are bipeds⟩ will be quite unsuitable. For since the phrase ⟨all men are bipeds⟩ can be used as a collective conjunction of order zero, as an entailment of first order, and as an empirical law of nature—which is a conjunction of a proposition of first order and a proposition of order zero—the formula does not exhibit those distinguishable features whose emphasis is considered important. It is desirable that one type of formula correspond to one type of proposition. This reasonable requirement, that ambiguity in the exhibition of differences which one wishes to emphasise be avoided, is a far cry from the view that one and only one way of distinguishing types of proposition, and one and only one way of exhibiting the corresponding differences by formulae, is *the* way, and intrinsically preferable to all others.

There are as many ways of describing the form of propositions as there are views about what differences it is logically important to distinguish. Yet as far as logical propositions are concerned their form is usually described in essentially similar ways. The following definition of the form of a logical proposition will be seen to come near to definitions of logical form in terms of logical constants and variables. It is, I believe, sufficiently general to be relevant to most views according to which valid logical propositions are valid *in virtue of* their form, or according to which certain forms of logical propositions are validating forms.

To describe a logical proposition *relating concepts* is to identify the concepts of its antecedent and consequent, and the manner of their combination by means of 'and', 'not', 'or'. To describe a logical proposition *relating propositions* is to identify the concepts and the bases of the related propositions. If we describe, not the logical proposition itself but merely *its form*, then instead of identifying the different concepts we merely indicate that they are different, and instead of identifying the different bases we again merely indicate that they are different.

It is usual to exhibit the form of a logical proposition by modifying a phrase which is used as a logical proposition, and thus to turn the phrase into a formula. I shall do this by replacing the signs which are used as concepts such as ‹green›, ‹P›, etc., by ‹X›, ‹Y›, ‹Z›, and the signs which serve to identify bases such as ‹this›, ‹that›, ‹my pen› by ‹x›, ‹y›, ‹z›. I shall thus say that '('x is X' entails 'x is Y')' exhibits the logical form of '('my pen is black' entails 'my pen is coloured')' and that the form of '('Triangle' entails 'plane figure')' is exhibited by '('X' entails 'Y')'.

Before turning to our main question, namely, the relation between validity and form, some comments on the above definition of logical form may be permissible. First, it must be kept in mind that it is in practice often difficult to decide whether a formula indicates all the different concepts which are related by the logical proposition. This difficulty, however, will not affect our argument. Secondly, in speaking of the form of logical propositions we shall consider only propositions by whose statement only one logical relation is applied. The discussion of compound logical propositions would add nothing essentially new and would be technically more complicated. Thirdly, instead of replacing identifiable concepts and bases separately by "variables", it is sometimes sufficient to replace identifiable propositions as wholes by "variables".

Whenever the logical form is sufficiently clearly exhibited by means of "propositional variables" only, it is not less clearly exhibited by the method described above. Conversely, however, replacement of whole propositions does not always exhibit the form of logical propositions. It is, for example, not available for simplifying logical propositions which relate inapplicable concepts.

In considering the relation between form and validity I shall avoid the ambiguous phrase "in virtue of". Instead, I shall ask whether the concepts 'being of ... form' (the dots indicating a description or exhibition of the form), and 'being a valid logical proposition' can be related as the protasis and the apodosis of an empirical law of nature, or as the antecedent and the consequent of an entailment. In other words, I shall ask whether the form of a logical proposition is ever a natural sign, or a sufficient reason, of its validity.

Now the form of a logical proposition is never a natural sign of its validity in the sense that 'having ... form' is the protasis of an empirical law and 'being a valid proposition' its apodosis. For an empirical law of nature relates ostensive and therefore zero-order concepts, while of the two concepts 'having ... form' and 'being a valid proposition' only the first is a concept of zero order. The second is of first order. For example, to describe the form of '('P' entails 'P')' is to state that ‹entails› is on either side flanked by the same capital letter. It is to state a factual proposition. On the other hand, to assert its validity is, as we have seen, to state a compatibility-proposition of first order.

It will further strengthen the general argument here being urged if we consider the widely held theory that the form of excessive entailments, with self-entailments as cores, is a natural sign of their validity. There is, indeed, a stronger form of the view, namely, that all *and only* such entailments (and certain compounds of them) are valid. But it will be enough if we deal with the weaker and less assailable of the two. Take, for example, the assertion that the logical form '('(x is X) and (x is Y)' entails '(x is X)')' is a natural sign of the validity (a) of the proposition '('(my pen is black) and (my pen is round)' entails '(my pen is black)')'; and (*b*) of the proposition '('(my pen is round) and (my pen is square)' entails '(my pen is round)')'. We have seen (in Chapter XII) that the validity or invalidity of these propositions depends on our second-order commitments. If, as we well may, we refuse to admit any excessive entailments, then neither entailment is valid; if we admit all excessive entailments, then both entailments are valid; if we admit excessive entailments whose antecedents are consistent, then the first, but not also the second, entailment is valid. Yet whatever our commitments, that is, whatever rules we accept, the form of the excessive entailments remains the same. It is therefore *not* the natural sign of their validity, in the sense in which sign and thing signified are connected by an empirical law.

We have likewise seen that a conceptual thinker may or may not be committed to all second-order logical propositions of form '('(' X ' entails ' Y ')' entails '(' X and Z ' entails ' Y ')')'. Yet whether or not these propositions are appropriate depends not on their form, but on the rules governing the use of the related concepts. Although valid with respect to one set of rules and invalid with respect to another the form of these propositions is the same. It cannot therefore be a natural sign of their validity.

That the logical form of at least some valid propositions is not a natural sign of their validity can perhaps most easily be seen in the case of logical propositions of first order relating ostensive concepts. Thus though '('green' entails 'coloured')' and '('green' entails 'round')' are both of form '(' X ' entails ' Y ')', the first of these propositions is valid but the second is not.

We have here shown by a general argument that the logical form of a valid logical proposition is not a natural sign of its validity, and we have illustrated the argument by examples. That the logical form of a valid logical proposition is not a sufficient reason for its validity can be shown in a precisely similar way. First of all, since 'having ... form' is a concept of order zero it does not entail 'being a valid logical proposition', which is a concept of first order. This general argument can be strengthened by discussing the view that the form of excessive entailments with self-entailments as their cores is the reason of their validity, and by using the same examples as were used in arguing that logical form is not the sign of logical validity.

If it is agreed that no valid logical proposition is valid *in virtue of its form*, in the sense that logical form is either a natural sign of or a sufficient reason for logical validity, we may ask next as a point of some interest how a view to the contrary could have arisen. The following seems a likely explanation. Most deductive arguments put forward in ordinary language contain much that is irrelevant to their validity. Attempts to formulate precepts for the separation of the relevant from the irrelevant lead to the discovery that this procedure can often be paralleled by a gradual transformation of phrases used as logical propositions into formulae which can be used to exhibit the relevant features of the logical propositions. If one overlooks the fact that a phrase which can be used in accordance with certain rules as a proposition is itself not a proposition, one may easily overlook the circumstance that any feature of the phrase considered apart from these rules is not a feature of the proposition. The step from this to the belief that a feature of the phrase is a natural sign or sufficient reason for a feature of the proposition is then easily taken.

It is, of course, highly convenient always to use the same phrase as the same proposition, and phrases of the same visual or auditory pattern as propositions of the same type. If we adhere to the convention to use only phrases of certain patterns as valid logical propositions then these patterns are *conventional* signs of their validity.

Many text-books of logic pour scorn on the belief that words or signs as such, that is, apart from rules accepted for their use, are natural signs or even sufficient reasons of the properties of the things to refer to which they are used. Yet by the doctrine of validity in virtue of form, the same text-books seem to imply or to suggest that patterns of word-sequences or sign-sequences are as such the natural signs of or even sufficient reasons of the validity of the propositions as which they are used.

The visual patterns of most phrases in natural languages are only very rarely reliable (conventional) signs of the validity of the propositions as which the phrases are used. Logicians have always been concerned with pointing to the degree of correlation between linguistic patterns and logical validity, and have often suggested changes in the rules of natural languages in order to increase this correlation. But the attempts to construct perfectly logical languages, although sometimes described as attempts to discover *the* ideal logical language, have in fact always been attempts to make visual patterns fully reliable *conventional* signs of logical validity.

We must mention here the achievement of modern mathematical logic, in particular of so-called meta-mathematics or proof-theory, in establishing such correlations. It has been shown for a number of important formalisations of logical and mathematical theories that the visual shapes of formulae (or sequences of formulae) can be seen, either immediately or as the result of purely mechanical procedures, to be (conventional) signs of valid or of invalid logico-mathematical propositions—such propositions being called "formally decidable". Although the scope of these formalisms goes far beyond the conception of the older logic it is by no means even in principle unlimited.[1]

Logic is not formal in the sense that its valid propositions are valid "in virtue of" their form, although we can to some extent arrange matters so that visual patterns become conventional signs of validity. The propositions of logic are, however, formal in the sense in which "formal" and "non-empirical" are used interchangeably. The primitive logical propositions of second and higher order are, moreover, formal in the sense that every conceptual thinker is committed to them. In this respect they are unlike all other propositions.

If they are not valid in virtue of their form, why then are valid logical propositions valid? To ask why, for example, the logical proposition '$l('P_1' \ldots 'P_n')$' is valid is, we have seen, to ask why an accepter of '$r('P_1' \ldots 'P_n')$' would not violate this rule by stating the logical proposition. The answer that nobody can violate 'r' unless he has accepted it, is true by definition. But it evades the question, whatever its precise meaning. Perhaps it is more to the point to emphasise again that we can choose to satisfy or violate a rule,

---

[1] See, for example, Turing, 'On computable numbers with an application to the Entscheidungsproblem', *Proc. London Math. Soc.*, ser. 2, vol. XLII.

PART II

THE APPLICABILITY OF CONCEPTS

CHAPTER XIV

DIRECTLY AND INDIRECTLY GIVEN BASES
OF OSTENSIVE CONCEPTS

IN Part I our main concern has been with logical relations and logical propositions. In Part II we shall be chiefly occupied with factual propositions—in particular with the different ways in which the concepts we employ in factual propositions are linked to experience. Yet much of what has been said in dealing with more specifically logical questions is relevant to the chapters which follow. Thus in considering the possible logical relations between concepts it will be remembered that we were forced to recognise a fundamental difference between (*a*) ostensive concepts, exemplified in experience, and (*b*) non-ostensive concepts whose connection with experience is more tenuous. It seems, therefore, natural to enter upon the second stage of our inquiry with a more detailed discussion of those propositions the statement of which consists in the application of ostensive concepts.

Any ostensive concept is, at least *prima facie*, applicable not only to distinct bases, but also to bases which are given in different modes. For example, one basis of the concept 'white piece of paper' may be given now directly in perception, and another indirectly by being remembered. Even if we do not wish to prejudge the question whether a directly and an indirectly given basis can possibly be "the same", there can be little doubt that to characterise a basis as being either directly or indirectly given, is quite different from characterising it as a basis to which the concept 'white piece of paper' or any other ostensive concept is applicable.

Before considering the differences between the two modes of given-ness, it may seem proper and useful to ask first of all what they have in common, that is, what is meant by simply stating that a basis is given at all—no matter whether directly or indirectly. In this all we can do by way of an answer is to point out again (as has been done in the Introduction) that ostensive concepts and their bases are distinct features in familiar situations. We might add that by saying that a basis is given we mean that some ostensive concept is applicable to it; or that by applying some such concept to it, one would not violate the rules governing the concept. These "definitions" are, of course, circular. But they serve the purpose of drawing attention to the features to which we wish to refer.

Traditionally the question as to how the bases ($\acute{v}\pi o\kappa\epsilon\acute{\iota}\mu\epsilon\nu a$, *fundamenta*, subjects, etc.) of ostensive concepts are given, has been answered by reference to space and time or to some kind of apprehension. Thus, on the one hand, it has been said in many different ways that any basis of any ostensive concept is located in time, or in space and time, or that the basis of every ostensive concept is a cross-section of time or space-time. On the other hand, it has again been said in many different ways that the basis of every ostensive concept is given in some intuitive and sensuous kind of apprehension, such as sensation, perception, memory or imagination. Indeed, one usually distinguishes ostensive from non-ostensive concepts not by reference to ostensive rules but by pointing out that only ostensive concepts have bases located in time or space or that these bases are intuitively apprehended.

The two ways just mentioned of characterising ostensive bases are clearly connected. What is sensed or perceived is spatially and temporally present, while what is remembered or imagined is, if located in space or time at all, spatially or temporally remote. In both these classifications the main distinction is between bases directly given on the one hand and indirectly given on the other. What is directly given is sensed or perceived and spatio-temporally present. What is indirectly given is remembered, expected, or imagined and spatially or temporally remote. In due course I shall discuss the various kinds of spatio-temporal location on the one hand and the various kinds of intuitive apprehension on the other. But first we must try to have the dichotomy between directly and indirectly given bases made more precise.

Some help can be derived from considering linguistic usage. There can be little doubt that the word ‹this›, for example, is often an indication that the basis of an ostensive concept is directly given, and there is similarly little doubt that the word ‹yesterday› frequently indicates that the basis of an ostensive concept is indirectly given. One might thus feel inclined to distinguish the cases where a basis is directly given by compiling a catalogue of words headed by ‹this›. Such a list would, of course, be very unreliable unless accompanied by a general description of the use of the words in identifying bases. One would have to say, for instance, that they are used as pointers. This way of describing their function would give rise to the question what, apart from literally pointing, constitutes pointing to a directly given basis.

Doubtless in learning the use of ostensive predicates we are at first wholly and in the later stages largely dependent on having some of their bases literally pointed at. On the other hand, much that is directly given is not capable of being pointed at, except in a sense which is so little reminiscent of literal acts of pointing, or so vaguely, that an explanation of the meaning of "directly given" in terms of pointing does not make the former notion clearer. It is, therefore, desirable to try to formulate the distinction between directly and indirectly given bases in some other way.

Let us assume that we are applying an ostensive concept ‘P’ to some basis b. And let us say that b is a directly given basis of ‘P’ if, and only if, we can apply ‘P’ to b without at the same time applying to b some other concept, say ‘Q’, which neither entails nor is entailed by ‘P’. Correspondingly we shall say that b is an indirectly given basis of ‘P’ if, and only if, ‘P’ cannot be applied to b unless at the same time there is applied to it some other concept, say ‘Q’, which neither entails nor is entailed by ‘P’. The former definition covers what can be literally pointed at. It similarly covers the cases in which we identify the basis of an ostensive concept by means of ‹this›, ‹that› or other demonstratives or with the help of gestures without applying concepts.

By characterising a directly given basis as one which can be identified without applying a concept to it, I do not imply that a basis which can be identified without the application of a concept cannot also be identified with its help. Thus whether or not, in applying the concept ‘black’ to this directly given basis, I identify the basis as my pen or whether I simply point does not affect the manner in which the basis is given. Our way of distinguishing directly and indirectly given bases, is, I believe, more precise than definitions in terms of pointing, whether literal or otherwise, or in terms of sensation and perception on the one hand and other kinds of apprehension on the other. It nevertheless leaves room for borderline cases, in particular for the gradual transition from the indirect mode of being given to the direct, and vice versa, that is, it leaves room for the appearing and disappearing of bases.

The proposition that a basis b has the ostensive property 'P' does not entail that the basis is directly, or for that matter indirectly, given. Thus, pointing to what I now see in front of me I may state that this is a chair. In doing so I am applying 'chair' to a directly given basis, but I am not also applying a concept 'directly given' to it. Similarly, in stating that yesterday's dinner was tasty I am applying 'tasty', but not also 'indirectly given', to the indirectly given basis of 'tasty'.

The way in which the basis of an ostensive concept is given is, *prima facie* at least, different from any ostensive property of the basis. Just as one would find it unnatural to regard 'chair' and 'sensed' as concepts of the same kind, so one would find it equally unnatural to regard 'chair' on the one hand and 'directly given' on the other as concepts of the same kind. It would hardly occur to anybody to say that the concepts 'chair' and 'indirectly given' or 'chair' and 'directly given' overlap; or that there are two mutually exclusive and jointly exhaustive kinds of chairs, namely, the directly and the indirectly given ones.

That the way or mode in which a basis is given is not an ostensive property of it can be shown by a stricter proof. Every ostensive concept has, or conceivably could have, some indirectly given bases. So if 'directly given' were an ostensive concept it would have indirectly given bases. Such bases would be characterised as being directly and indirectly given, which is absurd. It is similarly absurd to assume that 'indirectly given' is an ostensive concept and that consequently some of its bases are directly given. The feeling is thus justified that modes and ostensive concepts are entirely different notions—a feeling which arises when one considers, however superficially, the statement that a basis is green and sensed, or green and remembered, or the like.

The distinction just discussed is a distinction of two modes, in either of which the bases of ostensive concepts of *every* kind can be given. It is not a distinction between some kinds of ostensive concept and others. However much the ostensive concepts 'green patch', 'chair', 'action' may differ in other respects, the bases of any one of them can be either directly or indirectly given. Similarly, the difference between 'appearing to be a chair but possibly being an illusion' and 'chair' is not a difference of the mode in which their bases are given. The bases of either concept can be given in either mode.

In order the better to guard the distinction between directly and indirectly given bases against possible misunderstandings, it must be contrasted with some other distinctions, especially with the distinction between knowledge by acquaintance and knowledge by description.[1] "Known by acquaintance" and "directly given" on the one hand, and "known by description" and "indirectly given" on the other, are neither synonymous nor logically equivalent. To see this it is sufficient to note that on Russell's theory we cannot be acquainted with physical objects, while according to the above definitions a basis, and consequently an instance, of 'physical object' can be either directly or indirectly given.[2] Moreover, according to Russell we can be acquainted with past sense-data, while according to the above definitions what is past is without doubt indirectly given.

Again, our distinction is unrelated to the distinction between sense-data and logical constructions. This follows from considering the meaning of "sense-datum", which, in spite of considerable variations of use, refers only to directly given bases or instances of a special kind of ostensive concept of which 'green patch' is an example, but not 'chair'. As against this, the distinction between directly and indirectly given bases is not limited to the bases of any particular type of ostensive concept.

---

[1] See, for example, Russell, *The Problems of Philosophy* (London, 1912), and elsewhere.

[2] For the definition of "instance" see Chapter III, p. 26.

Lastly, it is not the case that 'directly given basis' and 'impression' or, on the other hand, 'indirectly given basis' and 'image' or 'idea' are synonymous notions or logically equivalent: for a basis or instance of 'image' may be directly or indirectly given. Moreover, according to one of the two main uses of "image" every ostensive property 'P' of an image corresponds to a different ostensive property 'Q' of the corresponding impression. According to the other use an image and its corresponding impression must differ in the possession of at least one ostensive property. An example of the former alternative is the view that of any two corresponding properties that of the image is fainter than that of the impression. An example of the second alternative is the view that images, but not impressions, possess a property "image-like". On either view it is self-contradictory to say that all ostensive concepts which are applicable to images are also applicable to impressions. As against this, our position is that the same ostensive concepts are applicable to directly and to indirectly given bases.

In applying an ostensive concept, say 'green', to a directly or to an indirectly given basis, one is satisfying the same ostensive rule. There are not two ostensive rules and consequently two ostensive concepts, say 'green-for-directly-given-bases' and 'green-for-indirectly-given bases'. It is not the sort of greenness which distinguishes what I saw yesterday and what I now see in front of me, but the modes in which the bases are given. There is hardly any need to prove, for example, that the ostensive concept 'green' cannot be split into an exclusive alternation, of the concepts 'green-for-directly-given-bases' and 'green-for-indirectly-given-bases', both of which would be non-ostensive. To see the absurdity of this we need only to note that it would imply that an exclusive alternation of two non-ostensive concepts entailed and was entailed by an ostensive concept.

Of the results of this chapter those which are important for what follows are the distinction between modes and ostensive properties and the distinction between the modes of being directly given and being indirectly given. Since what is directly given would usually be regarded as either sensed or perceived, the question arises whether 'being sensed' and 'being perceived' are two determinate kinds—in other words, submodes of 'being directly given'. The answer to this question must be in the negative. We can see this if we consider that, for example, any directly given instance of 'green patch' would be regarded as sensed and not as perceived, whereas, for example, any directly given instance of 'chair' would be regarded as perceived but not sensed. The difference lies not in the way in which a basis is given, but in the concept which is applied to it.

What is directly given is spatially and temporally present. What is indirectly given may be spatially and temporally remote or only spatially remote or only temporally remote. Moreover, what is temporally remote may be past or future. Are these characteristics submodes of 'indirectly given'? Are they ostensive concepts? Or are they characteristics of a third kind? Though this question will be considered presently we may prepare the ground for its discussion by illustrating the distinction between the direct and indirect mode of being given, by the examples of 'precedes' and 'distant from'.

'Precedes' is an ostensive concept. In exemplifying it we can literally point to examples and anti-examples. Instances of directly given precedence, for example, of lightning immediately followed by thunder, are frequent. Indeed every instance of directly given change is an instance of directly given precedence. The proposition that one occurrence precedes another does *not* entail that at least one of the two is not directly given. Examples of indirectly given bases of 'precedes' are again easily produced. If we state that yesterday's lunch preceded yesterday's dinner or that tomorrow's lunch will precede tomorrow's, or even that yesterday's lunch preceded this movement which we are now observing, we are applying the ostensive concept 'precedes' to indirectly given bases. According to our definition the basis of the last example is indirectly given, although we can distinguish a directly given part of it.

As with 'precedes', so with 'spatially distant'. It would, I believe, be generally agreed that among the rules which govern the use of 'spatially distant' there is an ostensive rule, and that its bases can be directly or indirectly given. I can, for instance, apply the concept to two houses in a remote town as well as to two fingers on this hand now in front of my eyes.

By applying the concepts 'precedes' and 'spatially distant' we do not characterise their bases as directly or as indirectly given. That this is so follows from their being ostensive. It is worth noting that by applying the concept 'precedes' we do not characterise its basis as past, present or future, and by applying 'spatially distant' we do not characterise its basis spatially, as either present or remote.

CHAPTER XV

STATEMENTS ABOUT THE REMOTE, THE REMEMBERED AND THE IMAGINED

WE have seen that the distinction between directly and indirectly given bases of ostensive concepts roughly speaking corresponds, on the one hand, to the distinction between the spatially and temporally present and the spatially and temporally remote and, on the other, to the distinction between what is sensed or perceived and what is apprehended in other ways.[1] In the present chapter I shall be concerned with spatial and temporal remoteness, and the ways of apprehending the spatially and temporally remote, in so far as these topics fall within the framework of an inquiry into conceptual thinking. Thus I shall not be attempting a detailed phenomenological description of remembering, anticipating or imagining, but considering the application of concepts to what is remembered, anticipated or imagined. Similarly, I shall not attempt a phenomenology of time and duration, but inquire into the logical structure of propositions about the past and the future. The main problem of this section, arising from the difference between ostensive concepts and modes, is to determine the role of ostensive concepts and modes in propositions about the spatially remote, the past and the future, the remembered, the anticipated and the imagined.

It is tempting to regard 'being spatially remote' and 'being temporally remote' as unanalysable submodes, of the mode of being-indirectly-given, and to regard 'being past' and 'being future' in turn as unanalysable submodes of 'being temporally remote'. Yet whenever a concept is stated to be "unanalysable" one feels the need for an explanation of the precise sense in which it is so regarded and some proof that it is really in this sense unanalysable. The meaning of "philosophical analysis" is too

---

[1] I am using the term "remote" in the special sense in which what is remote is not perceived.

ambiguous (see Chapter XXXIII) to warrant my saying that in considering the interrelation of modes and ostensive concepts, in propositions about the remote, I am or am not engaged in an analysis of them.

For our purpose it is necessary on the one hand to remember that a certain basis may be indicated as indirectly given without anything's being implied as to whether it is spatially remote or past or future. On the other hand, it is equally important to recall that the concepts 'precedes' and 'distant from', by whose application we establish temporal and spatial ordering, are ostensive. To state their applicability to this or that basis does not imply any information about the mode in which such bases are given. It therefore seems plausible to assume that in order to characterise the application of a concept 'P' to what is past, one must apply the ostensive concept 'precedes' *and* indicate the mode of the basis of 'P'. This assumption I hold to be justified.

All memory propositions are about the past, but not all propositions about the past are memory propositions. The person who tells us that yesterday's dinner was tasty is not necessarily stating a memory proposition, and the person who tells us that Brutus killed Caesar is obviously not stating a memory proposition. All historical propositions are propositions about the past. Yet if it is the task of the historian to give historical explanations, then some historical statements are not merely statements about the past. It is, to say the least, a necessary preliminary of any philosophy of history to give an account both of propositions about the past, and of historical explanation. (For some brief remarks on the latter question see Chapter XXVI.)

In stating that Brutus killed Caesar one is not only applying the concept 'kills' but also at the same time characterising its basis as past. We might emphasise the twofold use of <killed> by saying that Brutus killed Caesar in the past. There can be no doubt that the basis of 'kills' in 'Brutus killed Caesar' is indirectly given, in the sense in which we explained the mode of being indirectly given. We cannot identify the basis by pointing to it, but have to identify it by the application of other concepts, for example, 'member of the Roman Senate', etc. It is convenient to call 'kills' the *principal* concept of the proposition, and the concept or conjunction of concepts which is applied in order to identify the basis of the principal concept, the "identifying concept" or "identifier" of the basis in the proposition. The same basis of a statement about the past may be identified by means of different identifiers. It is further convenient to have a name for the concepts which are entailed by an identifier of a basis. We shall call them "partial identifiers".

A partial identifier which is common to all statements about the past is the ostensive concept 'precedes'. Thus in stating that Brutus kill*ed* Caesar one partially identifies the basis of 'kills' by stating or implying that the killing precedes anything, or at least something, that is directly given, for example, this movement of my pen. While the partial identifier 'precedes' is common to all propositions about the past, the function of the concept 'being a movement of a pen' can be fulfilled by any concept 'Q' provided that its basis is directly given.

It is best to consider, somewhat schematically, the proposition '$P(a)$ and (a precedes b) and $Q(b)$', where 'P', 'Q' and, of course, 'precedes' are ostensive. To apply the concepts 'P', 'precedes' and 'Q' is not to give any information about the modes in which their bases are given. Yet once we indicate these modes we thereby also indicate whether or not the basis of 'P' is past. Thus if the bases of 'P' and 'precedes' are indirectly given while the basis of 'Q' is directly given, the basis of 'P' is characterised as past. It is not sufficient to indicate that the bases of 'P' and 'precedes' are indirectly given, since this information does not preclude the possibility that the basis of 'P' is characterised as future. In making statements about the past it is, of course, neither necessary nor usual to specify a concept 'Q' whose basis is directly given. However, by dropping the assumption that 'Q' is specified we should only complicate the presentation of the argument without adding anything essential to it.

To sum up: every proposition about the past, for example '$P(a)$ in the past', entails and is entailed by (1) a proposition '($P(a)$ and (a precedes b) and $Q(b)$)' in which 'P' and 'Q' and, of course, 'precedes' are ostensive and (2) a proposition that the bases of

'P' and 'precedes' are indirectly given whereas the basis of 'Q' is directly given. (Our definitions of the modes in the previous section imply that a basis which is partly directly and partly indirectly given should be called "indirectly given".) 'Q' may be any more or less specified concept, as long as its basis is directly given.

The characteristic of pastness is thus explained in terms of ostensive concepts and modes. It neither is an ostensive property nor is it an unanalysable submode of 'indirectly given'. Very roughly we might say that the notion combines that of temporal ordering, which is ostensive, with that of the two modes.

It is sometimes assumed that for a radical empiricist every proposition about the past must be logically equivalent to a proposition about the present. At least, the principle that the meaning of a proposition is the method of its verification, although highly obscure in many respects, seems to warrant this conclusion. If our account of 'pastness' is correct, the conclusion is clearly false. To see this we assume that in asserting a proposition about the past we apply an ostensive concept 'P', and in asserting a supposedly equivalent proposition about the present we apply an ostensive concept 'Q'. Even if 'P' and 'Q' are logically equivalent, the propositions that the basis of 'P' is directly given, and that the basis of 'Q' is indirectly given, are logically independent. Consequently the proposition about the past does not entail the proposition about the present.

In stating a memory proposition we seem to be characterising a basis not only as past but also as remembered. Just as in discussing propositions about the past it was not necessary to describe experiences of the flow of time or of pastness, so in discussing memory propositions one need not go deeply into the phenomenology of remembering. For our purpose we may agree that to remember is to repeat what one has learned in the past, to recognise what one has encountered in the past, or to recall what one has experienced in the past. It is not necessary to decide how far these activities are different from each other, or which if any of them is more fundamental than another. Moreover, in the present context the difference between the dispositional and the non-dispositional use of <remember> is not important. Whatever is said about the latter will apply with obvious modifications to the former. (Disposition-statements will be discussed in Chapter XIX.)

It is quite proper to say that in remembering we *somehow* apprehend the past. This manner of speaking, however, does not justify the paradoxical and false conclusion, that in applying a concept 'P' to a now remembered basis b we are applying 'P' to a basis which is at one and the same time indirectly given because characterised as past, and directly given because *now* remembered. No basis can be directly and indirectly given at the same time.

The concept 'remembered' is ostensive, since its bases can be directly or indirectly given. Thus I may now remember something and I may have remembered something a year ago. In discussing propositions about the remembered, in each of the three senses of the term, I shall always assume that what is being remembered is *now* being remembered and that the basis of 'remembered' is thus directly given.

Consider first the proposition that a certain action, say a jump which I am now performing, is now remembered in the sense of being a learned repetition of past jumps. To state this proposition is to state of some directly given basis b that it is a jump and that it is a learned repetition of $c_1, ..., c_n$ which are past jumps. It would thus seem that in stating the memory-proposition we state the incidence of a relation, 'learned repetition', between b on the one hand and the indirectly given bases $c_1, ..., c_n$ on the other. It seems, in other words, that the basis of 'remembered', in the sense of 'learned repetition', is indirectly given, which is contrary to our assumption that what is being remembered is now being remembered and is thus directly given. The difficulty can be overcome by noting that in stating that b is a learned repetition of $c_1, ... , c_n$ we may be mistaken in assuming that there have been past jumps of which b is a learned repetition. In other words, b may *appear* to be a learned repetition of past jumps whether or not there have been past jumps. If there have been then the statement that b *appears* to be a learned repetition of past jumps is veridical; if there have not been past jumps it describes a delusive repetition.

To state a delusive memory-proposition of the type which we

are discussing is to state (1) that the directly given b is a jump, (2) that b appears to be a learned repetition of past jumps, (3) that there have *not* been any such past jumps. To state a veridical memory-proposition of the type discussed is to state the propositions (1) and (2) and the proposition that there *have* been past jumps. This shows that by asserting that something is being remembered in the first sense of the term, we do not apply a concept 'remembered' or any other concept to a basis which is wholly past *and* also present. It also shows that the basis of 'being (veridically or delusively) remembered' need not even partially lie in the past. That the difficulties which we thus avoid are not invented is witnessed by the doctrine that in memory we are in direct cognitive contact with the past.

Our account certainly admits of much refinement, especially as regards the second proposition. But it is important to note that if 'P', say 'being a jump', is ostensive, then '(appearing to be a learned repetition of past P's)' is also ostensive. Its bases may be directly or indirectly given. The *ostensive* rule governing the use of '(appearing to be a learned repetition of past P's)' is the same as that which governs the use of 'P'. The latter concept is unilaterally entailed by the former, which, in a sense to be made more precise in the subsequent chapters, is an ostensive concept of higher level than 'P'.

Secondly, let us consider the memory-proposition that something, say a certain person, encountered in the past is *now* being recognised. The difficulties and their solution are similar to those of the previous example. To state our memory-proposition is to state: (1) that a directly given basis b is a certain person, that is, has the properties of being a person and properties which distinguish b from all other persons, though not from all other bases; (2) that b appears to share with past bases the property of being a person and the distinguishing properties mentioned; (3) that there have been such bases in the past. If (3) is false then our memory statement describes a delusive recognition. In the present context it is not necessary to deal with the difficulty of determining the properties which distinguish one person from another. If our memory-proposition is true then we recognise the same *person* as we have encountered in the past—but not the same basis of 'person'—and certain distinguishing properties. A directly and an indirectly given basis may be the same person, that is, they may be bases of a certain conjunction of concepts; but the same basis cannot at the same time be directly and indirectly given.

Consider thirdly the proposition that a certain experience, say yesterday's dinner, is now being recalled. To state this proposition is to state: (1) that a certain directly given basis b is what might be called a "dinner-memory"; (2) that b appears to share, or to "reflect", certain properties of a basis c which is a past dinner; (3) that there has been such a dinner. While this account shows that we need not assume that 'recalled' is applied to a basis which is directly and also indirectly given or which lies at least partially in the past, it leaves many questions unanswered. Prominent among them is the question as to the nature of a dinner-memory, or more generally a P-memory, and the question as to the properties which the dinner-memory shares with the dinner. I do not feel competent or called upon to answer these questions, but I am inclined to believe that the nature of 'P-memory' and of 'appearing to share...' varies from person to person and varies even with the same person under different circumstances.

The remaining types of proposition about the remote, and the ways in which it is apprehended, can be discussed more briefly. Propositions about the future are analogous to propositions about the past; propositions about what is imaginatively anticipated are analogous to propositions about the remembered in the sense in which what is remembered is recalled.

Using again the terminology used in discussing propositions about the past, we note that a common partial identifier of every basis which is characterised as future, is again the ostensive concept 'precedes'. I omit the comments which lead to a general account of propositions about the future and assume them as being implied in the remarks already made on propositions about the past. To state, schematically speaking, that '$P(b)$ in the future' is to state: (1) '$Q(a)$ and (a precedes b) and $P(b)$', where 'P', 'Q' and, of course, 'precedes', are ostensive concepts; (2) that the bases of 'P' and 'precedes' are indirectly given whereas the basis of 'Q' is directly given.

'P' is the principal concept of the proposition about the future, and 'Q' may be any property as long as its basis is directly given.

To state that a certain experience, say tomorrow's dinner, is imaginatively anticipated is to state: (1) that a certain directly given basis b is what might be called a "dinner-anticipation"; (2) that b appears to share, or to "reflect", certain properties of a basis c which is a future dinner; (3) that there will be such a dinner. This account avoids the same kind of difficulties as the account of memory-propositions of the third type. It also leaves similar questions unanswered. There is, however, little temptation to assume that in stating that tomorrow's dinner is now imaginatively anticipated, one is applying a concept to a basis which is directly and at the same time indirectly given. There is likewise little temptation to assume that the basis of 'imaginatively anticipated' must at least partially lie in the future. In anticipating the future one is more prepared to admit the possibility of delusion than one is in recalling the past. This difference would, among other things, make the phrase "precalling the future" seem unsuitable.

It is, however, conceivable that some people should precall the future just as reliably as most of us recall the past. They might precall tomorrow's dinner as we recall the dinner which we ate yesterday. If there is such precalling, it may be well to point out that though the same *dinner* may now be precalled and tomorrow eaten, that is, though a directly and indirectly given basis may have certain common properties, the same basis can as little as ever be conceivably directly *and* indirectly given.

What is spatially remote is indirectly given. Yet spatial remoteness, like temporal remoteness, is not an unanalysable submode of 'being indirectly given'. In all propositions about the spatially remote we can, as in all propositions about the indirectly given, distinguish between a principal concept and an identifying concept. All identifying concepts in these propositions entail the ostensive concept 'distant from' as a partial identifier. To state '$P(b)$ remote in space' is to state (1) '$Q(a)$ and (a is distant from b) and $P(b)$', and (2) that the bases of 'distant from' and 'P' are indirectly given whereas that of 'Q' is directly given. 'Q' need not be specified as long as its basis in the proposition is directly given.

What has been said concerning propositions about the imaginatively anticipated applies (with the obvious modifications) to propositions about that which is imagined to be spatially remote. There is, however, no danger at all of anybody's thinking that in stating that something, say a mountain, is spatially remote we apply a concept 'spatially remote' or some other concept to a basis which at the same time is directly and indirectly given.

In one sense of the term "imagined", whatever is a P-memory, say a dinner-memory, a P-anticipation and, of course, whatever is represented as spatially remote, *is also imagined*. In this sense of the term what is imagined can conceivably be veridical or delusive. Thus a dinner-memory is veridical if it not only appears to share or to reflect certain properties of a past dinner, but if there has in fact been a past dinner. There is another use of the term "imagined" in which what is imagined cannot possibly be veridical.

In stating that I recall a certain horse I am applying the concept 'horse' to an indirectly given basis. In stating that I merely imagine a horse, or, to take an inapplicable concept, a centaur, I am not applying 'horse' or 'centaur', nor am I even implying the applicablity of these concepts. To state that somebody imagines something that has the property 'P' is to apply not 'P' but the concept 'imagining a P'. The applicability of, for example, the concept 'imagining a centaur' does not entail the applicability of 'centaur'. However, though the argument from the applicability of the former to the applicability of the latter concept is fallacious it is equally wrong to assume that centaurs do not exist *because* the argument is fallacious.

In closing this chapter I should like to emphasise again that the above discussion is logical, not phenomenological. I have not been concerned with the phenomenology of time and the apprehension of bases, but with propositions, that is, the application of concepts to bases. What I have tried to show is that propositions about the spatially and temporally remote and the intuitively apprehended are logically equivalent to conjunctions of propositions whose statement is nothing over and above the application of ostensive concepts and the indication of whether their bases are directly or indirectly given.

CHAPTER XVI

DESCRIPTIONS, EXPLANATIONS AND INTERPRETATIONS

HAVING dealt in outline with the ways in which the bases of ostensive concepts are given, we now turn to an examination of the different types of ostensive concept. For this purpose we can take as starting point a useful, if imprecise, distinction which, in many fields of theoretical thinking, is drawn between description, explanation and interpretation; also, correspondingly, between descriptive, explanatory and interpretative propositions. After some brief and perhaps obvious remarks about explanatory propositions in a very wide sense of the term, I propose to inquire into the relation which holds between any two ostensive propositions (or concepts), of which the one can be properly regarded as an interpretation of the other. In terms of this relation I shall then distinguish between such concepts as are relatively descriptive and such as are relatively interpretative. This distinction is of philosophical interest in itself, and it will be needed throughout the remainder of this essay.

Whether a proposition is explanatory or not depends, not only on the rules which are satisfied by stating it, but also on the attitudes and the general outlook of the person requesting the explanation. If this person is intellectually sufficiently articulate he will not only be able, in every particular case, so to respond as to indicate whether or not he regards a proposition as explanatory; he will also be able to formulate general requirements which must be fulfilled by every explanatory proposition. Much of what is called a person's philosophical or metaphysical position can be described by simply stating what for him are the criteria of an explanatory proposition.

In our own civilisation most explanations are scientific ones. This means, roughly speaking, that most people would be well satisfied if told, in answer to their question why b has 'Q', that *b* has '*P*' and that by an empirical law of nature what has '*P*' has (or must have) '*Q*'; and it further means that they would be all the more satisfied if this law could also be shown to be a logical consequence of some comprehensive hypothetico-deductive system. We have seen (in Chapter XI) that an empirical law is a conjunction of an inclusion-or-overlap proposition (exclusion-or-overlap proposition), say between '*P*' and '*Q*', and a factual proposition that no *P* is, has been, or will be a not-*Q* (no *P* is, has been, or will be a *Q*). It is needless to add that a person satisfied with empirical laws as answers to his requests for explanation is not therefore also able to exhibit the type of rule which is satisfied by the statement of such laws.

While there have been and are people who would not regard any statement of an empirical law as an explanation and who would, for example, hold that laws of nature tell us only *how* but not *why* what happens does happen, there are others who would regard certain kinds of empirical law as the only explanations. The requirement that explanations be empirical laws of a certain type, say mechanistic laws, is—like the more general requirement that they be empirical laws—metaphysical in a clearly determinable sense (see Chapter XXX).

Others again would ask for causal explanations in a sense in which to give one is not to state an empirical law of nature of any kind. The use of the term "causal" is so highly ambiguous that every kind of explanation is in *some* of its many senses a causal explanation. How wide the use of the term is can be seen from the controversy as to whether causal propositions are logical or factual.

A type of explanation which distinctly consists in stating logical propositions might be called "explanation by convention". To explain why a certain basis *b* has the property '*Q*' is in this sense of "explanation" to draw attention to the appropriateness of a proposition that *b* has '*P*', and to the (perhaps forgotten) acceptance of a rule which is satisfied by stating that '*P*' entails '*Q*'. It happens, I think, quite often that we are satisfied if our request for an explanation of why something has a certain property is answered by reference to a convention. The view, however, that every explanation is of this type would hardly be defended by anybody, unless he held not only that every explanation consists in a statement of entailments but also that all entailments are conventional in a sense in which primitive entailments are not (Chapter VI).

Yet another type of explanation consists in stating what are sometimes called "synthetic *a priori* propositions". This term covers, as we have seen, a great variety of propositions, legitimate and spurious. Among the legitimate are various types of entailment and various types of rule to the effect that certain categories be applied rather than others. The latter will come up for discussion in due course, under the name of "directive" propositions (in Chapter XXX). These examples of types of proposition which might for some persons be found explanatory do not, of course, exhaust all possibilities.

A logical inquiry can exhibit the rules which are satisfied by various kinds of proposition, but it is not concerned to show why some groups of people regard certain types of proposition as satisfactory answers to their requests for explanation. It can exhibit, for example, the rules which are satisfied by empirical laws, but not *explain* why such propositions are satisfactory explanations to some people and why propositions about final causes are satisfactory explanations to others.

From the explanatory propositions discussed so far we can distinguish a type of proposition which differs sufficiently from all of them to deserve a distinct title. I shall call them "interpretative" and contrast them with "descriptive" propositions. Under various names this contrast has been especially significant in philosophy. Thus when we wish to outline the general position of a philosopher and to indicate the tenets which are most characteristic of his view of knowledge, we often cannot do it better than by drawing attention to what, if anything, he regards as mere description of the immediately given, and what he regards as interpretation. The distinction between the immediately given and the interpreted is, however, drawn in so many different ways that one cannot help suspecting that the notion of 'what is immediately given' is either a question-begging term or too vague to be usefully employed.

Let us suppose that we are faced with something which looks like a chair, but which for some reason may be suspected of only being an appearance of a chair. To state in such a case that what looks to be a chair is one would be to interpret the proposition 'this looks like a chair' by the proposition 'this is a chair'. It would be, we might say briefly, to interpret the former proposition by the latter. As a matter of fact we very rarely are aware of interpreting propositions about *apparently* external objects by propositions about external objects. Furthermore, I see no reason at all to assume that whenever we state a proposition about an external object we subconsciously interpret a proposition about appearances. There is no logical need to assume that what we consciously would do in the work-room of an illusionist, we always do subconsciously in the normal course of life. Whether or not we ever in fact interpret consciously or otherwise propositions about apparently external objects by propositions about external objects is irrelevant to the logical relations between these propositions. It is these relations in which we are interested.

Although we are not concerned with any conscious or unconscious activity of interpretation, we shall, for convenience, say that of the pair of propositions 'this is a chair' and 'this appears to be a chair', the former is interpretative and the latter is interpreted. We shall similarly say that of the pair of concepts 'chair' and 'appearing to be a chair', the former is interpretative and the latter is interpreted. What, then, is the relation between them? Clearly the interpretative concept entails but is not entailed by the interpreted concept. Since, however, 'green' unilaterally entails 'coloured' and yet nobody would regard the statement that a certain leaf is green as an interpretation of the statement that it is coloured, we must look for further characteristic features of the relation between interpretative and interpreted concepts.

It is useful to remember here the notion of purely ostensive concepts and purely ostensive derivatives of them (Chapter v). An ostensive concept is purely ostensive, we said, if its use is governed only by an ostensive rule. If the use of a concept 'P' is governed by an ostensive rule, say 'r', and by other rules besides, then the concept whose use is governed only by the ostensive rule is the purely ostensive derivative of 'P'. Now, comparing 'chair' and 'appearing to be a chair', we note that the two concepts have the same purely ostensive derivative, or that their ostensive derivatives are governed by the same ostensive rule. Let us call two ostensive concepts with the same purely ostensive derivatives "co-ostensive".

We can now characterise a pair of ostensive concepts 'P' and 'Q', in which 'P' is interpretative and 'Q' is interpreted, as follows: (1) 'P' unilaterally entails 'Q', (2) 'P' and 'Q' are co-ostensive. The difference between the pair 'green' and 'coloured' and the pair 'chair' and 'appearing to be a chair' is that the latter but not the former is a pair of co-ostensive concepts.

Just as two ostensive concepts may stand in a unilateral entailment relation without being co-ostensive, so two concepts may be co-ostensive and yet neither entail the other. Thus, for example, the concepts 'being a chair in accordance with Hume's conception of physical object' and 'being a chair in accordance with Plato's conception of physical object' are co-ostensive although neither entails the other. I shall call two co-ostensive concepts 'P' and 'Q' "dependently co-ostensive" if 'P' entails 'Q' or if 'Q' entails 'P'; and I shall call two co-ostensive concepts 'P' and 'Q' "independently co-ostensive" if neither concept entails the other. 'Chair' and 'appearing to be a chair' are dependently co-ostensive. Of any two dependently co-ostensive concepts the entailing concept is interpretative, or as we may say higher, and the interpreted concept is lower. Two independently co-ostensive concepts may or may not be incompatible. For example, the independently co-ostensive concepts 'Humean chair' and 'Platonic chair' are incompatible. Either of two independently co-ostensive concepts is always dependently co-ostensive with at least one common concept, namely, their common purely ostensive derivative.

So far the notion of interpretative and interpreted concepts has been defined only with respect to a pair of dependently co-ostensive concepts. It is possible, mainly in terms of "dependently co-ostensive concepts", to define "absolutely interpretative" and "absolutely interpreted" concepts. Since an absolutely interpreted concept is not interpretative of any other concept it may be also called "absolutely descriptive".

An ostensive concept, say 'P', is absolutely descriptive if the following two conditions are fulfilled: (1) 'P' does not entail any lower co-ostensive concept; (2) for any pair of dependently co-ostensive concepts 'Q' and 'R' (in which 'Q' is higher than 'R') if 'Q' entails 'P' then 'R' also entails 'P'. An ostensive concept which is not absolutely descriptive is absolutely interpretative. In other words, 'P' is absolutely interpretative if (1) 'P' entails some lower co-ostensive concept or (2) if for some pair of dependently co-ostensive concepts 'Q' and 'R' (in which 'Q' is higher than 'R'), 'Q' entails 'P' whereas 'R' does not entail 'P'.

These definitions of absolutely interpretative and absolutely descriptive concepts are, I believe, clearer than definitions in terms of the elusive notions of the immediately given or of immediate experience. Yet they are unsatisfactory, since we have not any means of deciding in practice whether a concept which we believe to be absolutely descriptive really is so. For it is quite conceivable that we simply have not noticed that a concept which we believe to be absolutely descriptive entails some lower co-ostensive concept. Philosophy is full of disputed examples of propositions which are alleged to be absolutely descriptive, that is, of propositions whose statement is the application of allegedly absolutely descriptive concepts. One only needs to think of the propositions describing Descartes' indubitable, clear and distinct perceptions, the propositions describing Hume's impressions, or the propositions describing what remains after Husserl's phenomenological reduction has been performed.

Instead of relying on the unrealistic absolute distinction between interpretative and descriptive concepts, we shall use a relative distinction which pertains only to concepts which are explicitly accepted by a conceptual thinker, that is to say, concepts of whose acceptance he is more or less clearly aware. An explicitly accepted concept is explicitly or relatively descriptive if, and only if: (1) it does not entail a lower explicitly accepted concept, and (2) for any pair of explicitly accepted and dependently co-ostensive concepts 'Q' and 'R' (in which 'Q' is higher than 'R'), if 'Q' entails 'P', then 'R' also entails 'P'. An ostensive concept which is not explicitly or relatively descriptive is relatively interpretative.

If a concept is explicitly interpretative it is also absolutely interpretative. A concept which is explicitly descriptive for one group of thinkers may be explicitly interpretative for another group. In the following it will often be useful to show that certain concepts are absolutely interpretative by showing that they entail lower co-ostensive concepts. I shall, however, never attempt a proof that a concept is absolutely descriptive.

It follows from the definition of interpretative concepts that the applicability of a lower concept is a necessary but not a sufficient condition for the applicability of any of its higher concepts. Thus in applying the higher of two dependently co-ostensive concepts the risk of being mistaken is greater than in applying the lower. The application of an absolutely descriptive concept, if one could be sure of its absolute descriptiveness, would involve the lowest possible risk of being mistaken. The question of the kind of risks which are involved in applying various kinds of interpretative concept and the question for what purposes the risks are being undertaken will be discussed in Part III.

In considering, for example, the pair of dependently co-ostensive concepts 'chair' and 'appearing to be a chair', we note that only the higher of them entails 'persisting when not perceived', 'external', 'public'. These and similar concepts have been regarded as characterising particular entities called "substances" which have been postulated in order to account for the identity of physical objects and persons through time. The distinction between higher and lower co-ostensive concepts and between instances and bases will permit us to avoid the postulation of substances.

No conjunction of descriptive concepts entails any interpretative concept. This follows from the definitions of interpretative and descriptive concepts. The concepts which are entailed by an interpretative concept 'P' are either descriptive or interpretative. Let us assume that the conjunction of all descriptive concepts entailed by 'P' is 'D_1 and D_2 ... and D_n'. Among the concepts entailed by 'P' there is at least one lower concept 'P_1' which is co-ostensive with 'P' and which entails all the descriptive concepts entailed by 'P' but does not also entail 'P'. (For example, if 'chair' is our interpretative concept, then 'appearing to be a chair' entails all descriptive concepts entailed by 'chair', but not also 'chair'.) If 'D_1 and D_2 ... and D_n' does not even entail 'P_1' then it does not entail 'P'. If, on the other hand, it does entail 'P_1', then, since 'P_1' entails the conjunction, 'P_1' is logically equivalent to 'D_1 and D_2 ... and D_n'. But a conjunction equivalent to 'P_1' cannot entail 'P' since 'P' entails 'P_1' unilaterally.

It follows almost immediately that no alternation of conjunctions of descriptive concepts, say '(D_1 and D_2 ... and D_m) or (D_{m+1} and D_{m+2} ... and D_n)' entails an interpretative concept 'P'. For to state that an alternation of concepts entails a concept is to state that each member entails this concept. The case of the alternation is thus reduced to the case of the conjunction where, as usual, "conjunctions" of one member are also admitted.

Lastly, no negation of a descriptive concept 'D' is an interpretative concept. If 'D' is descriptive then it is ostensive. The negation of an ostensive concept is, however, not ostensive (Chapter v). If the negation of a descriptive concept is not even ostensive, it cannot be interpretative because every interpretative concept is ostensive. The above remarks about the logical relation between conjunctions, alternations and negations of descriptive concepts on the one hand and interpretative concepts on the other, apply equally to absolutely and to relatively descriptive and interpretative concepts.

At least since the time of Berkeley some philosophers seem to have tried to prove the following incompatible theses. On the one hand that physical-object concepts entail *lower* concepts, whose applicability to a basis is therefore never a sufficient condition for the applicability of physical-object concepts. This thesis, which is often formulated in vague and obscure ways, I have argued to be correct. On the other hand, the same philosophers have often also believed and tried to prove that lower concepts, for example concepts characterising sense-data but not also physical objects, nevertheless entail physical-object concepts. This thesis we have seen to be false. Since no conjunction of (absolutely or explicitly) descriptive concepts entails any (absolutely or explicitly) interpretative concept any attempt to prove the thesis must fail. The apparent impossibility of solving the "problem of the external world" which haunts the systems of many empiricists, seems mainly due to the belief that its solution would consist in proving that physical-object concepts are entailed by conjunctions of lower concepts which they entail. One may, of course, substitute for this view a weaker and vaguer thesis by holding that physical-object concepts are relations between instances of descriptive concepts, for example, concepts characterising sense-data. However, such relations are either descriptive concepts, which therefore do not entail interpretative concepts, or else they are interpretative and thus, of course, equivalent to interpretative concepts.

More recent attempts to "analyse" physical-object concepts by showing their alleged equivalence to lower concepts have made use of the techniques of symbolic logic. They amount to alleged proofs that a physical-object concept is an alternation of finite or possibly infinite conjunctions of descriptive concepts. We have seen that no higher concept is entailed by an alternation of finite conjunctions of descriptive concepts, and the unsuitability of the notion of "possibly infinite conjunctions" for the clarification of concepts has already been emphasised (Chapter x).

In discussing the modes in which the bases of ostensive concepts are given we have noted that what we have called directly given bases are usually characterised as sensed or perceived. We have pointed out that 'being sensed' and 'being perceived' cannot be regarded as submodes of the mode of 'directly given' since, for example, the instances of certain concepts, say, 'physical object', although directly given, would never be regarded as sensed, whereas the instances of other concepts, for example, 'green patch', would, if directly given, always be regarded as sensed. We therefore concluded that the difference between the sensed and the perceived is a difference in the applied concepts and not or not only in the mode in which their bases are given.

The distinction between the sensed and the perceived is connected with the distinction between the immediately given and that which is merely inferred or interpreted. If we tried to make the former distinction less obscure by translating it into the language of modes, interpretative and descriptive concepts, we should say that to be sensed is to be a directly given instance of an absolutely descriptive concept, and to be perceived is to be a directly given basis of an interpretative concept. The difficulties involved in the distinction between absolutely interpretative and absolutely descriptive concepts are thus also involved in the distinction between the sensed and the perceived. Though, however, the merely relative distinction between relatively or explicitly interpretative and relatively or explicitly descriptive concepts will prove useful, a distinction between the relatively sensed and the relatively perceived would seem pointless. For the main purpose of the distinction between the sensed and the perceived is to characterise the immediately given in an absolute manner.

It is hardly necessary to emphasise that a person who accepts both relatively interpretative and relatively descriptive concepts is not thereby enabled to formulate the rules for their use and to state their mutual relations. The acceptance, however, of both descriptive and interpretative concepts requires no more subtlety than is possessed by a child who accepts the concepts 'chair' and 'coloured'.

CHAPTER XVII

INTERPRETATIVE LEVELS AND HIERARCHIES
OF OSTENSIVE CONCEPTS

IN the preceding chapter we have to some extent justified and made more precise the rather vague distinction between the description and the interpretation of the immediately given. It is by applying absolutely descriptive concepts that we describe experience and by applying interpretative concepts that we interpret it. Since, however, we have no means of deciding in practice whether a concept which, *as far as we know*, does not entail any lower concept is absolutely descriptive, we have to be content with a distinction between relatively descriptive and relatively interpretative concepts. This naturally raises the question whether there are degrees in descriptiveness and how they are measured.

So far we have not compared interpretative concepts in general with respect to the degree to which they are interpretative, although that some are more interpretative and others less is almost immediately clear. The need for a method of comparing concepts in respect to the degree to which they are interpretative is felt by those, for instance, in ethics, who want to distinguish non-natural, moral characteristics from natural characteristics such as a 'physical object'; or again the same need is suggested by some of those who, however vaguely, speak of different levels of thought and of analysis.

The attempt to provide a method of comparing different interpretative concepts with regard to their being more or less interpretative will be made at first with the help of some rather unrealistic assumptions, assumptions which do not really hold good for conceptual thinking in general. I shall try to show, however, that even when we drop these some useful distinctions are still left. Lastly I shall contrast the transition from less to more interpretative concepts, on the one hand with increasing "specification", that is, the transition from more to less general concepts; on the other hand with increasing "particularisation", that is, the transition from judging something to be a thing of a particular kind to judging it to be a particular thing of this kind.

The difference in the degree to which concepts are interpretative is quite obvious in the case of dependently co-ostensive concepts. Thus 'appearing to be a chair', 'chair', 'chair-as-understood-by-Plato' clearly form a sequence in which the later members are more interpretative than the earlier. Again, of two independently co-ostensive concepts, whether they are compatible or not, it can safely be said that either of them is more interpretative than the lower concepts which are co-ostensive with both of them. Thus the mutually compatible co-ostensive concepts 'chair-thing' and 'chair-event' are each of them more interpretative than 'chair' and still more interpretative than 'appearing to be a chair'. Similarly, the incompatible co-ostensive concepts 'Platonic chair' and 'Humean chair' are more interpretative than 'chair' and still more interpretative than 'appearing to be a chair'.

Even concepts which are not co-ostensive seem, *prima facie* at least, comparable as to the degree to which they are descriptive or interpretative. To see this consider again the co-ostensive concepts 'chair' and 'appearing to be a chair'. It is reasonable to regard those concepts which are entailed only by the higher of two co-ostensive concepts as more interpretative than those which are entailed only by the lower of them. For example, 'physical object' is entailed by 'chair', but not also by 'appearing to be a chair'. On the other hand, 'coloured' is entailed by both 'chair' and 'appearing to be a chair'. Although 'external object' and 'coloured' are not co-ostensive, the former concept can reasonably be regarded as more interpretative than the latter. We might similarly feel inclined to regard 'chair' and 'table' as being interpretative to the same degree. Everything considered, it seems worth while to attempt a stratification of concepts into different interpretative levels.

To do this let us introduce first the notion of difference between two concepts, of which one entails the other. This notion will be easily recognised as similar to the traditional *differentia* and to the notion of remainder which was used (in Chapter v) to bring out the contrast between Boolean class-algebra on the one hand and the logic of ostensive concepts or "classes" on the other. If 'P'

unilaterally entails 'Q', then I shall call 'R' a difference between 'P' and 'Q' if, and only if, (1) 'Q and R' entail 'P', and (2) 'P' entails 'R'. For example, the concept 'chair' entails the concept 'piece of furniture' unilaterally. The concept 'appearing to be a chair' is a difference between them. To characterise 'appearing to be a chair' more precisely, we assume that it entails whatever 'chair' entails with the exception of 'physical object'; and that it does not entail what 'chair' does not also entail. Whatever is a piece of furniture and appears to be a chair is necessarily a chair; for 'being a piece of furniture' entails 'being a physical object'. Moreover, whatever is a chair necessarily appears to be a chair in the above sense of the words.[1] The conditions for a concept's being a difference are thus fulfilled.

Let us now assume for a moment that we can be sure that no entailment between concepts is going to escape our notice and, in particular, that we can rely on a concept which on close scrutiny seems absolutely descriptive being absolutely descriptive. A stratification of ostensive concepts into different interpretative levels can now be achieved. We can say that an interpretative concept is of *first level* if, and only if, it entails descriptive and interpretative concepts, *and* if the difference between it and any interpretative concept which it entails is a descriptive concept. If concepts which characterise both physical objects and illusions of them—concepts such as 'green', 'round', 'coloured', 'appearing to be a chair' in the sense described above—are absolutely descriptive, then 'chair' is an ostensive concept of first level. It clearly entails descriptive and interpretative concepts. Examples of the latter are 'piece of furniture' or 'physical object'. The difference between 'chair' and 'piece of furniture' and between 'chair' and 'physical object' is, of course, 'appearing to be a chair'.

In a similar way we should define an interpretative concept as of *second* level if it fulfils the following conditions: (1) that it entails descriptive concepts, interpretative concepts of first level and interpretative concepts which are not of first level; and (2) the

---

[1] It is, of course, true that a piece of furniture which "appears to be" a chair may turn out to be a table. But in order to avoid lengthy and philosophically unimportant qualifications, I am using ‹appearance of a chair› only in the restricted sense in which what appears to be a chair either is a chair or not a physical object at all.

difference between it and any interpretative concept which is not of first level is an interpretative concept of first level. We could define concepts such as 'action', 'behaviour' and 'apparent behaviour' in such a manner that 'action' would be a concept of second level, 'behaviour' a concept of first level and 'apparent behaviour' a descriptive concept.

The definitions of concepts of third level and higher would be analogous. In general, a concept of nth level entails descriptive concepts, concepts of first, second...$(n-1)$th level, and other interpretative concepts; the difference between it and any of the last-mentioned concepts is a concept of level $n-1$.

The taking of concepts as stratified into different interpretative levels in the manner just described exhibits an important difference between two kinds of entailment: (a) horizontal, that is, entailment between concepts of the same level, and (b) vertical entailment, that is, entailment between concepts of different levels. From the definition of interpretative levels—ultimately, from the nature of co-ostensive concepts—it follows that the direction of vertical entailment is always downwards, from the higher interpretative level to the lower. For example, 'green' entails 'coloured' horizontally, while the entailment between 'chair' and 'coloured' is vertical as proceeding from a concept of first level to a descriptive concept or, at any rate, from a concept of some higher interpretative level to one that is lower.

If we consider a system of stratified concepts, it may be the case—it normally is the case—that a number of concepts of a given level entail a certain concept which also belongs to that level. For instance, each of the concepts 'table', 'chair', 'piece of furniture', etc., all of which belong to the same level, entail 'physical object'. We might say of these concepts that they belong not only to the same level, but also to the same category. By "category" we may mean here either the entailed concept 'physical object' or the set of concepts entailing it. If all concepts of a given set (say those accepted by some person) which belong to a certain level belong also to a certain category, we might say that they are centralised with respect to that category.

Without trying to provide a measure of the degree to which, in a set of concepts, the concepts of a certain level are centralised, we can reasonably say that nevertheless different degrees of centralisation of a level are possible. For example, if the concepts of first level in a given system of concepts contain only physical-thing and physical-process concepts, then these concepts of the first level are centralised with respect to the category 'physical'. If, on the other hand, all concepts of first level in a given system are physical-object concepts, then these concepts are centralised with respect to the category 'physical object'. In the latter example the concepts of first level are more centralised than in the former.

A system of concepts in which every level is centralised with respect to one category might be called "a hierarchy of concepts". Different conceptual hierarchies might be built on the foundation of the same descriptive concepts. For example, a hierarchy of conceptual levels whose first level is centralised with respect to the category 'physical process' is certainly different from a hierarchy which is centralised with respect to the category 'physical thing'. Yet it is quite possible that nevertheless all descriptive concepts which are entailed by any interpretative concept of one hierarchy are also entailed by some interpretative concept of the other.

To be useful in any limited formalised system of ostensive concepts the above sketch of a method of stratifying them into interpretative levels would undoubtedly have to be refined. On the other hand, however, the stratification outlined is much too neat and tidy to do justice to the complexities and imprecisions of non-formalised conceptual thinking. The almost disturbing tidiness of hierarchies of concepts in which each concept belongs to a numbered level is due to the assumption that nothing entailed by the concepts which we are considering escapes our notice, and, in particular, that we can be sure of our absolutely descriptive concepts.

If, as we must, we drop this assumption, it becomes immediately impossible to assign a number unambiguously to any interpretative level and consequently to any concept belonging to this level. We cannot, for instance, in comparing 'Platonic chair', 'chair' and 'appearing to be a chair' say that 'Platonic chair' is an interpretative concept of second level. All we can say is that 'Platonic chair' is of higher level than 'chair', which is again of higher level than 'appearing to be a chair'. We might also say that 'Platonic chair' is at least of second level.

The effort to separate naturalistic and non-naturalistic concepts in ethics seems to play with a distinction of interpretative levels. More precisely, some so-called non-naturalistic ethical theories seem to imply that non-naturalistic moral concepts are at the lowest of second level. They are certainly of higher level than physical-object concepts, these again being regarded as of a level higher than concepts of apparently physical objects.

Apart from the uncertainty about absolutely descriptive concepts and consequently about the exact interpretative level of any concept, we have the further uncertainty as to whether two concepts which, after careful application of our definition of interpretative levels, seem to belong to the same level, really do belong to it. By constructing a formalised system we could, of course, guard against error in this respect; but we are here concerned with concepts which we find ourselves using outside such systems. It might, for example, seem that the concepts 'voluntary action' and 'moral-or-immoral action', as we use them, belong to the same level, while closer inspection might reveal the latter concept to be of a level higher than the former.

Our method of stratification does, however, allow us to compare even concepts which are not co-ostensive in respect to the degree to which they are interpretative. Moreover, while we can hardly ever be sure, especially where highly interpretative concepts are concerned, that two such concepts belong to the same interpretative level, we can often show conclusively that they belong to different levels.[1]

Interpretation, as we have called the application of a higher interpretative concept to what is also the basis of a lower one, is always specification (transition from *genus* to *species*) but not every specification is necessarily an interpretation. For example, in applying 'chair' to a basis of 'appearance of a chair' we specify and interpret this basis. On the other hand, in applying 'appearance

---

[1] It should not be necessary to add that whatever the interpretative level of an ostensive concept, its *order* is always zero: for to apply an ostensive concept is never to state or to deny a logical proposition.

of a wooden chair' to a basis of 'appearance of a chair' we stay within the same interpretative level. We specify the basis, but do not also interpret it. Using the distinction between horizontal and vertical entailment we might say that by applying a concept 'P' to the basis of a concept 'Q' we specify this basis if 'Q' vertically or horizontally entails 'P'; but only if 'Q' vertically entails 'P' do we interpret this basis.

Interpretation and specification are thus ways of determining a basis or characterising it in greater detail by applying further concepts to it. Either must be distinguished both from the identification of bases and from what might be called the "particularisation of things". It is clear that interpretation and specification of bases are different from the identification of them, whether with or without the help of concepts: for a basis must have been identified before it can be specified or interpreted.

In order to explain and discuss "particularisation" it is best to consider an example. Let us, therefore, compare the proposition that some identified basis is a chair, with the proposition that it is a particular chair, for example, the chair on which Napoleon sat after the battle of Waterloo. We might, of course, simply say that the particular chair about which we are speaking not only is a chair but also has the property 'having been sat upon by Napoleon after the battle of Waterloo'. But is this, however true, quite satisfactory, without further discussion of the nature of this type of property? In any case, I propose to approach the problem—the nature of the transition from judging something to be a chair to judging it a particular chair—from a different angle.

First of all it should be noted that, as has often been pointed out, when we say that something is a chair we speak imprecisely. We should readily agree that what we mean is better expressed by saying that a certain basis belongs to a chair, is part of a chair, or, as I shall say, an aspect of a chair. The concept 'aspect of a chair' is interpretative. It is co-ostensive with 'appearance of an aspect of a chair'. Whatever is a chair-aspect, say a frontal view, stands necessarily in certain typical relations to other chair-aspects, for example, to side-views, tactual aspects, etc. We might call these relations "unifying aspect relations" or "aspect-fusions". On the other hand, whatever is, as we shall say briefly, an apparent chair-aspect does not necessarily stand in these relations to other apparent chair-aspects. For example, if anything is the apparent frontal view of a pink elephant, seen by a drunkard, then it is not necessarily fused with an apparent side-aspect in the way in which frontal views and side-aspects of "real" elephants are fused.

When we say that a certain basis "is a chair", we wish to state that a certain directly or indirectly given basis is an aspect of a chair and therefore necessarily is standing in aspect-fusion to other bases, some of which are less clearly identified than others whereas some are not identified at all. Since a physical object has a past and a future, and since even the number of its indirectly given present aspects is unlimited, it is impossible to identify all its aspects.

The question whether a certain basis which is a chair-aspect is an aspect of a particular chair, say the one on which Napoleon sat after the battle of Waterloo, is a request for the identification of further bases to which the given basis stands in aspect-fusion. The greater the number of bases which are identified as being fused with the given bases, the better acquainted do we become with the chair, of which the originally given basis is an aspect.

The concept 'chair' and more generally the concept 'physical object' are examples of concepts of aspect-continua. To particularise a given basis of 'aspect of a chair' is to identify further bases to which this one stands in the relation of aspect-fusion. It is not to specify this basis by applying concepts to it which are more specific than 'aspect of chair', for example 'aspect of wooden chair'. It is consequently also not to interpret this basis by applying to it concepts of higher interpretative level, for example 'Platonic chair'.

That a chair is an aspect-continuum explains how two different bases, for example a directly and an indirectly given one, can belong to the same particular chair. Particularisation of an aspect of a chair is the identification of further bases with which it is fused. There attaches no mystery to the statement that everything of a kind is necessarily a particular thing of this kind and vice versa. If two chairs could have all their *ostensive* properties and relations in common, we could still account for their numerical difference, as being a difference in the fused bases. The difference in the directly or indirectly given bases is what makes one particular chair different from another. It is their true *principium individuationis*.

Physical objects are not the only aspect-continua, and 'aspect of a physical object' is not the only aspect-concept. All such concepts are necessarily interpretative: for 'aspect of a P' is always co-ostensive with a lower concept 'apparent aspect of a P' which, unlike the former, does not characterise bases as standing necessarily in unifying relations to other bases. On the other hand, not all interpretative concepts are concepts of aspects. Thus 'beautifully green' might be regarded as a concept of higher interpretative level than 'green'. If so, it is certainly not an aspect-concept. However that may be, for the understanding of the function of concepts in the manipulation of things, in moral behaviour and even in historical and aesthetic judgment, a close consideration of aspect-continua and aspects of different kinds is fundamental.

While the function of these concepts will be discussed in some detail in Part III, it might be useful to illustrate by a further example here the notions of interpreting the basis of an ostensive concept by applying a concept of higher interpretative level to it; and of particularising an aspect of an aspect-continuum by identifying further aspects of it. I have chosen the notion of a self, or person or mind because I believe that certain difficulties connected with this notion can be clarified if we note that a self is a continuum of aspects and that each aspect of a self is an instance of an interpretative and thus *a fortiori* of an ostensive concept.

The concept 'self' is, like the concept 'chair', a concept of an aspect-continuum. The unifying relations, of course, which unify, say, the frontal view of a chair with its side view, are different from the unifying relations which unify, for example, my bodily feelings with my observed bodily movements. The concept 'self' is, again, like the concept 'chair' and any aspect-continuum, non-ostensive and not exemplifiable. What can be exemplified is always only 'chair-aspect', for example a frontal view of a chair, or 'self-aspect', for example a bodily feeling or a bodily movement, never a whole chair or a whole self.[1]

---

[1] I have, as is usual, often spoken of, say, 'chair', when 'chair-aspect' would have been the correct term. Only in this loose way of speaking is 'chair' ostensive.

'Self-aspect', like 'chair-aspect', is interpretative. By applying to a bodily feeling or a bodily movement the concept 'self-aspect' we interpret it as being fused, with other bodily feelings or aspects, to a continuum of aspects. To judge that a basis is an aspect of a self is not to imply that we can identify every other basis with which it is fused. It may, moreover, be that some of these bases cannot be directly given. For example, we can judge that a person's bodily feelings are fused with his bodily movements as aspects of the same self, although his bodily feelings cannot be directly given to us. We can similarly judge that a chair's frontal view is fused with its rear view even though it is not directly given to us and in the case of some chairs *cannot* be given to us.

The statement that a feeling is an aspect of my self, like the statement that a feeling is an aspect of your self, is interpretative. The former statement differs from the latter in that the basis of 'aspect of self' is in the first statement directly given whereas in the second it is indirectly given. The difference is analogous to the difference between saying that a directly given and that an in-directly given basis are frontal views of different chairs. The difference between my self and your self lies, thus, not in the unifying relations between bases of 'self-aspect' but in the bases which are related and in the modes of some of them.

The main topics of this chapter have been the logical relations between interpretative concepts and the concepts of lower level which they entail, for example between 'chair-aspect' and 'ap-parent chair-aspect'; or between 'self-aspect' and 'apparent self-aspect'. By saying that the applicability of 'apparent chair-aspect' is a necessary condition of the applicability of 'chair-aspect' I have not implied that we must or in fact do apply the former concept before applying the latter. Similarly, it is not implied in anything here said that we ever appeal to the applicability of concepts of lower level as evidence for the applicability of concepts of higher level. Yet if we do appeal to such evidence we appeal to necessary but not to sufficient conditions.

CHAPTER XVIII

ON SOME ALLEGED PROOFS OF THE APPLICABILITY OF INTERPRETATIVE CATEGORIES

WE are not as a rule concerned with establishing the applicability of our interpretative concepts in principle. Indeed, in normal circumstances we not only take their applicability for granted, but we apply them without appealing to any evidence and without feeling any need to do so. In unfamiliar surroundings we might feel the need to justify, for example, that what appears to be a physical object is a physical object, but not also that 'physical object' is in principle applicable, that is, not empty. (In strictness we should, of course, speak of aspects of physical objects, rather than speak of physical objects. Yet unless the relation between such aspects is relevant to the discussion, it is preferable to speak in the usual less precise and less cumbersome manner.)

On the other hand, to consider philosophically whether the external world exists is to ask the question whether 'physical object' is applicable at all—whether we are right in assuming its applicability. When the ordinary person and the slightly less ordinary psychologist ask whether something is a physical object or an illusion, they assume that 'physical object' is not an empty concept. When a philosopher asks whether the external world is real or an illusion, he questions the assumption which is taken for granted by the ordinary person and the psychologist. The term "illusion" is thus used in entirely different senses in the first and in the second question. To overlook this is to invite much confusion.

The philosophical question whether a moral order exists is similarly the question whether the category 'moral action' is in principle applicable or empty, and not whether, on the assumption of its applicability, it is appropriately applied to a particular action. Philosophical questions as to whether something exists are normally questions about the applicability or emptiness of categories, and not questions about the appropriate application to particular bases of categories presumed to be applicable.

The purpose of this chapter is mainly negative. It is to show that certain arguments which purport to prove the applicability of interpretative concepts are fallacious. The fallaciousness of deductive arguments from the applicability of lower concepts follows clearly from the discussion of interpretative levels and vertical entailments. On the other hand, probability-arguments which are intended to show the applicability of interpretative categories are less obviously fallacious. By examining unsuccessful justifications of the belief in the applicability of interpretative categories, the ground will be prepared for a closer consideration of the belief itself (Chapter XXI). Although I shall mostly refer to the interpretative category 'physical object' any other example would serve equally well.

Whether one feels the need to justify a belief will depend on one's temperament and on many other circumstances. Whether the belief is justifiable will depend on the nature of the belief and the conditions which a justification would have to fulfil. Thus to justify the belief in an external world is not one single problem. It may well be that in some sense of justification our belief in the existence of an external world can be justified in more ways than one, whereas in some other sense of justification it is impossible because the conditions of its success are self-contradictory.

We have seen that it is logically impossible to deduce the applicability of 'physical object' to a basis, from the parallel applicability to it of a concept of lower interpretative level, for example 'apparent physical object'. Such a deduction would imply the possibility of vertical entailments from a lower to a higher interpretative level, which we have seen to be absurd. If we cannot even deduce the applicability of an interpretative concept to a particular basis in this manner, we can still less deduce in this way its applicability in principle.

The main merit of Hume's discussion of the external world is, I believe, to have shown that *if* to justify the belief in an external world is to deduce the applicability of 'physical object' from the applicability of interpretative concepts of lower level, then it is logically impossible to produce such justification. Hume, of course, does not use the terminology of interpretative concepts, and my exegesis may, for this or other reasons, be regarded as mistaken—the question is not of importance in the present context. If to "justify" the applicability of an interpretative concept is to deduce it from the applicability of lower concepts, then such justification is logically impossible whatever the correct reading of Hume.

Hume does, however, seem to be mistaken in arguing from the logical impossibility which he recognises to scepticism. If it is logically impossible to justify our belief in the external world in a self-contradictory sense of "justification" (involving vertical entailment from the lower to the higher level), then the recognition of this logical impossibility gives no support to scepticism. One does not become a sceptic if one finds that a thing cannot be at once green and not green all over. I think what influenced later philosophers in Hume was not so much his correct doctrine that the "existence" of the external world cannot be demonstrated on the assumption that impressions "exist". It was rather his wrong belief that the logical impossibility of a demonstrative justification was an argument for scepticism. Their real difficulty was their failing to see that they should not have accepted this.

The impossibility of demonstrating that 'physical object' is applicable because concepts of lower level, for example 'impression', are applicable could easily lead to attempted proofs that 'physical object' is *probably* not empty if some concepts of lower level are applicable. The hopelessness of such attempts might appear obvious. I shall nevertheless try to show that probability-arguments to the effect that a category is not empty, whether in terms of an entailment-notion of probability or in terms of a frequency-notion, must fail.

By an entailment-notion of probability I understand any notion of it which is definable in terms of entailment. By a frequency-notion I understand any notion of probability which is definable in terms of relative frequencies. Entailment-notions of probability are not defined only in terms of entailment, frequency-notions not only in terms of relative frequencies. For our purpose, however, we shall be able to ignore the other features of probability-notions, especially those which, in the various theories, provide for the possibility of measuring degrees of probability. It is equally unimportant for our purpose to decide which of the two types of probability-notion is used in scientific inquiries, and which comes nearer to ordinary usage.

The fundamental idea of all entailment-theories of probability can be easily illustrated by assuming that the probability-premiss and the probability-conclusion are both conjunctive propositions (including under this also "conjunctions" with one member only). By dropping this assumption we should, apart from purely technical complications, introduce no new problem.

We assume, then, that an internally consistent conjunction 'p_1 and p_2 ... and p_n' entails 'q'; that all propositions in its antecedent and consequent are essential[1]; that by stating 'p_1', 'p_2', ..., 'p_n' and 'q' one applies respectively the concepts 'P_1', 'P_2',...,'P_n' and 'Q' to some basis. It makes good sense to say that on the assumption that 'p_1 and p_2 ... and p_n' are true, 'q' is certainly true, or certain. To assume the truth of 'p_1 and p_2 ... and p_n' is to assume that 'P_1', 'P_2', ..., 'P_n' are applicable. On the other hand, 'P_1', 'P_2',..., 'P_n' may well be applicable though 'p_1 and p_2 ... and p_n' is false, since by stating this conjunction we not only state the applicability in principle of the concepts, but apply them to particular bases.

It is useful to tolerate for a while the term "evidential conjunction". It will be used only in this chapter. I shall say that 'p_1 and p_2 ... and p_n' is a complete evidential conjunction for 'q' if it entails 'q' and if the concepts 'P_1'...'P_n' are not empty. Thus a complete evidential conjunction need not be true. On the assumption that it is true, 'q' is certain. On the assumption that only some members of the complete evidential conjunction are true, 'q' is not certain but, in one sense of the term, probable.

Even on this rudimentary theory some probabilities can be compared. For example, if of two subconjunctions of the same complete evidential conjunction for 'q' one unilaterally entails the other, then the former makes 'q' more probable than the latter. There may be more than one complete evidential conjunction for 'q'. Consequently, if a member of such a conjunction is false it

[1] See p. 24.

does not follow that 'q' is false, or that 'not-q' is certain. To provide for the possibility of measuring probabilities of the kind described (by assigning real numbers to them in the usual manner) we should have to amplify our rudimentary theory in many ways. This would involve raising many controversial questions without proposing any answers. For our purpose it is mainly necessary to remember that in stating that the assumption 'p_1 and p_2' makes 'q' probable it is presupposed that 'p_1 and p_2' is a subconjunction of a complete evidential conjunction for 'q'.

It is supposed that a conjunction of propositions whose statement is the application of lower-level concepts makes probable the applicability of 'physical object'. What is involved in a proof of it? Any proof of it would have to show first of all that a complete evidential conjunction entails the applicability of this concept to some basis. Now it cannot be that such a conjunction has only lower-level concepts as its members; for this would imply the possibility of entailment in the direction from lower to higher level. But if, on the other hand, we assume the conjunction to have applicable concepts of the same level as 'physical object' or of higher interpretative level, then we assume as being certain that of which we set out to establish the probability.

On the assumption that 'physical object' is in principle applicable, we can show that the applicability of it *to a particular basis* becomes the more probable, the greater the number of different lower-level concepts entailed by 'physical object' which are applicable to this basis. We cannot, however, in this manner, make probable the applicability of 'physical object' in general. The point is that since the applicability of no conjunction of lower-level concepts entails the applicability of any higher-level concept, no complete evidential conjunction consisting of lower-level concepts entails any higher interpretative concept.

Next we turn to frequency-concepts of probability. Theories of this type define probability either directly as a relative frequency, or as a limit of a convergent series of relative frequencies. It is again not necessary for our purpose to raise controversial questions as to the nature of further assumptions about the convergence of series of frequencies, and the possibility of measuring different degrees of probability. Consideration of the notion of relative frequency is sufficient.

Let us assume that we are considering a sequence of bases each of whose members has a certain property 'P'. Let us assume further that one can find out for any member of an initial section of the sequence, whether it has a certain property 'Q' or not. The frequency of 'Q' in an initial section of the sequence is obtained if one divides the number of members of the section which have 'Q' (and, of course, 'P') by the number of all the members of the section. The uselessness of a frequency-concept of probability for the purpose of justifying, for example, the belief in the applicability in principle of 'physical object' can be seen very easily. If we ask, for instance, for the frequency of 'being a physical object', in any series whose members have the property of 'appearing to be a physical object', we clearly assume that the former concept is not empty. We must thus once again run into fallacy. We must have assumed, concerning what we wished to prove probable, that it was already certain.

It would seem that all the great variety of probability-theories are built round either an entailment-concept of probability, or a frequency-concept. Justification of a belief in the applicability of an interpretative category, for example 'physical object', might be sought in another direction. A justification might be sought which would not, or would not obviously, belong to either type of probability-notion. If not, we shall be well advised always to inquire closely whether the tacit assumption that the category is *certainly* not empty be not hidden somewhere among the premisses from which we infer that it is *probably* not empty.

So far, then, we have seen that arguments in justification of a belief in the applicability of an interpretative category, by deduction from the applicability of concepts of lower level, are self-contradictory; and that probability-arguments which proceed from the applicability of concepts of lower level to the probable applicability of interpretative concepts of higher level, are circular. One can show, in refutation of professed demonstrative and probability-justifications of the types described, that the requirements in terms of which these justifications are defined cannot conceivably be fulfilled. The possibility of showing this implies of course that the requirements be made reasonably clear.

This is not the case in certain other justifications which are offered of the belief in the applicability of 'physical object', 'moral action' or other interpretative categories. These are the justifications in terms of so-called "synthetic *a priori* propositions" or "synthetic necessitation". It is, indeed, difficult to examine so vague a doctrine. But if by "synthetic *a priori* propositions" we understand vertical entailments from lower to higher interpretative level, then the assumption that we can justify anything by such means is self-contradictory. It would seem that writers on ethics use ‹synthetic *a priori* propositions› in this sense whenever they declare that propositions describing an action in terms of naturalistic concepts necessitate its being moral (immoral or morally indifferent), and then proceed to compare this kind of necessitation with entailment.

Some arguments in favour of such "synthetic" necessitation are obviously fallacious even if it is difficult to see what precisely they are meant to prove. The fact, for instance, that we judge, with a feeling of self-evidence, that some basis is a physical object, does not by itself point to any necessary applicability of the concept resulting from the applicability of lower concepts. It is, of course, quite true that the consideration of some logically necessary propositions is accompanied by feelings of self-evidence. But it does not follow that, therefore, every feeling of self-evidence points to some logically necessary proposition. A similarly unconvincing argument in favour of synthetic necessitation consists in saying that we know that the interpretative categories which we are using are applicable, and that this knowledge can be explained only by assuming synthetic *a priori* propositions.

The failure to justify belief in an external world in the above senses of "justification" does not, of course, preclude the possibility of showing that this belief fulfils other requirements and can therefore be "justified" in a sense of the term which is defined by means of these requirements. Thus one might say that it is better policy to assume that 'physical object' is in principle applicable than that it is empty. But while such a pragmatic justification is unobjectionable so far as it goes it does, as I hope to show, evade some questions which can be answered.

Instead of looking for a justification in terms of requirements which cannot be satisfied without self-contradition or circularity, I shall inquire more closely into the nature of our belief in an external world and similar beliefs involving interpretative categories. It will, I hope, be seen that the unsatisfactory character of deductive, of probability, and of pragmatic justifications of these beliefs is at least partly due to a misconception of the *sort* of belief we are entertaining in believing that the external world is real or that there is a moral order or, in general, that an interpretative category is not empty. Before, however, discussing these topics we must consider some other questions whose discussion had to wait until the notion of interpretative levels had been explained more fully. These questions concern disposition-statements and the "privacy" of immediate experience.

CHAPTER XIX

DISPOSITION-STATEMENTS

WHOEVER reflects on the nature of conceptual thinking has at some stage to face the problem of clarifying the notion of disposition-statements. This is so, not only because a great deal of conceptual thinking consists in stating or considering propositions about dispositions, but because conceptual thinking itself cannot be characterised without the help of such propositions. Indeed, some understanding of disposition-statements had to be presupposed, and could reasonably be presupposed, at the outset of the inquiry; but the more detailed discussion which we require had to be postponed until after empirical laws of nature had been discussed and the notion of interpretative levels introduced.

That some disposition-statements are closely related to empirical laws of nature is almost immediately obvious. The connection between the application of interpretative concepts, for example 'physical object', and a certain kind of disposition-statements is less clear. Yet the view that seemingly categorical statements about physical objects are really disposition-statements, and the metaphor that physical objects are stores of dispositions, are symptomatic of a connection, however obscure, between a kind of interpretative concept and a kind of disposition-statement.

From a purely philological point of view we are entitled to put the name "disposition-statement" to a very great variety of statements, including some whose triviality makes it unprofitable to discuss them. It is thus advisable to restrict the field of disposition-statements by replacing the purely philological criterion of the grammatically correct use of the word, by other criteria. The statements which satisfy these latter criteria can then be alone called "disposition-statements". It will mean narrowing the sense of the term. We are the more justified in this restriction inasmuch as it is among disposition-statements in the narrow sense that we find the very types with which philosophers have been chiefly preoccupied.

Before, however, laying down restrictive conditions it will be well to survey quickly the whole field of statements about dispositions.

"Disposition" is, of course, a familiar term of ordinary language. And grammatically it would be quite correct to speak of a momentary disposition or inclination, say, to laugh or to weep. In this way we can use "disposition" for an occurrence. It would nevertheless be a pity to let considerations of philological usage deprive us of a very useful distinction. I suggest, therefore, that we use "disposition" as incompatible with "occurrence", and thus that we regard statements about so-called "felt" and, more generally, "occurrent" dispositions, as statements about pseudo-dispositions and not as disposition-statements at all.

Again, when we refer to the dog Pluto's disposition to bark, we are usually remembering that he is a dog. We ascribe this to him because he is a dog. It is to him *qua* dog and not *qua* individual that we ascribe it. Similarly, in saying that every dog has the disposition, we are ascribing the disposition not to individuals as such, but to individuals as members of the species. One is nevertheless speaking perfectly correct English if one ascribes the disposition to Pluto as an individual. It could even in certain circumstances be an interesting piece of information, to be told that the individual called "Pluto" has the disposition to bark, for example if it has turned out that this animal is not a dog at all and that zoologists are unable to determine his species. A person who ascribed to such a creature the disposition to bark might explain what he meant by providing us with a list of the stimuli to which it reacted by barking. The information conveyed by the list might be that it barks when given food, when shown a brightly coloured flag, and so on. Such a statement and list might be called a "reaction-statement". Reaction-statements are far from trivial or unimportant. Indeed, formulations of reaction-statements often, if not always, precede the formulation of laws of nature. I shall nevertheless find it convenient to adopt a definition of "disposition-statements" which excludes reaction-statements, although to use the word "disposition" in referring to them would, as has already been conceded, be perfectly good English.

Further, it is quite true that when a person tells me that dogs have the disposition to bark he will as a rule be able to indicate some condition under which any dog will bark. I will expect a person who makes a disposition-statement intelligently and seriously to be ready to indicate such further conditions if asked for them. Yet it would again be logically and grammatically quite proper in anyone to say that dogs have the disposition to bark although we are not able to state the conditions. To say that dogs have the disposition or tendency to bark, and add that one does not know the conditions under which they will bark, is not self-contradictory. The statement really amounts to saying merely that dogs do in fact sometimes bark. It will be convenient and methodologically advantageous to exclude this type of grammatically correct and sensible statement also from what we are going to call "disposition-statements" in our narrow sense of the term.

Another necessary departure from common usage had better also be noticed. In stating that dogs have a disposition to bark we usually imply that although, of course, not all dogs are constantly barking, some have been observed to do so. We imply in other words that the concept 'barking dog' is known not to be empty. A person might, on the other hand, make the statement that fish have the disposition to bark *and* be content to point out, in spite of all evidence to the contrary, that the conditions under which fish bark have merely never been realised. But again we hardly need to argue the reasonableness of considering as disposition-statements, only such as we have got in the statement that dogs have the disposition to bark, which implies that barking dogs have actually been observed.

One last example of correct English usage falling outside the scope of our intended definition: we frequently meet with statements in the social sciences of the following general sort. A social situation of a certain kind is said to develop under "favourable socio-economic conditions" into one of another kind. This amounts very nearly to saying nothing more than that the change described sometimes does happen. Often, however, the sentence is used not only for the proposition that the change sometimes happens but also, and even primarily, as an exhortation to look out for certain features, however vaguely characterised, of social situations.

It seems again clear that it would be inviting confusion not to exclude propositions of this type from being considered in the present context.

I turn, then, to disposition-statements in a narrower and more interesting sense of the term. In laying down the conditions such statements have to fulfil, it will be convenient to fall back, again, upon a few technical terms. Supposing that we use <dogs have the disposition to bark> for a disposition-statement, I shall say that we are using <dogs> for the *explicit condition*, and <bark> for the *consequence* of the disposition-statement. "If dogs," as we might say, "then they bark." But dogs are not always barking, and to say that it (the barking) is a "disposition" in them, is to say that the conditions under which they bark are for the moment suppressed, that is, they are left unexpressed. Now a statement which contains on the one hand the explicit condition and some or all of the suppressed conditions, and on the other hand the consequence, will be called a "statement supporting the disposition-statement" or briefly a "supporting statement".

It will be seen that the supporting statement is nothing but the disposition-statement made clearer and fuller. It would therefore be a mistake to assume, when first a disposition-statement is made and then one which supports it, that two propositions are being stated, of which the one unilaterally entails the other. Their connection is much more intimate, since to state one is to re-state the other. Whether we can speak of logical equivalence, that is, bilateral entailment, depends on whether or not we have admitted self-entailments. The answer to this question is in the present context not important.

The following conditions are, I believe, fulfilled by all disposition-statements except those which I deliberately wished to exclude because of their being useless or better discussed in another context. First condition: if the explicit condition of a disposition-statement is applicable to a certain basis, then its consequence need not be necessarily also applicable to this basis. For example, although dogs have the disposition to bark, it is not self-contradictory to state that a particular dog or indeed any dog whatsoever is at the moment not barking.

Second condition: The explicit condition, the consequence and the suppressed conditions of a disposition-statement must be concepts and not particulars. This condition, which, I believe, is generally recognised by writers on the subject, excludes reaction-statements which ascribe dispositions to particular bases *qua* particular bases.

Third condition: the conjunction of the explicit condition and the consequent must be applicable to some basis. To state that dogs have the disposition to bark is to imply that "barking dog" is applicable to some directly or indirectly given basis. This condition excludes, for example, the case of the "disposition-statement" that fish will under unknown and unknowable conditions bark.

Fourth condition: to state that either the explicit condition is *not* applicable to a basis or that the consequence *is* applicable to it, must not be to state a logically necessary proposition. For example, if we assume that all dogs have the disposition to bark, then it is not logically necessary that Pluto should be either not a dog or else barking. Indeed, the proposition is sometimes true and sometimes false.

No disposition-statement is fully understood unless we can replace it by a supporting statement which, apart from the explicit condition and the consequence, also displays (*a*) the suppressed conditions and (*b*) the relation of the explicit and the suppressed conditions to the consequence. From our account of empirical laws (in Chapter XI) it will be clear that some disposition-statements can be supported by statements of empirical laws. That statements of such laws support disposition-statements has generally been assumed. The difficulties which have arisen in explaining the nature of disposition-statements have, I believe, been mainly due to the further assumption that empirical laws are either formal implications or entailments.

Let us assume that ‹if anything is a body deprived of support then it falls downwards› is used for an empirical law of nature. The statement of this law supports the disposition-statement that any body has the tendency (disposition) to fall downwards. Clearly "body" is used for the explicit condition, "falls downwards" for consequence, and "deprived of support" for the suppressed condition. The nature of the relation between these concepts has been discussed.

A disposition-statement which is supported by the statement of an empirical law clearly satisfies the conditions which we have taken as fulfilled by disposition-statements. It is thus in particular not self-contradictory to assume that a body with the disposition to fall downwards is not now falling downwards. Bodies have, moreover, been observed to fall downwards. Lastly, in stating that something is either not a body or else is falling downwards, one is not stating a logically necessary proposition.

The conditions fulfilled by disposition-statements are on the whole weaker than those laid down for statements of empirical laws (Chapter XI). This is so mainly because the protasis of an empirical law contains all conditions for the applicability of the apodosis, and not only the explicit ones. It is thus reasonable to ask whether some disposition-statements are not supported by statements other than empirical laws of nature.

It can be shown schematically that disposition-statements can be supported by entailments. Assume that 'P' and 'Q' are two concepts which jointly but not singly entail a third concept 'R'. We might suppress 'Q' and state that whatever possesses 'P' has the disposition to possess 'R'. The entailment that 'P and Q' entails 'R' supports a disposition-statement if, first, the applicability of 'P' to some basis is compatible with the inapplicability of 'R' to this basis; if, secondly, 'P', 'Q', 'R' are concepts; if, thirdly, 'P' and 'R' are applicable to the same basis, that is, if their conjunction is not empty; and if, fourthly, one is not stating a logically necessary proposition by stating that either something has 'not-P' or it has 'R'. It is not at all difficult to satisfy these conditions. An example would be the proposition that authors have the disposition to be poets, which could be supported by the statement that 'being an author composing verse' entails 'being a poet'. Here 'composing verse' is, of course, the suppressed condition.

It can similarly be shown that disposition-statements can be supported by the statement of formal implications of order zero. Assume for this purpose that 'P and Q' formally implies 'R' and that at the same time 'P and not-Q' formally implies 'not-R'. We might again suppress 'Q' in the first and 'not-Q' in the second formal implication. From what has been said about Russellian formal implications and similar implications of order zero in particular (Chapter x), we can assume that the applicability of 'P' to a basis is compatible with the inapplicability of 'R' to it; that 'P', 'Q', 'R' are concepts; that 'P' and 'R' are applicable to the same basis; and, lastly, that '(something has either 'not-P' or it has 'Q')' is not logically necessary. Since these conditions can be satisfied by some conjunctions of formal implications, we could regard any such conjunction as supporting the statement that whatever has 'P' has the disposition to have 'R'. The proposition that bipeds have the disposition to be mammals would be an example, if supported by the conjunction that 'being a featherless biped' formally implies 'being a mammal'; and that 'being a biped but not featherless' formally implies 'not being a mammal'. Here 'being featherless' is the suppressed condition. The possibility of disposition-statements' being supported not only by empirical laws, but also by entailments and formal implications, is not incompatible with the view that the disposition-statements which are typical of scientific theories are supported by empirical laws of nature.

It would be rash to assume that all disposition-statements which satisfy our conditions are in fact supported only by statements of empirical laws, of entailments or of factual implications. Other kinds of supporting statements, in particular combinations of the types so far discussed, might be found. What would make them interesting would, of course, be the contingency that they, or statements closely resembling them, should be found to be in actual use.

One variety of disposition-statements supported by entailments is of special interest. Consider the proposition that a visual appearance of a chair has the disposition to lead (as a result of certain operations, for example, of sitting down) to a tactual appearance of a chair. We assume that the disposition-statement is supported by the entailment that 'being a visual *appearance* of a chair and being an *aspect* of a chair' entails 'leading to a tactual appearance of a chair'. Here 'being a visual appearance of a chair' is the explicit condition, 'leading to a tactual appearance of a chair' is the consequence and 'being a visual aspect of a chair' is the suppressed condition.

The suppressed condition entails both the explicit condition and the consequence. It is of higher interpretative level than are either the explicit condition or the consequence, and it is co-ostensive with the former. A visual appearance *which is also a visual aspect* of a chair does indeed necessarily lead to a tactual appearance of a chair, while a mere visual appearance of a chair may well not. The applicability of the interpretative concept 'aspect of a chair' is the (suppressed) condition for the connection of different appearances of a chair. Aspect-concepts are frequently used in this way. It would be a mistake, however, to confuse the categorical statement that a certain basis, say *b*, is an aspect of a chair, with a conjunction of disposition-statements such as: 'if *b* is a visual appearance of a chair then it has the disposition to lead to a tactual appearance of a chair'.[1]

---

[1] See also Chapter XXVI.

CHAPTER XX

ON THE PRIVACY OF IMMEDIATE
EXPERIENCE

ANOTHER topic which, like that of disposition-statements, pre-supposes the chapters on interpretative concepts, is the privacy of immediate experience. Yet it would not be unreasonable in anyone to object to any account of immediate experience in any such terms. The objector might emphasise the contrast between the discursive or generalising function of conceptual thinking and the individual character of immediate experience. He might hold that even by reflecting on our immediate experience we necessarily deprive it of its immediacy, and that by applying concepts to it—explaining it in terms of differences between kinds and levels of ostensive concepts—we may be changing it out of all recognition.

Whatever the clear meaning of these familiar charges, it hardly seems that those philosophers who characterise immediate experience by the applicability to it of certain concepts, use the term "immediate experience" in such a manner that to state the applicability of a concept to it is to be guilty of a contradiction in terms.

Once we take this use of the term for granted, it does not seem implausible to think that the nature of immediate experience might be characterised by means of distinctions between different kinds of concepts. Indeed, the question whether all immediate experience is sensed and whether what is perceived is interpreted, has been discussed above in this manner. We have noted that the term "sensed" refers to directly given bases of descriptive concepts, the term "perceived" to directly given bases of interpretative concepts. Since, however, concepts of different interpretative levels may have the same basis and since no criterion of the absolutely descriptive character of concepts is available, we had to conclude that the distinction between the sensed and the perceived is also only relative and consequently worthless for most of its usual purposes.

In the present chapter I shall try to use the distinction between interpretative concepts of different levels and a further distinction between impersonal, personal and strictly personal concepts, in considering the question whether immediate experience—perhaps all experience—is private; and, if so, how its privacy is to be transcended. I shall, first of all, argue that the doctrine of the privacy of all experience or of immediate experience, as it is usually formulated, is neither self-evident nor clear. I shall then propose some definitions for the terms "personal", "impersonal", "private", which will be used in reformulating and criticising the doctrine of privacy. The first two of them will also be needed in later stages of the discussion.

Both Descartes and Hume, to choose two otherwise widely differing philosophers, hold that immediate experience is essentially private. According to Descartes the meditating philosopher who uses the method of doubt becomes necessarily aware of this handicap but, if he continues to meditate in the right way, does overcome it. According to Hume the meditating philosopher who becomes aware of the private nature of immediate experience cannot conceivably transcend it. He can believe that he experiences a public world, but only by ceasing to meditate correctly on the nature of his experience.

Without a thorough discussion of the theories of Hume and Descartes and some other philosophers, the connection between the present discussion of immedate experience and the traditional treatment of it is perhaps not too obvious. Two quotations, however, must take the place of many, and the use of italics in them must take the place of detailed textual criticism.

"In any case", says Descartes in the second Meditation, "it is certain that *I seem* to see light, hear noise and feel heat; this cannot be false and is what *in myself* is properly called perceiving...." Hume insists similarly on the private character of immediate experience: "We may observe that 'tis universally allowed by philosophers, and is besides *pretty obvious of itself*, that nothing is ever *really* present with the mind but its perceptions or impressions and ideas...'tis impossible for us so much as to conceive or form an idea specifically different from ideas and impressions."[1] The

---

[1] *Treatise*, Bk. I, Pt. II, Section VI.

doctrine expressed in these and other passages has been regarded by many thinkers as important, as generally accepted or even as self-evident.

Yet the clarity of the doctrine leaves much to be desired. Terms such as "perception" and "experience" are transplanted from non-philosophical contexts into philosophical without much effort to safeguard their use against the dangerous ambiguities which are the frequent result of such transposition. And these are not dangers that exist only in pedantic minds. To show this we only need recall the different meanings of "illusion" in (a) the question whether, on the assumption that 'snake' is *not* an empty concept, the snake, seen by the drunkard, is an illusion; and (b) the question whether *the world* is an illusion for the reason that 'physical object' (and therefore 'snake') *is* an empty concept.

An equally dangerous ambiguity in the use of "experience" is of course the familiar one. Does it refer to the experienced or to the experiencing? In a similar way "perception" in its many senses refers to perceiving and the perceived. In most non-philosophical contexts the differences in the use of such terms can be safely ignored or, at least, need not be emphasised. That we must not ignore the distinction in discussing the doctrine of the privacy of immediate experience is often preached, but less often practised.

Experiencing is, by definition—more precisely, by the definitions which most people would give if pressed—private in a sense in which nothing else is. Whatever is my experiencing is necessarily not another person's experiencing. Indeed, another person is, precisely, a being whose experiencing is different from mine. However, another person is also a being who can either share what is experienced by me or who experiences something similar to what is experienced by me. A being whose experiencing is not different from mine would not be *another* person. A being who could not share what is experienced by me, or who could not experience anything similar to what is experienced by me, would not be another *person*. The distinction between 'experiencing' and the 'experienced' is thus not only implicit in a widespread use of the term "experience", it is also demanded by widespread uses of "person".

Since experience in the sense of experiencing is by definition private though in the sense of the experienced it may be private or public, we are in danger of confusion if we try to support the doctrine of the privacy of the experienced by an irrelevant appeal to the privacy of experiencing. This mistake seems to have been committed by Hume, at least in some passages of his *Treatise*. If ordinary uses of the critical terms can be said at all to embody any doctrine about the nature of the experienced, then they point to the view that some experiences, in the sense of what is experienced, are public. It is quite proper to say that our enjoying a piece of music is a kind of experiencing and therefore private and incapable of being shared, and that nevertheless two people may enjoy the same or a similar musical experience. The assumption that the enjoyed music can be shared, although enjoying it is private, is an assumption common to composer, conductor and concert-goer.

The issue as to whether privacy attaches to everything that is experienced or to any part of it, can be translated into the terminology of ostensive concepts, and in particular into the terminology of ostensive concepts of different interpretative levels. What we have to do here is to replace "experience" (in the sense of the experienced) and "private" with terms whose meaning is clearly defined and yet is adequately linked to the vaguer common uses of these rejected terms. It must be emphasised again that the definitions to be given will be used not only in the necessarily uncertain reformulation of the doctrine that all or some "experience" is "private", but also in later discussions, which are independent of the correctness of the reformulation.

In attempting to define the meaning of "empirical proposition" in a way which would do justice to the use of the term by Kant and other philosophers (Chapter XI) we defined a proposition which describes possible experience as an ostensive or a negated ostensive proposition, or an internally consistent conjunction of such propositions. To state such a proposition is thus to describe what is possibly experienced.

The term "immediately experienced" would have to be defined differently for different philosophers. I believe, however, that the definition which would correspond to perhaps the most frequent use of the term would be the following: the term "immediately experienced" refers to a directly given basis in so far as it is characterised by an absolutely descriptive concept. Some philosophers might be prepared to waive the demand for characterisation by an absolutely descriptive concept, and be satisfied with the weaker requirement that the directly given basis be characterised by an interpretative concept of low level.

I believe that the above definition of "immediately experienced" is a fair approximation to its use by those philosophers who do not treat the statement, about something immediately experienced, that it can be characterised by concepts as a self-contradictory statement. With other meanings of this term I am not here concerned. How that which cannot be conceptually characterised can nevertheless be made the topic of a philosophical discussion is consequently not a question which will have to be answered or which arises from the discussion.

I feel less confident that the definition of "private" to be proposed approximates to the intentions of its various users as closely as do the above definitions of "possibly experienced" and "immediately experienced". It is convenient to start with a representative example. Let us consider the statement that a certain feeling of pain is private. A person who makes this statement does not, or does not normally, state two logically independent propositions, namely, that a certain basis is a feeling of pain and that it is private: for every feeling of pain is necessarily private.

On the other hand, by saying that every feeling of pain is necessarily private one also does not wish to imply that the ostensive concept 'a feeling of pain' entails another ostensive concept 'private'. The necessary connection is different from that between 'green' and 'coloured', both of which are ostensive, since ⟨private⟩ is not used for an ostensive concept when pain is called "private". In explaining its meaning we cannot give examples and anti-examples as we do in explaining the meaning of "green", "chair", "pain". True, a tooth-ache, which is private, and a feeling of anxiety, which is equally private, are both ostensive. Yet this does not imply that 'private' itself is an ostensive concept.

Though we cannot compare the statement that a feeling of pain is necessarily private with the statement that what is green is necessarily coloured, we might be able to compare it with the statement that what is green is necessarily ostensive. In the latter statement ⟨ostensive⟩ is not used for an ostensive concept, but to characterise 'green' as an ostensive concept. By making it we do not characterise a basis of 'green' but the concept 'green' itself. Similarly, by stating that a feeling of pain is private, we may be characterising not the basis of 'feeling of pain' but the concept itself. This would be an explanation why any feeling of pain is necessarily private, though 'private' is not an ostensive concept. It is not the only explanation, but one which does justice to many uses of ⟨private⟩ by philosphers and others. Even apart from possibly reformulating an obscure theory in a clearer manner, it will be convenient to consider 'private', like 'ostensive', as a characteristic of concepts and not, like 'green', as a characteristic of bases.

I do not deny that ⟨private⟩ is often used for an ostensive concept and not for a characteristic of ostensive concepts of a certain type. There may, indeed, be exemplifiable feelings of privacy which can be distinguished from feelings of lack of privacy or of publicity. It must, however, lead to considerable confusion if in talking of immediate experience we use ⟨private⟩ for an ostensive concept and also for a characteristic of a type of ostensive concept. The danger of such confusion is the greater, the less clearly the fundamental distinction between ostensive and non-ostensive concepts is noted.

Instead of defining directly a use of ⟨private⟩ for a characteristic of a type of ostensive concept, I propose first to define a weaker notion for which I shall use the word "personal". I shall say that an ostensive concept, say 'R', is personal if, and only if, the following two conditions are fulfilled: (1) to apply the concept 'R' to a basis, say b, is to state a relation between b and a basis, say a, of 'person' (more precisely, of course, of 'aspect of a person'); (2) the proposition that 'R' holds between a and b does not entail the proposition that 'R' holds between any other person and b. A concept 'R' is accordingly impersonal if (1) to apply 'R' is not to state a relation between b and a person or if (2) the proposition that 'R' holds between b and some person does entail that it holds between b and any other person.

According to the preceding definitions 'a feeling of pain' would be a personal concept but 'chair' would be an impersonal concept. Thus the proposition that a directly or indirectly given basis is a chair (more precisely, an aspect of a chair) does not entail that the basis is related to me or some other person in some peculiar way. I may, of course, believe that the basis is so related to me; or even that I could otherwise never know, believe or judge that the basis is a chair. However, to state these beliefs is to state propositions which jointly and singly are logically independent of the proposition that the basis is a chair. On the other hand, if anything is a feeling of pain it is necessarily the pain of some person. Moreover, that it is the pain of some person does not entail that it is the pain of any other person. (As is permissible within the scope of a mere logical inquiry I have ignored the fact that animals feel pain.)

A concept 'R' is private or, as I prefer to say, *strictly personal* if, and only if, the following two conditions are fulfilled: (1) to apply 'R' to a basis, say b, is to state a relation between b and another basis, say a, of 'person'; (2) the proposition that 'R' holds between a and b entails the proposition that 'R' does not hold between any other person and b. The first condition, which must be fulfilled by every strictly personal concept, is identical with the above-mentioned first condition fulfilled by all personal concepts. The second condition for strictly personal concepts is, however, stronger than the corresponding condition for personal concepts. A comparison between these corresponding conditions shows that while every strictly personal concept is personal, not every personal concept is also strictly personal or private.

The concept 'a feeling of pain' is an example not only of a personal concept but also of a strictly personal concept. According to our normal use of ‹feeling of pain›, ignoring other sentient beings, if anything is a feeling of pain it is necessarily the pain of a person. Moreover, if it is a feeling of pain of one person it is necessarily not the feeling of another person. Even if we adopt Schopenhauer's use of ‹pain›, according to which in a sense anybody's pain is everybody's pain, we should still have to use ‹pain› or perhaps some other word for a strictly personal concept. The distinction between personal and impersonal concepts will help us to avoid the use of the terms "objective" and "subjective" whose ambiguity unnecessarily obscures some otherwise unproblematic questions in ethics.

If we accept the above definition of "immediately experienced" on the one hand and of "private" on the other, as corresponding more or less to the use of these terms in the formulation of the doctrine of the private character of immediate experience, then we can reformulate the doctrine in a clearer fashion. To state that whatever is immediately experienced is private is to state that all absolutely descriptive concepts, or all ostensive concepts of low interpretative level, are strictly personal.

To disprove this statement it is sufficient to give a counter-example. For that purpose we consider a purely ostensive concept, for example, the purely ostensive derivative of 'green'; the level of which is certainly as low as we can wish. To apply it to a basis is not to state a relation between this basis and a person. Consequently it is a mistake to say that all ostensive concepts of low interpretative level are strictly personal.

If therefore we interpret "the immediately experienced" and "the private" in the above manner, then the doctrine of the privacy of all experience or even of all immediate experience is false and the problem as to whether and how this privacy can ever be transcended does not arise. According to our interpretation of the terms in which the doctrine is formulated, we have to defend the unexciting thesis that part of what is immediately experienced, for example, a pain, is private, and part of it, for example, a coloured patch, is public. If the interpretation is considered to miss the point of the doctrine I can only plead the obscurity of its usual formulations.

CHAPTER XXI

ON THE ONTOLOGY OF OSTENSIVE CONCEPTS

I RETURN now—after the justifiable digressions of Chapters XIX and XX—to philosophical problems about existence. These have been long and well represented both in their perplexity and in their futility by the question: does a physical world exist? Two sources of confusion have been removed already without much difficulty. First of all we have noted the difference between, say, the zoological question whether sea-serpents exist and the philosophical question whether physical objects exist. It is simply that the zoologist in asking his question assumes that 'physical object' is not empty while the philosopher calls this very assumption in question. Secondly, it has been shown that demonstrative arguments in justification of the assumption are self-contradictory and that probability arguments are circular (Chapter XVIII).

We are now prepared to consider in a more positive manner the nature of statements to the effect that a concept is not empty or that what can be characterised by means of it exists. The choice between speaking of the non-emptiness or emptiness of concepts on the one hand and of the existence or non-existence of particulars on the other is largely a matter of taste. There are, however, cases where the term "existence" is used and where yet a straightforward translation into the idiom of empty and not empty concepts is not possible. For example, the question, whether, if the set of natural numbers exists, there exists also the set of all its subsets, is— at least very often—only another formulation of the question whether a certain abstract algebra or calculus is or is not consistent. Another example is the use of the term "existence" by some existentialists, who imply by it that human beings "exist" but not things. These examples could be easily multiplied, and in view of them I shall, as a rule, speak of the emptiness or otherwise of concepts, rather than the existence or non-existence of particulars.

It is often assumed that science and common-sense presuppose an ontology (doctrine of categories, theory of objects), the implications of which are largely hidden from scientists and ordinary people in their common pursuits. On this view it is the business of the philosopher to make the fundamental categories of scientific and common-sense thinking explicit. Sometimes the even more radical claim is made that ontology or metaphysics is an inquiry which may lead to the discovery of those categories which are characteristic of reality—a reality which may have little to do with common-sense or science. In this way it is characteristic of Plato to speak of the reality of numbers and of the unreality of physical objects.

A scientist *qua* scientist will regard as not empty those categories which he can successfully use in the construction of theories from which empirical laws can be deduced. If this attitude is elaborated by philosophers it gives rise to the metaphysics of logical positivism, pragmatism and similar philosophical doctrines. Other types of metaphysical theory are obviously in the habit of using different criteria of the emptiness or non-emptiness of categories. There are, then, different senses in which categories are asserted to be empty or not-empty, and it must be philosophically important to distinguish between at least some of these senses.

For this purpose some of our earlier distinctions will stand us in good stead, in particular those between ostensive and non-ostensive concepts, between different levels of ostensive concepts, and between bases and instances of them. As regards this latter distinction we may recall that an ostensive basis is anything to which *some* ostensive concept is (appropriately) applicable. An ostensive concept, say 'P', is applicable to a basis, say b, if a person by applying 'P' to b would not be violating the rules governing 'P'. The fact that some particular person, or anybody at all, has or has not accepted the concept or applied it to the basis, is here irrelevant. An instance, on the other hand, has reference to a person. A basis is an instance of a concept only with respect to the person who in fact has applied the concept to the basis. As I put it earlier, to speak of concepts and their bases is to consider concept-basis relations, and to speak of concepts and their instances is to consider concept-basis-thinker relations.

The distinction between instances and bases carries over into a distinction between two senses of empty concepts—namely, concepts empty of instances, and concepts empty of bases. In addition, there is a generally acknowledged third sense of empty concepts, namely, that of logically empty, or internally inconsistent concepts. Any such concept is logically equivalent to a conjunction of concepts, of whose members one at least is incompatible with some other. It is thus empty because of a certain concept-concept relation. These remarks suggest a convenient order in which to consider (1) definitions of emptiness in terms of concept-concept relations or of internal inconsistency, (2) definitions of emptiness in terms of concept-basis relations or of the applicability of concepts to bases, (3) definitions of emptiness in terms of concept-basis-thinker relations or of the application of concepts to bases by certain thinkers.

As regards the logical emptiness of concepts there is little more to be said. We might, if we like, distinguish between different types of logical emptiness according to the different definitions of internal consistency, and according to the different types of incompatibility propositions or entailments which are the ground of the logical emptiness.[1] Thus, we might distinguish between the emptiness of 'P and Q' according to whether 'P entails not-Q' is or is not a primitive entailment, etc. Clearly a logically empty concept is not (appropriately) applicable to any basis, and since it can have no bases it also can have no instances. Those philosophers who hold that a category, say 'physical object', is empty do not wish to imply that it is logically empty as is, for example, 'female father'. There is no need to argue this point.

Turning now to the definition of emptiness in terms of concept-basis relations, I first of all propose to call a concept descriptively empty if it is not (appropriately) applicable to any ostensive basis. Of a concept which is so applicable I shall say that it has descriptive content. All ostensive concepts have, of course, descriptive content. This is not necessarily the case with compounds of ostensive concepts, in particular with conjunctions which may or may not be descriptively empty. For example, 'wooded mountain' has descrip-

_____
[1] See, for example, Chapter XII.

tive content but Meinong's 'golden mountain' or 'unicorn', that is, 'horse-like animal with one horn', is descriptively empty.

In stating that there are no unicorns or golden mountains we often wish to state less than that the concept is descriptively empty, namely, that we believe it to be so because no basis of it is known or will ever be found. We may also, however, wish to say more, for example that the emptiness of these concepts rests on some empirical law of nature. Thus in saying that 'unicorn' is empty we do as a rule imply on the one hand that the concept is descriptively empty, and on the other, that if anything is a horse-like animal then it cannot have a horn. The term "cannot" indicates here the type of necessity, explained (in Chapter XI) as being characteristic of empirical laws of nature.

When a subjective idealist proclaims that 'physical object' is an empty concept because *esse est percipi* and because the alleged *esse* of a physical object is not, or not only, *percipi* he does not wish to imply that the concept 'lion' is empty in exactly the same sense as the concept 'unicorn'. There is, according to Berkeley, no harm in speaking with the vulgar to the effect that lions exist. But we should not even be speaking with the vulgar if we stated that unicorns exist. The concept 'lion' (as entailing 'physical object') is empty in some non-vulgar, metaphysical sense; whereas the emptiness of 'unicorn' is not only metaphysical. We can, I believe, help the subjective idealist in expressing his intention more clearly by stating that 'physical object' is not descriptively empty whereas 'unicorn' is.

It does seem to me that Berkeley and his followers and opponents, sometimes at least, fail to distinguish precisely between the descriptive emptiness of 'physical object' which they do not and cannot reasonably assert and an emptiness of another type the nature of which they have not quite recognised—and which has to do with instances, that is, concept-basis-thinker relations and not with bases, that is, concept-basis relations. If, therefore, Berkeley is attacked by opponents who are lacking in subtlety or charity or both, for holding that both unicorns and lions are in one and the same sense of the term non-existent, the fault does not always lie with the attackers.

Just as Berkeley cannot, I think, reasonably be regarded as denying descriptive content to 'physical object', so we cannot accuse Plato of denying this: for Plato is careful to distinguish between the existence of physical objects and the real existence ($ὄντως εἶναι$) of the Forms. Indeed, in our terminology, Plato's 'physical object' has descriptive content whereas 'number' and other Forms have not since they are non-ostensive concepts. To these examples of implicit distinction between the descriptive type of emptiness and some other type which yet is not logical, we could add many others taken from philosophers of the most varied kinds. Such further examples would illustrate this distinction not only with regard to 'physical object' but with regard to any interpretative category.

What then is this third sense in which ostensive concepts and their compounds can be said to be empty, yet without being either empty descriptively or logically? As I have indicated, it must be defined in terms not of concept-concept relations or of concept-basis relations but of concept-basis-thinker relations. *It is emptiness of instances and not of bases.* Let us say, then, that a concept is ontologically empty with respect to a person who either has not (appropriately) applied the concept at all, or who having applied it previously no longer intends to do so. For such a person the concept has never had any instances, or no longer has any. Of a concept which for a certain person is not ontologically empty, I shall say that it has ontological content for him.

There are many species of ontological emptiness or ontological content. As this is not the place to attempt a thorough classification I shall merely submit a few examples pointing towards it. Consider the concept $ἀρετή$ as used in fourth-century Athens. For any person who does not know the rules governing its use this concept is ontologically empty. It is also ontologically empty, though in a different sense, for the Greek scholar who knows how the Greeks applied it and thus could, therefore, apply it himself, but who only as it were pretends to apply it, for example when explaining its use to his pupils. Or take the example of a person who, let us say, has been a philosophical realist and accepted the rules governing 'physical object', in the version of perhaps a particular realist philosopher, but who has undergone a philosophical "conversion" to some variety of phenomenalism. This person will not have ceased to know the rules governing 'physical object'. Neither will he have ceased to be able to apply them. All that has happened is that the concept which he did recognise, and still recognises, as having descriptive content has for him changed from being a concept with ontological content to being one ontologically empty. These examples suffice, I think, to show the variety of sorts of ontological emptiness and content which concepts may exhibit.

The connection between the three types of empty concept is briefly this: logical emptiness entails descriptive emptiness which in turn entails ontological emptiness for all thinkers. If, on the other hand, for any particular thinker a concept has ontological content it must have descriptive content; and if it has descriptive content then it cannot be logically empty. In other words, if a concept is internally inconsistent it cannot be applicable to any basis and in such a case it cannot have instances for anybody. On the other hand, if a concept has instances for some particular thinker, then it must have bases to which it is appropriately applicable; and in this case it cannot be an internally inconsistent conjunction of concepts.

Clearly, if a concept has ontological content for one thinker it can yet be ontologically empty for another. Again, if a concept has ontological content for a particular thinker then all lower-level concepts entailed by it will also have ontological content for him. For example, to the Platonist, for whom 'chair-as-conceived-by-Plato' has ontological content, 'chair', 'chair-appearance' etc., have ontological content. On the other hand, obviously the fact that a concept has ontological content for a thinker does not imply that the higher-level concepts by which it is entailed have ontological content—even if they are descriptively not empty.

It is usual to distinguish between two kinds of empty concepts only, namely, the logically and the factually empty. This distinction is insufficient, because insensitive to the difference between the descriptive emptiness of 'unicorn' on any philosophical view, and the ontological emptiness of some interpretative concepts which are not descriptively empty.

Let us now consider again the perplexing question: does an external world exist? or (an only slightly less provocative form of the same) the question: is the concept 'physical object' empty? If we assume that the concept is on all hands agreed to be internally consistent then the question can be understood in two different ways, namely, (1) is the concept descriptively empty? and (2) is the concept ontologically empty?

The perplexity arises from the fact that people for whom 'physical object' is ontologically not empty take a philosopher (often not without his fault) to be asking the first question when in fact he is concerned with the second. Now the first question—is the concept descriptively empty?—is, indeed, an extremely odd one to raise. It amounts to asking whether 'physical object' has any basis to which it could be appropriately applied or, more explicitly, whether if anybody *were* to accept the rules governing 'physical object' he *would* be violating them by applying them to any ostensive basis. The answer is so obvious that the question seems preposterous. If a person *were* to accept the rules governing 'physical object' he would not be violating them by applying the concept, for example, to his pipe. No more is needed to show that 'physical object' is not *descriptively* empty.

What we have said about the alleged proofs of the applicability (descriptive content) of 'physical object' from the applicability of lower-level concepts remains, of course, unchanged. We cannot in this manner establish that 'physical object' has descriptive content. But that a thesis cannot be established in one way is no proof that it cannot be established in another.

We come now to the second question: is 'physical object' ontologically empty? The first point here is again an obvious one. For some people, mainly philosophers, it is ontologically empty, but for most others it is not. These empirical facts can be established by an empirical inquiry. What we have to find out is whether as a matter of fact a certain person does or does not accept the rules governing 'physical object' and does or does not intend to apply them. In the case of Berkeley we should, on the evidence of his published works, come to the conclusion that for him the concept is ontologically empty.

Now Berkeley is, of course, not content to convey to his readers that for him 'physical object' is ontologically empty. Metaphysics would, indeed, be a dull subject if metaphysicians merely habitually put it on record that for them certain categories had ontological content whereas others were ontologically empty. What they also, and mainly, do is to give reasons why they have accepted and are applying some categories, why they have rejected others and why other people should follow their example.

Roughly speaking, whether their metaphysics be operationalist, Hegelian, or any other, what metaphysicians do when they argue that a category is not empty is to recommend the acceptance of certain categories and the rejection of others. Such recommendation is, moreover, supported by an appeal to general principles. The nature of these principles, at least of those of them which in a way regulate the acceptance and rejection of categories, will be examined in Part III. Discussion of them will presuppose a clear distinction between the descriptive and the ontological emptiness of interpretative concepts, particularly those of the latter which (with respect to a given system of concepts) are categories.

CHAPTER XXII

ON THE ONTOLOGY OF NON-OSTENSIVE
CONCEPTS

So far we have been concerned with different types of statement to the effect that ostensive concepts and their compounds are or are not empty, or that they do or do not characterise what 'is real' or 'exists'. Accordingly, we have been concerned with lions, unicorns and physical objects rather than with numbers, propositions and unobservable entities. In this chapter we shall consider the emptiness or otherwise of non-ostensive concepts.

The relation of non-ostensive to ostensive concepts has already been discussed (in Chapter VII). It was there argued that in exhibiting the rules governing the use of non-ostensive concepts, one is not helped by postulating ideal particulars to which they would be applicable in a manner analogous to that in which ostensive concepts apply to their bases. If the postulation of ideal particulars is at all harmful, it is perhaps so, chiefly, by creating the false impression that a problem which cannot be solved by mere postulation has in fact been solved in this way.

If of two philosophers one holds that what is characterised by certain non-ostensive concepts cannot conceivably be real, while the other holds that what is real must be so characterised, then their disagreement is usually due to their acceptance of different criteria of "the real". If changelessness and absence of spatial and temporal location is characteristic of the real, then physical-object concepts and their co-ostensive concepts do not characterise it. If changeability and space-time location are criteria of the real, then non-ostensive concepts do not characterise reality.

Once the different criteria accepted by the opposing thinkers are brought to light, the disagreement may vanish. It may, however, turn out that the disagreement concerns the justification of one set of criteria in preference to another. In this, as in many similar cases, the disputants might appeal to ordinary language as embodying their criteria. Ordinary language, or rather the languages of groups of non-philosophers who are in the habit of conveying information to each other by spoken or written words, does not, however, embody any of these criteria. It is, I believe, neutral, and takes no sides even as between criteria as widely divergent as are those of Plato and Hume; although it suggests refinements of the use of "real", for example inclining towards a Platonic or towards a Humean concept of reality.

By saying that arguments in favour of one set of criteria rather than another cannot be settled by appeal to ordinary usage, I do not wish to imply that the matter is beyond the reach of rational argument. As I have indicated, the nature of reasoning about criteria of reality, the reasoning often called "metaphysical", will be discussed in Part III (especially Chapter XXXIII).

In discussing statements to the effect that ostensive concepts are empty in different, though not clearly distinguished, senses of "empty" (existence, reality), we accepted the usual distinction between logically and factually empty concepts. We have, however, found it necessary to distinguish within the latter group between descriptively and ontologically empty. Without this or some similar distinction we could not even explain, with regard to any philosophy for which the physical world is "unreal", the difference between the emptiness of 'unicorn' and that of 'physical object'. In discussing statements to the effect that some non-ostensive concepts are empty, whereas others are not, we shall equally have to recognise, over and above the distinction between logical and factual emptiness, a distinction between different species of factual emptiness.

Non-ostensive concepts are by definition descriptively empty: no such concept could be appropriately applied to any ostensive basis. Nevertheless, although non-ostensive concepts do not directly characterise possible experience, they are used in the characterisation of possible experience. Their connection with experience or, as we shall say, their quasi-applicability is mediated by their relations to ostensive concepts. We have (in Chapter VII) distinguished between simplifying and completable non-ostensive concepts. We distinguished between them according to the different relations which they bear to ostensive concepts. Simplifying concepts, of which those of geometry and arithmetic are examples, differ from the concepts which they simplify, by standing in relations of exclusion or of inclusion, where the latter stand in the relation of overlap. The simplifying concepts which we have considered were at best, of course, only rudiments of arithmetical and geometrical concepts. They were only the first stage in a gradual transition from ostensive concepts to the concepts of arithmetic and geometry.

Completable concepts, on the other hand, are such non-ostensive concepts as can be combined with ostensive to form ostensive concepts. They are either governed by rules to which ostensive rules can be added without inconsistency (and are thus in a way provisionally non-ostensive) or else they are necessarily non-ostensive. Provisionally non-ostensive concepts are, for instance, some concepts of particles. Completable concepts, whose non-ostensive character could not possibly be lost by an addition of an ostensive rule to the other rules governing them, are in particular the epistemological concepts such as 'proposition' and 'concept'. 'Asserting a proposition' is indeed an ostensive concept which is co-ostensive with 'producing a series of signs of a certain specified kind'. But 'proposition' itself is not ostensive.

With regard to the question whether they characterise what is real the three sorts of non-ostensive concepts, viz. simplifying concepts (for example, some concepts of mathematics), ideal-constituent concepts (for example, concepts of so-far-unobservable particles in physics), and epistemological concepts (for example, 'proposition') are usually discussed separately.[1] I shall keep to this practice, although what I have to say about them will be very similar in each case.

The question whether *any* simplifying concept characterises what is real must be answered, and affirmatively answered, before we can go on to ask which simplifying concepts do and which simplifying concepts do not characterise what is real. Yet I do not propose to raise the former question, and for this reason. If some general criteria of reality are accepted the answer is already given.

[1] There are others which would be susceptible of similar treatment.

If no such criteria are forthcoming, then the question seems to be a request for a more or less rough indication of the rules governing simplifying concepts, a request which loses its point once these rules are clearly exhibited. In a similar way the question whether a person's politics are progressive or reactionary is a request for a rough indication of what his political views are. This request also loses its point when this person's particular views are known. To add to a detailed account of anyone's political views the information that he is "progressive" is at best to add nothing and at worst to produce confusion.

The question as to which simplifying concepts characterise "what is real" and which do not can be made clearer. It is possible, and for the clarification of certain problems useful, to distinguish between two senses in which simplifying concepts may be empty. Just as a subjective idealist may hold that 'physical object' is not descriptively empty but is ontologically empty, so a defender of Kant's Transcendental Aesthetic might hold that 'non-Euclidean triangle' although not empty in one sense is yet empty in another.

In order to distinguish more clearly between two senses of the emptiness of simplifying concepts, I shall first of all say that a simplifying concept is quasi-applicable with respect to a set of ostensive concepts, if it occurs at least in one concept-concept relation which simplifies a concept-concept relation between the ostensive concepts of the set. Thus, for example, the concept 'geometrical circle' is quasi-applicable with respect to the concepts 'visual circle' and 'visual ellipse' because the proposition that 'geometrical circle' excludes 'geometrical ellipse' (with two distinct foci) simplifies the proposition that 'visual circle' overlaps with 'visual ellipse'. I am speaking of the quasi-applicability of 'geometrical circle' because this concept, although it has no ostensive basis, is yet linked with the bases of 'visual circle' by way of the simplifying relation between the two concepts.

The contrast between quasi-applicable simplifying concepts and such as are not quasi-applicable is analogous to the contrast between applicable, that is, not-descriptively-empty, and descriptively-empty ostensive concepts or compounds of ostensive concepts. Thus the quasi-applicability of a simplifying concept is logically not dependent on whether a person employs the simplifying concept or intends to employ it. To state the quasi-applicability of a simplifying concept is, in other words, to state how this non-ostensive concept is connected with ostensive concepts and *through them* linked to ostensive bases. It is not to state concept-basis-thinker relations, but, as it were, mediated or indirect concept-basis relations.

Moreover, just as the undisputed, and indisputable, applicability of, for example, 'physical object' leaves room for disagreement about its ontological emptiness or otherwise, so agreement about the quasi-applicability of, for example, 'non-Euclidean triangle' leaves room for ontological disagreement. A defender of Kant's Transcendental Aesthetic might, as is proper, admit the quasi-applicability of this concept and yet hold that, unlike 'Euclidean triangle', it characterises nothing real, or is ontologically empty. What he means, or something approximating his meaning, might be expressed by defining a simplifying concept as *ontologically* not empty *for a person*, if, and only if, it is not only quasi-applicable but the person also has satisfied the rules for its use, or at least intends to do so.

The metaphysical arguments for or against the "reality" of Euclidean space (as distinct from the quasi-applicability of the concepts of Euclidean geometry), frequent about the beginning of the present century, have, I believe, died down. One should note here that in accordance with our definitions both the concepts of Euclidean geometry *and* the concepts of a non-Euclidean geometry not only are quasi-applicable but also may have ontological content for the same person. An applied mathematician may indeed be in the habit of employing the two types of simplifying concept for different purposes.

Concerning the question whether ideal-constituent concepts characterise what exists or is real one may again ask the two questions, namely, first, whether such concepts are *in general* empty and, secondly, which of them are so or not so. Since the second question presupposes an affirmative answer to the first, the term "emptiness" and its cognates are being used differently in the two questions. As has been pointed out for simplifying concepts, a detailed exposition of the rules governing ideal-constituent concepts makes any answer to the first question superfluous. Its purpose is, I believe, often only to serve as an inducement to exhibit these rules, and their relations to those governing ostensive concepts.

It is again possible and helpful for the understanding of certain problems usually regarded as metaphysical or ontological, to distinguish between two senses in which ideal-constituent concepts are or are not empty. The distinction is similar to that which has been drawn between the quasi-applicability or otherwise, and the ontological emptiness or otherwise, of simplifying concepts. Like the latter distinction it is analogous to the opposition of descriptive and ontological emptiness, in the case of ostensive concepts.

When Kant wrote the Transcendental Aesthetic he ignored the possibility of a non-Euclidean geometry. Yet an apologist in search of a defence for him could at least hold, as we have pointed out, that although 'non-Euclidean triangle', like 'Euclidean triangle', must be allowed to be quasi-applicable, yet only the latter is (for him and should be for everybody) also ontologically not empty. Precisely so a defender of a mechanistic philosophy might hold that although a certain concept of 'field' and a certain concept of 'ideal particle' are both quasi-applicable, only the latter is ontologically not empty.

The definition of "quasi-applicability" for ideal-constituent concepts, and consequently of "ontological emptiness", is suggested by the relation which holds between these concepts and ostensive ones. A non-ostensive concept is a quasi-applicable ideal-constituent concept with respect to a set of ostensive concepts if, and only if, it can be combined with ostensive concepts of the set, to form ostensive concepts, *and* the rules of combination be the same as govern the combination of ostensive concepts, *and* lastly, the ostensive concepts which result from the combination belong to the category of physical objects or processes (Chapter VII).

It is shown by writers on the methodology of physics how, as it is sometimes put, what is in itself unobservable can be indirectly observed through its effects, or how the presence of what is in itself unobservable is inferred from what is observed. Thus a line on a photographic plate is within a certain experimental and theoretical context "inferred" to be the trace of an ideal particle. In judging that the basis of 'line on a photographic plate' is also a basis of 'line on a photographic plate made by an ideal particle' we have made use of the quasi-applicability of 'ideal particle'. We have combined it and the ostensive concept 'line on a photographic plate' into an ostensive concept, in the same way as we should combine the two ostensive concepts 'line on a photographic plate' and 'being made by a needle' into 'line being made on a photographic plate by a needle'. I believe that it would make for clarity if instead of speaking about indirect observation, or about inference to the presence of ideal-constituent concepts, we spoke about making use of their quasi-applicability. Obviously, however, there is no need for present purposes to argue this point.

An ideal-constituent concept, say some concept of 'field of force', which allows us to do without 'ideal particle', is ontologically not empty for a person if, and only if, it be in the sense above described quasi-applicable, *and* the person have satisfied or intend to satisfy the rules governing its use. If a philosophising physicist says he understands but does not accept the view that 'particle', but not 'field', characterises ultimate physical reality, he may mean, or may mean very nearly, that for him only the former concept is not ontologically empty.

Lastly we turn to epistemological concepts such as 'concept', 'proposition'. The question whether or not, for example, 'concept', or as it has been put 'species' or 'genus', characterises what is real has been asked again and again and has, I believe rightly, become an often-quoted example of sterile philosophical discussion. Some philosophers, I believe, still ask, as if they were asking a profound question, whether propositions exist. They ask, moreover, whether propositions or only meaningful sentences exist. That at least the question about the existence of concepts is profoundly important has been proclaimed by Porphyry and has been accepted by many medieval and modern philosophers. Porphyry, in his Introduction to Aristotle's *Organon*, asks whether genera and species have real existence or whether they are only in our thoughts, whether if they do exist they are corporeal or not, and whether they exist separately from perceptible objects or in these objects only.

The question whether genera and species really exist is the question whether the non-ostensive concept 'concept' characterises what is real. The preceding discussion should have more than prepared us for an answer. Unless we are given criteria for the use of "characterising what is real", the best we can do is to exhibit the rules governing 'concept', and show how it is related to ostensive concepts. A nominalist and a realist who accept this might still disagree as to how to answer Porphyry's question. The disagreement would concern the choice of criteria for applying "characterising the real".

It is more difficult to see what is meant by asking whether or not a genus is corporeal. If a corporeal concept is an ostensive concept, then we can confidently state that genera and species are not corporeal. I do not, however, think that this is acceptable as an interpretation of Porphyry. About the third part of his question I shall say nothing. It seems, however, that the difficulty of this question is not, as Porphyry himself thought, due to its profundity, but to the lack of any indication of the requirements which an answer would have to fulfil. It is, strictly speaking, not a question. It is rather the expression of an uneasiness which may lead to questions and has in fact done so.

Philosophers have often disagreed as to which epistemological concepts are empty and which are not. It may again help to reveal the nature of the dispute, if we compare quasi-applicable and not quasi-applicable epistemological concepts on the one hand, with epistemological concepts which are ontologically not-empty and those which are so empty on the other. A non-ostensive concept is a quasi-applicable epistemological concept, if it can be combined with ostensive concepts to form ostensive concepts, *and* the rules of combination be the same as govern the combination of ostensive concepts, *and* thirdly, concepts resulting from the combination be ostensive concepts used in describing conceptual thinking, for example the concept 'applying a concept to a basis' or some other. It will be observed that the whole definition is founded on the relation between non-ostensive and ostensive concepts used in characterising conceptual thinking (Chapter VII).

A non-ostensive epistemological concept is for a certain person ontologically not empty if, and only if, it be quasi-applicable and the person have satisfied or intend to satisfy the rules governing its use. In the Introduction I have argued that my choice of 'proposition' and 'concept' for the characterisation of conceptual thinking involves no grave commitments. The present account of the ontological emptiness or otherwise of epistemological concepts does, I believe, support this view. It further shows that statements to the effect that certain epistemological concepts are or are not ontologically empty form a very subordinate part of any inquiry into conceptual thinking; and that the substance of it is unaffected by translation from one system of epistemological categories into another. It is much to be feared, however, that a writer who undertook to translate his results from one such system to another in order to prove the invariance of his conclusions with regard to such a translation, would lay himself open to the justified reproach of being unnecessarily tedious.

CHAPTER XXIII

THE TRUTH OF PROPOSITIONS

A FAMILY of epistemological concepts which has received much attention from philosophers and logicians comprises the many different concepts of truth. Reflection upon them has led to various theories which seem to be incompatible with each other and are often so regarded by their protagonists. Generally speaking a theory of truth consists on the one hand of a set of rules governing the phrase ‹is true› (‹is false› and other phrases), and on the other of reasons why this set should be accepted in preference to others. I do not intend to develop and defend yet another "true" theory of truth but to discuss various types of theory, and in doing so to show that many apparent conflicts between them are not really conflicts at all, but misunderstandings. I shall briefly examine, first, the theories according to which ‹is true› is not used for a concept, next, the so-called "correspondence" theories, and lastly, the so-called "coherence" theories of truth. To these topics some earlier discussions (especially Chapter IX) are relevant.

There is no need to discuss the theories of truth put forward by logicians who assume that a notion of truth must satisfy a certain definite set of requirements which they clearly state, and about which they then proceed to show how they can be satisfied. Such thinkers hope that others too will be interested in their self-imposed problem because of its connection with other problems or for some other reason; and they are rightly not perturbed when chided because their theory does not satisfy requirements which others wish to see satisfied. To this class belong those "semantic" theories which stem from Tarski's classical work on the notion of truth in formalised languages.

It seems in general unreasonable to assume that one particular set of rules for ‹true› is for all purposes preferable to any other; since any such set, as long as it is internally consistent, is merely a more or less effective tool which, like any other tool, is useful in some contexts and useless in others. One cannot reasonably argue that a saw is in general preferable to a hammer because one cannot use a hammer for sawing wood.

It seems equally unreasonable to claim that one, and only one, notion of truth is implicit in "ordinary language", since this philosophical authority issues decisions which are too often conflicting and ambiguous. Just as customary uses of ‹real› suggest, but do not authorise, conceptions of reality as different as the Humean and Platonic, so do customary uses of "true" suggest many different reconstructions and refinements without embodying any of them.

This does not mean that the many different non-philosophical and non-technical uses have nothing in common or that there is not some one single condition to be fulfilled by every proposition if it is to be called "true". As far as I can see there is at least one such condition: to state that a proposition is true is to imply that it is appropriate, that is, that whoever were to apply the concept which is applied in stating the proposition, to the basis to which it is therein applied, would not violate the rules governing the concept. The truth of a proposition in any non-technical sense of the term entails its appropriateness.

Stating the appropriateness of a proposition is like stating that a move in a game is correct with respect to its rules, or that an action is legal with respect to the law of the land. To state the correctness of a move or the legality of an action is not to repeat the move or the action but to state a proposition about it; more precisely, it is to state a relation between the move or the action and a set of rules. Similarly, to state the appropriateness of a proposition is not to repeat it, perhaps with greater emphasis— it is to state a proposition about it by applying the concept 'appropriate'. A proposition about a move or an action is obviously different from the move or the action; and a proposition about a proposition is no less, though perhaps less obviously, different from the proposition about which it is stated. I have said that truth in any non-technical sense entails appropriateness, but for the subsequent discussion it will be sufficient to assume that the entailment holds for some non-technical senses of the phrase ‹is true›.

The modern prototype of all theories that truth is not a concept has been formulated by F. P. Ramsey.[1] He holds that ‹is true› and ‹is false› are not used as concepts "but for emphasis or stylistic reasons, or to indicate the position occupied by the statement in our argument". If all or some non-technical uses of ‹true› imply that a true proposition is necessarily appropriate, then Ramsey's theory must be rejected as an account of the non-technical uses of the term.

Ramsey's main point, however, was not so much to exhibit *the* customary use of ‹is true›, but rather to show that for many purposes of logic a thinker has no need to employ any *concept* of truth. Whether or not a thinker is right in this depends, of course, on the purposes in question. It is, moreover, quite possible that a person who could for his purposes do without such a concept should nevertheless prefer to use it. Using it in these circumstances is not in itself committing a mistake, although it would be one if the person had adopted Occam's razor or some similar principle.

Even as an account of customary uses the theory is not wholly inadequate, since in using "is true" as entailing "is appropriate" one often uses it also for other purposes which include those which Ramsey mentions. We sometimes say "how true!" to a statement in situations where we merely wish to emphasise it. But even in such situations we should not wish to say, and could not *in our sense* of "appropriate" without inconsistency say: "inappropriate, but how true!".

It is a curious fact that those who hold that truth is never used as a concept do not usually explain what they mean by a concept. I have (see Chapter II) given reasons for the decision to regard as a concept any sign which in accordance with the rules governing its use can stand in entailment relations to other such signs (and which is not used as a statement, proposition, or predicate). Since ‘appropriate’ is used as a concept, and since ‘true’ in many senses entails ‘appropriate’, ‘true’ is in this sense a concept.

Apart from arguments appealing to customary uses there are some others which also try to show that ‘true’ is not a concept. There are first of all arguments purporting to show that in applying

[1] *The Foundations of Mathematics* (London, 1931), p. 142.

'true' to propositions we are guilty of an infinite regress.[1] It is pointed out that 'p' is true only if '('p' is true)' is in turn true, and so on *ad infinitum*. Yet the mere possibility of proceeding in this manner does not imply that 'true' cannot be appropriately applied to 'p', unless it first has been appropriately applied, or is known to be so applicable, to "the last member of a series which has no last member". The regress is optional and thus not vicious.

Another type of argument purports to show that the use of <true> as a concept is incompatible with some generally accepted assumption. It is argued, for example, that since '('p' is true)' entails and is entailed by 'p', and since the empirical evidence for the antecedent is the same as the empirical evidence for the consequent, <true> is not used as a concept. As against this it must be said, first, that some coherence-theories of truth define the notion in such a way that 'p' does not entail '('p' is true)' because truth is regarded not as a characteristic of any single proposition but of a whole system of propositions. Secondly, if 'truth' is defined as a logical concept, empirical evidence is not relevant to its applicability in the same way as it is relevant to the applicability of empirical concepts.

A half-way position between theories according to which 'truth' is a concept and those which deny this, is occupied by theories according to which the phrase <is true>, although not used as a concept, is part of a sequence of words which is so used. Thus one might hold that in apparently stating that 'p' is true one is really stating that a person who considers 'p' in a certain manner, for example, clearly and distinctly (Descartes) or with self-evidence (*mit Evidenz*, Brentano) would not be able to deny it. On this view a spurious characteristic of propositions is confused with a genuine characteristic of persons judging. As far as I know this view is not put forward as an account of customary uses. As such it would have to be rejected.

<Truth> is then in fact used as a concept, although one can perhaps for many purposes do without applying it. A very simple definition of truth is to regard it as synonymous with appropriate-

---

[1] See, for example, L. Nelson, *Das sogenannte Erkenntnisproblem* (Göttingen, 1930).

ness. This definition would probably not correspond to any particular use of ‹true›, but it would exhibit what is common to all, or most, non-technical senses of the term and to many technical ones. The difference between empirically and logically true propositions lies, on this view, not in their appropriateness but in the different types and constellations of rules with respect to which they are appropriate.

I now turn to theories of truth according to which 'is true' entails not only 'is appropriate' but other concepts as well. According to whether those other concepts are concepts of order zero or of higher order, we can distinguish between factual and logical theories of truth. The most important representatives of the former type are the so-called correspondence theories. To state that 'Brutus killed Caesar' is on any such theory to state a relation between the proposition and an event or fact. The nature of this relation varies from one theory to another, and it may be that "correspondence" is often hardly a suitable name for it.

It has been objected against correspondence theories that they imply an unnecessary multiplication of entities and that one can characterise facts and events without employing the concepts 'true' or even 'proposition'. As has been said already on this point, the possibility of going about a certain task without using a concept is in itself no argument against using it. In any case, to state a proposition is not necessarily to describe an event or fact, since it is conceivable that 'event' or 'fact' may be ontologically empty for a conceptual thinker for whom 'proposition' is not ontologically empty.

Another argument against correspondence theories consists in pointing to the difficulty of accounting in terms of them for false propositions. This, it is often assumed, cannot be done except by assuming negative events. But a correspondence theory need not resort to negative events; and, this apart, the concept 'negative event' is itself quasi-applicable or, more particularly, completable (that is to say, it can be combined with ostensive concepts to form an ostensive concept), and there is no reason why it should be ontologically empty for everybody. We have seen (in Chapters XVIII, XXI and XXII) that alleged deductive and probability arguments to the effect that applicable or quasi-applicable concepts are or are not ontologically empty, are fallacious. We have also seen that alleged arguments to the effect that, for example, 'physical object' is, for every conceptual thinker, ontologically empty, are at best a recommendation to desist from using it. Similarly, it is no more than a recommendation to desist from employing the concept 'is true', when one argues to the effect that ‹true›, if used for a non-ostensive relation between events and propositions, is for every conceptual thinker ontologically empty. Arguments of this type show, it seems to me, a marked similarity to the type of argument which one might use in trying to convince a little boy, who wants an electric train for his birthday, that what he really wants is a Children's Encyclopaedia.

Although correspondence-concepts of truth are concepts of order zero, not all truth-concepts of order zero are correspondence-concepts. Thus if "truth of a proposition" is defined in terms of clarity, distinctness or other properties characterising the manner of its being apprehended, then ‹true› is being used for a concept of order zero, but not also for a correspondence-concept.

We now turn to the logical theories, that is to say, to theories according to which ‹true› is (or is to be) used for a logical concept. Some, but not all, coherence-theories of truth define coherence in terms of logical relations, in particular in terms of entailment and exclusion. Modern coherence-theories of truth seem to derive their inspiration from two disparate philosophical traditions, Hegelianism and symbolic logic.[1] Attempts at synthesising the Hegelian with symbolic logic by way of expressing the former in idioms of the latter seem to me especially unsatisfactory in this: that they fail to ensure the uniqueness of the perfectly coherent system. The almost immediate occurrence of triviality or absurdity which follows any formalisation of Hegelian dialectics in terms of strict implication or its variants should not, I believe, be regarded as necessarily a sign of the absurdity or triviality of dialectic. It rather points to an interpretation of its key-notions as, in our sense, non-logical relations. Here we shall discuss only some examples of logical coherence-theories.

[1] For example, Blanshard's *The Nature of Thought* (London, 1939).

Perhaps the simplest logical theory of truth is the view that truth is consistency. Here, truth is considered to be a property of a set of propositions, namely the mutual consistency of any two propositions or conjunctions of the set. Whether such a consistency-theory deserves the title of "coherence-theory" even by courtesy is of little consequence. It certainly does not conform to a widely accepted criterion of truth, inasmuch as since two sets of propositions each internally consistent may be mutually incompatible, it allows for the possibility of two mutually incompatible sets of propositions being both true.

The consistency-theory of truth gives rise to the question why from out of a number of mutually inconsistent and yet internally consistent sets of propositions, a particular one should be (or is in fact) selected as a guide for action. Any attempt to decide this question by biological or psychological propositions comes near to replacing the consistency-theory of truth by a pragmatic one which defines "truth" as usefulness. That some such theories involve an infinite regress does not mean that it cannot be avoided with ingenuity and patience.

If we wish to avoid the possibility of mutually inconsistent and yet true sets of propositions, but nevertheless insist upon defining truth and coherence as logical concepts, we must certainly strengthen the consistency-concept of truth by adding further conditions to it. A definition of this type would be the following: Let 'S' stand for an internally consistent set of propositions, 'p' for a member of the set and '$S-p$' ('S minus p') for the set which contains all the members of 'S' except 'p'. We now define a logical coherence-concept by stipulating that a set of propositions 'S' is coherent if, and only if, with regard to every proposition 'p' of the set, '$S-p$' entails 'p'.

Ewing rightly objects that such a definition is too weak to guarantee uniqueness.[1] It allows for the possibility of subsystems which are "altogether logically independent of each other". Such logical independence in turn allows for the possibility of sets of propositions which are coherent in the sense of the definition and yet mutually incompatible. He proposes what he believes to be a stronger definition by defining a set "S" of propositions as

[1] *Idealism* (London, 1934), p. 299.

coherent if, and only if, (1) every proposition 'p' of 'S' is entailed by '$S-p$' and (2) every subset of 'S' is dependent on the remainder of the set. He regards two sets as *in*dependent if, and only if, no proposition in one set entails or excludes (alone *or with some other propositions drawn from both sets*) any proposition of the other set. But this definition is not stronger than the one which it is supposed to strengthen.

To see this consider an internally consistent set 'S' of the propositions 'p_1', ..., 'p_n', and form the logical product of Ewing's two conditions. To state the first condition is to state:

(1) ('$S-p_1$' entails 'p_1') and ('$S-p_2$' entails 'p_2') and ... and ('$S-p_n$' entails 'p_n').

To state the dependence of two complementary subsets is to state an alternation such as: ('$S-p_r$' entails 'p_r') or 'a_1'. Here 'p_r' is one of the propositions of the set so that the first member of the alternation is also a member of (1), whereas 'a_1' embodies the alternative conditions for the dependence of the two subsets. Thus to state Ewing's second condition is to state a conjunction of alternations of the following kind:

(2) (('$S-p_r$' entails 'p_r') or 'a') and (('$S-p_s$' entails 'p_s') or 'b') and .... The first member of each alternation is a member of (1).

The logical product of (1) and (2) is therefore an alternation with (1) as a member. It is entailed by (1) and therefore not stronger than it. Since to state (1) is to state the coherence of 'S' in the sense which is criticised by Ewing, his proposed amendment does not strengthen the definition of coherence which he criticises for its weakness.

A desperate attempt to strengthen the logical definition of coherence has been made by Blanshard.[1] "Fully coherent knowledge would be knowledge in which every judgment entailed and was entailed by the rest of the system." If we interpret this statement in terms of any of the usual entailment concepts which differ from each other with regard to the non-primitive rules governing the use of "entails" or its cognates, then Blanshard's definition of coherence entails that any two propositions or conjunctions of the system would be logically equivalent.

This is hard to understand unless we assume that the intention

[1] Op. cit., vol. II, p. 264.

to define coherence as a logical notion has at this stage of the argument been forgotten. That this is so seems to follow from the reference to an idea of "integration" which is perhaps characteristic of Hegel and Bosanquet but not of C. I. Lewis and the other contemporary logicians to whom Blanshard appeals. "The integration", he says of a perfectly coherent system (p. 266), "would be so complete that no part could be seen for what it was without seeing its relation to the whole and the whole itself could be understood only through the contribution of every part."

In terms of any of the current notions of entailment this would be difficult to interpret. Thus it is not at all clear what would be the first step in a process of integration which would result in the logical equivalence of, for example, '$2+2=4$' and 'Socrates is a man'. This step would have to make these propositions more equivalent than they were before. There may be a perfectly legitimate sense in which one might speak of "degrees of equivalence". But a notion of degrees of equivalence has nothing to do with mutual entailment. The only process of integration compatible with logical equivalence in the usual sense would be a process of gradually conjoining all propositions, or all propositions of a given set, so that in the end only the conjunction of all propositions is asserted. This "integrated" conjunction would then, of course, be logically equivalent to itself. But this interpretation is too trivial to be taken seriously by anybody.

The above discussion of notions of truth was intended to show that no concept of truth is necessarily or in fact accepted or not accepted by every conceptual thinker. As regards coherence-concepts of truth, I have argued that attempts to define them in terms of logical relations do not guarantee the uniqueness of the ideally coherent system and do not live up to the Hegelian idea of dialectic, however obscure this idea may be otherwise. The contrast between entailment on the one hand, and the relation which accounts for coherence, whatever it may be, was clear to Bosanquet.[1] But neither he nor his successors have been able to clarify this relation. It seems plausible that it must be defined in terms of zero-order, or factual, concepts if it can be defined at all.

[1] See *Implication and Linear Inference* (London, 1920).

CHAPTER XXIV

ON THE NON-DISCURSIVE USE
OF SYMBOLS

THE discursive use of signs, that is, their use as statements, propositions, predicates or concepts, has been and will continue to be our main topic. Ostensive predicates, ostensive concepts, ostensive statements and ostensive propositions are the prototypes of discursively used signs. Other signs are discursive if the rules governing their use are sufficiently similar to those which govern the use of these prototypes. This characterisation, as has been emphasised in the Introduction, implies the impossibility of drawing a sharp distinction between discursive or conceptual thinking on the one hand and other types of thinking, or intelligent behaviour, on the other. Not all cases of discursive thinking, however, are borderline cases and, by means of various tests, one can keep well within the region of unambiguously discursive thinking.

In the present chapter I intend to move away from clear cases of the discursive towards the border-country between discursive and non-discursive thinking and beyond to uses of symbols which clearly are not discursive. After briefly discussing two tests which are passed by all discursive signs, I shall first of all consider so-called "combinatory" signs which, although not themselves discursive in our sense of the term, are used to combine discursive signs to form discursive signs. I shall say that discursive and combinatory signs have theoretical meaning, and contrast this type of meaning with other types of meaning or "meaning", namely, natural, representational and aesthetic meaning. Lastly I shall discuss "meaning" as used of works of art, only venturing on some tentative suggestions about it. For the aim of this chapter, it is important to note, is merely to show the room there is for such a theory and that much might be gained for it by comparing the discursive with the non-discursive uses of symbols. It is not intended to develop the theory.

If a sign passes the entailment-test, then it is certainly discursive.[1] A sign passes this test if it is possible to state an appropriate entailment or other logical proposition in whose antecedent or consequent the sign occurs essentially.[2] All discursive signs which we have so far treated, whether ostensive or not, clearly pass the entailment-test. "Green", "perfect triangle", "atom" and "proposition", to consider only predicates, can be appropriately used as antecedents or consequents of logical propositions.

All discursive signs, but also some non-discursive, pass a further test, namely, the test of interchangeability. This is easily explained by an example. Consider the predicative use of ‹green›. It is possible to accept a rule to the effect that henceforth ‹green› and some new sign, say ‹bla›, can be used interchangeably. If we decide to accept this interchangeability-rule, then whenever the rules governing the use of one of these signs would not be violated, the rules governing the use of the other would likewise not be violated. ‹Green› in its use as a predicate passes the test.

I hasten to add that ‹green› and most, if not all, words in English or any other natural language, which are used for predicates, are *not only* used in this manner. By stating that ‹green› in its predicative use passes the interchangeability test, I do not imply that it would also pass it if it were considered in all its uses. It is, indeed, sometimes believed that no natural language contains perfect synonyms or admits their introduction by definitional decree. If this thesis, which to me seems an exaggeration, were true, ‹green› and ‹bla› would still, even then, in their predicative use, be interchangeable. In practice we often rely on the interchangeability of predicates, especially when abbreviating predicative signs, for example, when we abbreviate ‹Master of Arts› into ‹M.A.› and use the two for interchangeable predicates.

It is not difficult to think of signs which pass the interchangeability test even though they are non-discursive, and of non-discursive signs which do not pass it. Thus, at least in some uses, "or" and "of the" are interchangeable with other signs already in use, or ones which are being freshly introduced as abbreviations.

---

[1] See Chapter III.
[2] "Essential occurrence" is more precisely explained in Chapter IV, p. 24.

On the other hand "hurrah" when used on the football-ground could hardly be abbreviated to "h". It might seem that the distinction between signs which pass the interchangeability test and those which do not is co-extensive with the current distinction between descriptive and emotive meaning. Since, however, the latter is held to have implications, for example concerning the nature of moral judgment, which the former certainly does not have, it is advisable to keep the two distinctions apart.

Of the signs which do not pass the entailment test, but do pass the test of interchangeability, I shall first of all consider so-called combinatory signs. A sign, we have said, is combinatory if, not being itself discursive, it is used to combine discursive with other discursive signs. Thus ‹or› is used, for instance, to combine the predicates "green" and "round" to form the predicate "green or round"; ‹of›, another combinatory sign, is used to combine "owner" with "a house" to form "owner of a house". Not only words, but word-order, tone of voice, or melody may be used as combinatory signs in this way.

Among combinatory signs we can distinguish two species: connective and uniting signs. The rules which govern the use of the connective (in combining discursive with other discursive signs to form discursive signs) can be formulated without reference to any *particular* discursive signs. If to the rules governing a connective sign we add those governing two discursive signs, then the conjunction of these rules governs the result of the combination of the two discursive signs by the connective. For example, the truth-functional connective "or" is a connecting sign: the rule for its use is formulated by saying that for any two statements 'x' and 'y', 'x or y' is false only if both 'x' and 'y' are false. If, now, to this rule we add the rules governing two particular statements, say "Brutus killed Caesar" and "Philosophy is not a kind of poetry", then the conjunction of all these rules governs the use of "(Brutus killed Caesar) or (Philosophy is not a kind of poetry)". All the so-called truth-functional connectives are connecting signs. Though it may be doubtful whether any natural language has purely connecting signs, some of its signs undoubtedly are used in this way, though this use of them may not exhaust their uses.

Uniting signs, although likewise combinatory, must be distinguished from connecting signs. Though uniting signs are also used to combine discursive signs with other discursive signs to form discursive signs, we still cannot formulate the rules governing their use without reference to *particular* discursive signs. Without reference, for instance, to "heart" and "matter" we could not explain the use of "heart of the matter". This discursive sign is not governed by the conjunction of separate rules governing "heart", "matter" and "of the" (in terms of, for example, "X of the Y", where "X" and "Y" are unspecified predicates). In combining "heart", "of the" and "matter", we, so to speak, create a new unity of parts not merely connected, but united.

Combinatory signs, whether connecting or uniting, are used to form new discursive signs by combining old ones. Although not essential to conceptual thinking, combinatory signs are in practice almost indispensable to the conceptual thinker. They enable him to economise labels and make it easier to keep track of them. Since combinatory signs are used in the service of discursive thinking, it is reasonable to group combinatory and discursive signs together under one name as "signs with theoretical meaning".

It is not difficult to see the indistinctness of the line between the use of uniting signs and the combination of discursive signs with discursive signs to form signs which are no longer discursive. "The heart of the matter" does, we may perhaps assume, still pass the interchangeability test. But "sessions of sweet silent thought" in the context of Shakespeare's sonnet is not a discursive sign any longer—or at least it is not purely discursive. In order to give any account of such a sign as this we need some theory of art; and even the most rudimentary theory presupposes the distinction between discursive or theoretical and other senses of "meaning". These different senses of the term need not be, and, as will become clear, are not species of a common genus.

Theoretical must be distinguished from natural meaning—the meaning of natural signs. When we say that dark clouds *mean* rain, lightning means thunder, and a frown means anger, we do not imply that dark clouds, lightning and the frown are theoretical signs (or more particularly discursive signs), or that they are governed by rules which we can accept, satisfy or violate. It is almost superfluous to state explicitly that these natural signs pass the test neither of entailment nor of interchangeability.

If we state, of two simultaneous or temporally distant events, that one is the natural sign of the other, we usually assume that the one which is the sign is directly given, whereas the signified event is indirectly given. We further assume usually that the two events are related by an empirical law of nature (Chapter XI). The implied relation may, however, at times be adequately expressed by disposition-statements, the supporting statements of which are not empirical laws. It is not necessary here to distinguish between these possibilities. In any of these senses, natural meaning is wholly different from theoretical meaning.

There are nevertheless reasons why natural and theoretical meaning may tend to be confused. First of all the same object may have meaning in both senses. A frown, for example, may be a natural sign of anger and may be deliberately used for a predicate, just as the word ‹anger›. Secondly, a human being who is in the habit of interpreting many words and visual appearances as discursive signs may easily think of natural signs too as discursive. He may believe that just as his neighbour uses ‹dog› for a discursive sign, so Zeus, at times, may use lightning to convey a proposition.

A third and again altogether different "meaning" is representational meaning. It may, indeed, be doubted whether we are ever well advised to say that, for example, a picture means what it represents. Yet it is a fact that some have considered representation as the prototype of all meaning. Indeed, all statements have been held to *mean* facts, in just the sense in which photographs, maps or sketches mean the originals which they represent. That the meaning of works of art is representational is perhaps the oldest of all the theories of art.

To state that a sign has theoretical, that it has natural or that it has representational meaning is not to state, or at least it is not only to state, that it has a certain structure; nor is it to state that when contemplated it affects us in certain ways. We might, nevertheless, regard as illuminating and by no means perverse the statement that a piece of music or a sunset means itself. To say that some works of art or nature mean themselves may be either a way of saying that strictly speaking they have no meaning or that they have "meaning" in a special sense of their own. There certainly are thinkers who hold that as far as art and even natural beauty are concerned, the symbol and the symbolised are one; or that the meaning of a work of art or nature is not its reference to something outside, but its internal coherence. This kind of meaning I shall call "aesthetic meaning" or "aesthetic coherence". The difference between aesthetic and all the other types of "meaning" is so great that the use of the term need not give rise to confusion.

I believe that all particulars have to a greater or lesser degree aesthetic meaning or aesthetic coherence and that great works of art have it to a greater degree than trivial ones. To give a pheno-menological description of aesthetic meaning is a difficult task and falls outside the scope of the present digression. Yet, I should say that a particular has aesthetic meaning in so far as it is or can be contemplated as having interdependent parts, none of which could be replaced by anything else. Aesthetic meaning thus admits of degrees. In a perfect work of art "the integration would be so complete that no part could be seen for what it is without seeing its relation to the whole and the whole itself could be understood only through the contribution of every part". This quotation when interpreted in terms of entailment as a logical coherence theory of truth we argued to be absurd or trivial (Chapter XXIII), but I take it to be singularly apt as a characterisation of aesthetic meaning or aesthetic coherence. The discursive meaning of a statement can be preserved even if one replaces the whole statement-sign or its constitutive signs by other signs according to interchangeability-rules. The aesthetic meaning of any object would be destroyed by such replacement. The possibility of *contemplating* a thing as having interdependent parts, where contemplation excludes the consideration of usefulness, is an essential characteristic of aesthetic meaning, although it is almost certainly not the whole of it.

The distinction between theoretical, natural, representational and aesthetic meaning does not imply the impossibility of one and the same sign's having all these "meanings". It might even be held that nothing is entirely without aesthetic and natural meaning so that any sign which has theoretical meaning, embodies theoretical, aesthetic and natural. This unity of different types of meaning in one sign is different from other kinds of unity, such as the unity of physical objects which can be physically divided, or of a concept which can be classified.

It is, I believe, to the unity of aesthetic meaning with others that a philosophy of art must turn its chief attention. There are differences in the degree to which representational, theoretical and natural meaning may be united with aesthetic. An important reason for this is that any work of art has recognisable parts which may severally have meaning in all the four senses of the term. It is thus quite possible that although the theoretical meaning of a work of art as a whole is negligible, it may be dominant in a part of it. To take an example at random, a novel might contain a competent lecture on any theoretical subject, although the function of the lecture in the novel as a whole might be merely to expose the vanity of the lecturer.

The possible unity of all or some kinds of meaning and the possibility that they may be present in different strengths leads, I believe, to a characterisation of the different arts and of the differences within the arts, which does not repel by artificial neatness. Every work of art possesses aesthetic meaning, that is, coherence of its parts, which reveals itself to contemplation. Not only works of art, but also natural objects and indeed all objects, possess such aesthetic meaning. What distinguishes a work of art from other particulars is, on the one hand, the degree to which it has aesthetic meaning; and on the other, that it or its interdependent parts possess, apart from and united with its dominant aesthetic meaning and its natural meaning, representational or theoretical meaning. In the latter respect the aesthetic wholes of nature are different, in that they lack representational and theoretical meaning. The distinction between works of art and other manufactured things is, of course, not sharp.

Music is the art whose works almost wholly lack representational and theoretical meaning. A passage in a Beethoven symphony may be representational as a faint memory of bird-song and perhaps even theoretical, for instance, by embodying the sound of a military signal. But these would be subordinate elements in the whole. Gradations downwards, from the great to the trivial, in works of music, as in the case of every art, are marked by decreasing coherence, that is, by the increasing possibility of replacing sounds and passages by others without loss. It is also in a different direction characterised by increasing emphasis on the representational element. A musical imitation of rain, even if so representational as to make one wish for an umbrella, would not be regarded as "good" music.

In painting, aesthetic meaning is united with representational and even with theoretical meaning. The latter enters, for instance, into surrealist paintings whose Freudian symbols tend to become discursive in the hands of those who paint according to theory. Although purely representational paintings would not be considered works of art, representational meaning can be united to a very high degree with a dominant aesthetic meaning. Yet a high degree of representational meaning is not, I believe, a necessary condition of a painting's being a work of art.

If the unity of representational with aesthetic meaning is characteristic of many paintings, the unity of a predominant aesthetic meaning with theoretical meaning is characteristic of almost all poetry. Yet some contemporary poets and some lyrical poets make little use of the theoretical factor. It becomes stronger as we pass from "abstract" and lyrical poetry to reflective poems and lastly to the poetical expression of facts and opinions.

It is not necessary for our purpose to consider the art of the novel and of drama. Their structure is more complicated and admits many variants. In a "good" novel or drama all four types of meaning may be more or less strongly emphasised, but must not predominate over its aesthetic meaning.

Failure to distinguish between the four different uses of ‹meaning›, to which perhaps some others might reasonably be added, leads to certain mistakes in aesthetics of which the intellectualist fallacy is perhaps the commonest. This is the view that since all meaning is theoretical, works of art have, or have predominantly, theoretical meaning. Philosophers whose aesthetic sensitivity prevents them from interpreting a work of art by a conjunction of factual propositions seem then to be driven to vague and unsatisfactory pronouncements, such as the declaration that every work of art expresses "*the* general in *the* particular".

The representational fallacy is perhaps less common now than before the general recognition of abstract painting and sculpture. It is the view that since all meaning is representational every work of art represents something. The frequent failure to find what is represented leads again to highly unsatisfactory theories, for example, to the view that what every work of art represents is Life.

The fallacy, in turn, that all meaning is natural leads to the view that works of art are meaningful in virtue of their being natural signs, for instance of their creator's mental states, his social status, or of the general economic situation. It leads to psychological, sociological and in general scientific theories, which may be interesting in themselves, but tend to detract attention from the dominant aesthetic meaning and its unity with other meanings which characterise objects as works of art.

The opinion, lastly, that all meaning is aesthetic meaning leads to difficulties even within aesthetics. In terms of it we can do justice to the dominant feature of all works of art. But we cannot by means of it justify the difference between works of art and works of nature, both of which have aesthetic meaning. We further cannot give a satisfactory classification of the arts, except perhaps in terms of the difference between sounds, words, colours, etc.

Similar fallacies are known in epistemology: the theory that discursive signs are really natural signs of the speaker's state of mind or intention; that discursive signs represent facts or at least the "structure" of facts; lastly, the aesthetic fallacy that discursive meaning is really and ultimately aesthetic meaning. The aesthetic fallacy in epistemology seems to be the root of the coherence theory of truth, the doctrine of concrete universals and indeed of Absolute Idealism.

PART III

THE FUNCTION OF CONCEPTS

CHAPTER XXV

THE APPLICATION AND ACCEPTANCE
OF CONCEPTS

WE had occasion to touch upon the application and acceptance of concepts at the outset of this essay. In opening Part III, as we turn our attention to the function of conceptual thinking in the context of some of the thinker's desires and purposes, which from now onwards will be our main subject, those notions become increasingly important. It is therefore advisable to introduce the topics of this part on the one hand by recalling the way in which the notions of application and acceptance have been presupposed in our discussion of the logical content of concepts (Part I) and of their applicability (Part II); and on the other hand by clarifying these notions further. This clarification becomes possible in the light of some relevant points arising out of the distinction between personal and impersonal concepts, the theory of interpretative levels and the account we have given of disposition-statements.

A person, it was explained in the Introduction, *accepts* a rule if he has, however vaguely, the intention to satisfy the rule. A person cannot satisfy or violate a rule without having accepted it, and conversely a person may accept a rule which at the moment he neither satisfies nor violates. The tests for the presence of the intention may be more or less reliable but are never absolutely certain. Of a person who has accepted a rule which governs the use of a concept we say not only that he has accepted the rule, but also that he has accepted the concept.

A person *applies* a concept if he accepts the rules governing its use and uses it in a statement. He applies it appropriately if in making the statement he does not violate these rules. Otherwise, he applies it inappropriately—or misapplies it. Strictly speaking we should distinguish between the application of ostensive concepts and the quasi-application of non-ostensive concepts. It will, however, suffice to consider ostensive concepts, since what will be said about them can with obvious modifications be extended to the non-ostensive.

The notions of acceptance and application have been presupposed in and have been sufficiently clear for the purpose of our previous discussions; and we have explicitly used them in characterising, for example, the aims of a logical inquiry, and in distinguishing it from empirical inquiries.

How we must have occasion to make use of the notions of the application and the acceptance of concepts, when engaged in considering the logical content of concepts (or, what amounts to the same, concept-concept relations), may not perhaps be immediately obvious. Let us consider the logical proposition that 'blue' excludes 'red'. The statement may seem to commit us to the suspicious assumption that 'blue', 'red' and concepts in general have a separate existence. If we are thus suspicious, if we hesitate to assume that concepts "exist", we can avoid the assumption if it happens that we have no qualms about assuming the separate existence of the people who accept and apply them. We can then regard, for example, the statement that 'blue' excludes 'red' as elliptical; and as obtaining completion in the statement "anyone who accepted the rules governing 'red' and 'blue', and yet applied both concepts to the same basis, would be violating the conjunction of rules which he had accepted".

The idea of the application and acceptance of concepts is in an analogous way involved when we consider the applicability of concepts, or concept-basis relations. That, for example, 'chair' is applicable to a certain identified basis b, again seems to commit us to the assumption that 'chair', and concepts in general, in some sense exist. We can avoid this by regarding the statement that 'chair' is applicable to b as elliptical. Its completion would be the statement that *if* anybody accepts the rules governing 'chair' he could apply it to b without violating these rules.

By assuming the separate existence of people who apply and accept concepts, but not also the separate existence of concepts, we make it possible to avoid overburdening our theory with ontological assumptions, and so the more readily make these assumptions a subject-matter of inquiry. The meaning of statements to the effect that concepts do or do not exist has already been discussed (Chapter XXII), and the nature of arguments for or against these and similar ontological statements will be considered later.

Concerning statements about concept-concept and about concept-basis relations, it is worth noting that the completed ones do not, any more than the elliptical, entail that anybody *has in fact* accepted or applied the concepts in question, or for that matter any concepts whatever. Moreover, the completed statements do not, any more than the elliptical, entail that the person who can choose to accept or reject a concept can also choose to make the concept satisfiable. In other words, the transition from the elliptical to the completed statements never implies that concept-concept relations and concept-basis relations become dependent on personal choice or any psychological facts about particular persons.

We can now consider some results of our previous discussion which may permit us to characterise the notions of applying and accepting concepts, more clearly and more fully. The distinction between personal and impersonal concepts (Chapter XX) which we used in considering the nature of immediate experience can be used also to bring out an important feature of the application and acceptance of concepts. 'Applying a concept' and 'accepting a concept' are themselves both personal concepts. In other words, application or acceptance is necessarily application or acceptance by a person; and one person's application or acceptance of a concept does not entail its acceptance or application by any other person.

Moreover '(accepting a concept '*P*')' and '(applying a concept '*P*')' are quite as much personal concepts when '*P*' itself is impersonal as when it is personal. To emphasise the necessarily personal character of acceptance or application of concepts, and to contrast it with the personal character of some and the impersonal character of others of the *accepted or applied* concepts, may seem unnecessary. Yet, especially when the term "subjective" is used in moral theory, a tendency can sometimes be observed to argue vaguely from the necessarily personal character of acceptance and application to the personal ("subjective") character of the applied or accepted concepts.

The statement that the acceptance or application of a concept by one person does not *entail* its acceptance or application by other people is, of course, quite compatible with the statement that *as a matter of fact* they are so accepted, and that prominent among the causes for our accepting most concepts is their acceptance by other people. Indeed, the common, although not logically necessary, acceptance of certain everyday scientific and moral concepts is one of the most important features of that co-operative enterprise which is a culture or civilisation.

The theory of interpretative levels and the account of disposition-statements (Chapters XVI, XVII and XIX) throws, I believe, further light on the application and acceptance of concepts. To state that one accepts a concept without actually applying it, that is, that one intends to satisfy a rule, is to make a disposition-statement and not a statement about any occurrence. On the other hand, the nature of the statement that one applies a concept is not uncontroversial.

Thus the statement that somebody, in performing an action, for example in uttering certain sounds, intends to satisfy a rule, might be regarded as a categorical statement. If so, we should have to account for the difference between the statement that somebody is performing an action *simpliciter* and the statement that in performing this action he is intending to satisfy the rule. It seems specially unnatural to regard the latter statement as a conjunction of two categorical statements, one about the performance and the other about a simultaneous act of intending.

To avoid this, one might feel tempted to regard the statement about the performance, as such, as a categorical statement; and to regard the statement about the performance intended to satisfy the rule, as a conjunction of (*a*) a categorical statement and (*b*) a disposition-statement about what the person who performs the action *would* do under certain circumstances. But it is difficult to replace an intention which is *simultaneous with the performance* by a disposition which is not simultaneous with it.

It is, I believe, mainly this difficulty which has led Ryle to assume that apart from hypothetical statements, which include disposition statements, we sometimes make what he calls "semi-hypothetical" statements.[1] The important philosophical problem

[1] *Concept of Mind* (London, 1949), pp. 139 ff.

upon which he has put his finger is that of the difference between statements such as 'By my performance of an action I intend to satisfy a certain rule' and 'I am performing an action'. He has shown that it is not a difference which can be explained in terms of conjunctions of categorical and hypothetical statements. However, Ryle's positive account does not go beyond the remark that it is the task of semi-hypothetical statements to straddle the gulf between categorical and hypothetical statements and that semi-hypothetical statements are hybrids between categorical and hypothetical statements. He does not exhibit the rules governing their use. The expression "semi-hypothetical statement" may thus claim the important function of having marked a question, but does not embody the answer.

I believe that the answer is implied in the theory of interpretative levels. To see this we may compare on the one hand 'verbally applying a concept' (or its logical equivalent 'intending to satisfy the rules governing a concept, by producing sounds') with 'producing (the same) sounds' on the other. It is clear that the two concepts are co-ostensive and that the former of them unilaterally entails the latter. The difference between the concepts is the one we discussed as a difference of interpretative levels between two dependently co-ostensive concepts. In terms of that discussion we can explain fully the difference between 'one verbally applies a concept' and 'one produces sounds', without any need to argue that the first of them is a conjunction of, or a hybrid between, a categorical and a hypothetical proposition.

Our account of the relation between co-ostensive concepts of different interpretative level (as discussed especially in Chapters XVI and XVII) need not be repeated here. It may, however, be worth remembering that the production of sounds is among the lower-level necessary conditions for the verbal application of concepts; and that no more here than elsewhere can any conjunction of lower-level concepts be logically equivalent to a concept of higher level. We may further point, here, to familiar phenomenalist accounts of physical-object concepts in terms of concepts of lower level (compounded by means of 'and', 'or', 'if...then', etc.) and to the analogy which they bear to behaviourist accounts of 'verbally applying concepts' in terms of compounds of 'producing sounds' and other concepts of lower level—both attempts being fallacious and for the same reasons.

The species of application of concepts which is perhaps most easily understood is their verbal application, though this is clearly not the only application. In principle, instead of producing verbal signs intended to satisfy rules which govern their use, people might have developed any other type of signs. The meaning of "sign" or, more particularly, "discursive sign" may be very wide—so wide as to include signs neither visual nor auditory, and signs invested with all the privacy and elusiveness of uncommunicated thought. Again the deliberate and the involuntary production of signs cannot be sharply distinguished. There is no clear line between the person who seeing a coming car which is to be avoided just avoids it and the one who apart from this action also applies a concept. A person's utterance of ‹help› may be a verbal application of a concept or it may be an automatic noise. It may also lie on the border between the two. Even without discussing the various species of the application of concepts, or their ways of shading off into each other or into automatic behaviour, we can see well enough that to apply a concept is to do something, and not merely to have a disposition.

The term "acceptance of a concept" covers both activities and dispositions, since a person accepts a concept if, and only if, he has the intention to satisfy the rules governing it. A person who by the performance of an action intentionally satisfies the rule certainly has the intention so to do. But a person may have the intention without actually applying the concept. In this case his acceptance is dispositional. To state that anyone accepts a concept without applying it is to make a disposition-statement which may be of any of the various kinds we have considered (Chapter XIX).

The type of disposition-statement which is most important in the present context is represented by disposition-statements whose supporting statements are empirical laws of nature. Schematically put, if '(P' has the disposition to be 'Q')' is the disposition-statement, then for example '(P and S' by a law of nature has 'Q')' would be the supporting statement. Here 'P' is the explicit condition of the disposition-statement, 'Q' its consequence, 'S' its suppressed condition.

When we say that a person accepts a concept without at the moment applying it, that is, that he has the *mere* intention to satisfy the rules governing the concept, we say more than that he has the disposition to do so. A newly born child may have the disposition to satisfy the rules governing 'Euclidean triangle' but not the intention. Again it is conceivable that a person who has the disposition to apply a concept has the intention not to do so. To say that a person has the intention to satisfy a rule is to imply that he has certain attitudes to the rule. This again implies that the person is *in some sense* aware of the rule or could at least be made aware of it. The awareness of a rule which is characterised by its accepter's ability to formulate it clearly, shades off into increasingly dimmer types of awareness and finally into situations where there is no awareness at all.

Thus when we say that a person accepts a concept which he does not at the moment apply we characterise this person by certain abilities and certain attitudes towards the concept which distinguish a disposition which is also an intention to satisfy the rules governing the concept, from a disposition which is not an intention. To draw a sharp line between dispositions which are also intentions and dispositions which are not intentions is impossible. For our purposes, therefore, it is fortunate that we do not need to have it drawn.

From the application and acceptance of a concept we can, although not always clearly, distinguish the pretended application and acceptance of the concept. Without recognising the possibility of a merely pretended application, it would be difficult to account for our understanding another person's conceptual thinking if it is different from our own. Part of our understanding, for instance, of obsolete concepts consists in our ability to pretend to apply them. To apply a concept, say verbally, is to produce certain sounds with the intention to satisfy the rules governing their use. To pretend to make verbal application of the concept is to produce these sounds, pretending thereby to satisfy the rules governing its use. The utterance may be the same in both cases. Indeed, the concepts '(applying a concept '*P*')' and '(pretending to apply a concept '*P*')' are co-ostensive. They are nevertheless incompatible since the former entails that '*P*' is accepted by the person who produces the utterance whereas the latter entails that '*P*' is not accepted by this person. The possibility of mutually incompatible co-ostensive concepts has been considered in general (Chapter XVI).

The above characterisation of the application and acceptance of concepts can be useful in clarifying a sense of the notions of belief and knowledge. A person who applies a concept, say '*P*', to a basis *b* believes, of course, that *b* is an instance of '*P*'. A person, however, may believe that *b* is an instance of '*P*' without verbally or otherwise applying '*P*' to *b*, provided that he has a disposition to apply '*P*' to *b*. Not every kind of disposition to do so will, however, constitute a belief. For example, the disposition to apply '*P*' to *b*, in a person who has done so before and who has not also the disposition to apply 'not-*P*' to *b*, will constitute the person's belief in the proposition that *b* is an instance of '*P*' even at a time when he does not apply '*P*' to *b*. On the other hand, the disposition to apply '*P*' to *b* in a newly born infant who has not yet applied any concept whatsoever would certainly not constitute a belief that *b* is an instance of '*P*' . Between these two extreme cases of disposition to apply a concept to a basis there lie others of which it may be doubtful whether or not they constitute belief that a basis is an instance of the concept.

A person who applies a concept appropriately to a basis (that is, who by his performance not only intends to satisfy the rules governing the concept, but succeeds in doing this), not only believes, but *knows* that the basis is an instance of the concept. A person may know this without appropriately applying the concept, provided that he has a disposition to do so. Dispositions which do and dispositions which do not constitute knowledge are again not always clearly distinguishable. According to this definition of "knowledge", knowledge unilaterally entails belief and need not be accompanied by any feeling of self-evidence. The definition seems to approximate to what is meant by those who, rightly or wrongly, say that knowledge is true belief.

From the belief that a *particular* basis is an instance of a concept we must distinguish the belief that a concept is not empty—be it descriptively or ontologically empty (Chapter XXI). To believe that a concept is not descriptively empty is either to state the applicability of the concept, or to have a certain type of disposition towards such a statement. The belief is knowledge if the statement is appropriate and if the disposition is one towards making an appropriate statement.

To believe that a concept is not ontologically empty is to believe that it is not descriptively empty *and* to accept it, that is, to have the intention of applying it. It would, however, seem that to speak of a belief to the effect that a concept is not ontologically empty is highly misleading. For the mere intention to do something, although it may be related to beliefs, is not itself a belief. If, in spite of this, we decide to say that a person who accepts a concept, *believes* that it is not ontologically empty, then we cannot distinguish this belief from knowledge; for the person who intends to apply a concept intends to apply it appropriately.

CHAPTER XXVI

THE UNIFYING FUNCTION OF
ASPECT-CONCEPTS

THE question of the possible function of a concept or of a kind of concept is a question of the way in which such a concept *can* serve a desire of those who accept or apply it. It is not the empirical question whether its accepters have in fact this desire. Even less is it the question how far they are aware of it. That, in fact, the desire is often present and that the concept is in fact being employed in its service will, however, lend interest to the question whether or in what way such function, for a concept, is possible.

Different kinds of concept may function in such a wide variety of ways, even the same kind of concept may function in so many different ways, that some selection of the functions which specially call for discussion becomes indispensable. The situation is analogous in this respect to that in which we found ourselves at the beginning of this inquiry. Then, the practically limitless variety of rules governing the use of concepts forced our discussion to proceed on some principles of selection of the rules calling for treatment. Our present discussion of functions must proceed upon similar principles.

To avoid trivialities in which pure chance selection might result, we decided to consider only, on the one hand, rules of conceptual thinking whose interest lay in their connection with traditional philosophical problems, and on the other hand, rules which are accepted, with the exception of small children and some mental defectives, by every human being. The latter requirement is fulfilled by ostensive rules, whose importance was further emphasised by the minimal definition of 'conceptual thinker' as 'person who accepts ostensive rules'.

As a result of our study of ostensive rules and in view of some obvious facts we could, if we wished, define a conceptual thinker more specifically without at the same time restricting the range of application of the concept. We could define a conceptual thinker as an accepter not only of ostensive concepts, but of interpretative or even of aspect-concepts, such as 'visual aspect of a chair', 'frontal aspect of a chair', etc. (Chapter XVII). For the accepter of a physical-object concept or of a physical-process concept accepts not only an ostensive concept, but at the same time also interpretative and even aspect-concepts. Although every person accepts aspect-concepts, which are interpretative and *a fortiori* ostensive, we must not forget that some ostensive concepts are not interpretative and that some interpretative concepts are not also aspect-concepts. Purely ostensive concepts are indeed not interpretative. Interpretative concepts are not, at least they are not by definition, necessarily aspect-concepts, although it might be difficult to give uncontroversial examples in support of this. But, again, whether there are such examples is for our purpose not important.

For the selection of functions of concepts for discussion I have adopted the following two principles: to consider, on the one hand, functions of concepts which are connected with traditional philosophical problems, and on the other hand, such as characterise the use made of concepts by nearly all adult human beings. Singly or jointly, these principles justify the discussion of the instrumental, the aesthetically contemplative (Chapter XXVII) and the practical function of concepts (Chapter XXVIII); that is, they justify us in considering the application or acceptance of concepts in the service of the desire to change what is given, or of the desire to contemplate it as an aesthetic whole (Chapter XXIV), and lastly of practical or moral desires.

All these desires are served by the application and acceptance of aspect-concepts. To apply an aspect-concept is to interpret an appearance as being not a *mere* appearance but an aspect which is fused with other aspects into an aspect-continuum. It is, in a sense which will presently be made clear, to unify appearances into aspect-continua. We cannot manipulate the bases of appearance-concepts which do not also belong to aspect-continua. Thus the drunkard cannot manipulate the basis of 'frontal appearance of a pink elephant' in order to make it give way to a side appearance in the same way in which he can manipulate, for example, the basis of 'frontal aspect of elephant'. We cannot contemplate a given basis as an aesthetic whole unless it is an instance of a fusion of aspects. Lastly, we cannot judge a basis to belong to a morally right action unless we judge it to be an aspect of an action.

If it is an ulterior function of the acceptance and application of aspect-concepts to serve manipulation, contemplation and moral conduct, then it is a more proximate function of their application and acceptance to serve the unification of appearances into aspect-continua. By speaking of the unifying function of aspect-concepts I imply that a person *can* by employing them satisfy a desire to unify appearances. I do not imply that whoever applies an aspect-concept has such a desire and, even less, that he is aware of it.

It would be highly unrealistic to believe, for instance, that whenever a person applies the concept 'frontal aspect of a physical object' he is aware (1) of a proximate desire to unify its basis with other aspects in order to satisfy (2) his ulterior desire to manipulate—say, to move—the chair and bring it nearer to the fire. It would be equally unrealistic to believe that awareness of this ulterior desire implies awareness of that proximate desire. Since we are concerned with the *possible* employment of concepts in the service of desires, there is no need to resort to the assumption of unconscious desires, however fruitful and unobjectionable such an assumption may be in other contexts.

Yet people *are* aware of a proximate desire to unify appearances into aspect-continua in the service of an ulterior manipulative desire, and very frequently. A scientist, for example, may be well aware of a desire to unify into *one* aspect-continuum the appearances of a chair and of the ashes of the chair after it has been burned down. He might have discovered or invented some concept of 'atomic arrangement', of which both chair-aspects and burned-chair aspects are aspects, and then explicitly state that this concept fulfils the unifying desire and that its application serves ulterior manipulative desires. I speak of discovery *or* invention since neither term alone is sufficient. To relate these terms to a more precise terminology, we might say that we "discover" a concept in so far as it is descriptively not empty, and that we "invent" it in so far as it is interpretative. Again, an artist who wishes to unify "the expression of unrelated feelings or thought" into "an integrated aesthetic whole" would be aware of a unifying desire.

The logical content of aspect-continua and to some extent their function has been discussed already (Chapter XVII). The terms "aspect" and "appearance" are borrowed partly from visual experience, and partly from the experience of handling physical objects. Their range of application, however, is not so restricted. For a better understanding of the function of aspect-concepts in all its generality it is necessary that we free ourselves from this limitation by a more general and detailed characterisation of the logical content of aspect-concepts and that we develop a rudimentary morphology of aspect-continua.

Instead of speaking about specified aspects of specified aspect-continua, for example, a frontal aspect of my fountain pen, I shall speak of unspecified aspects belonging to unspecified aspect-continua. I shall indicate different aspects of the same continuum by means of capital letters, speaking, for example, of an A-aspect, a B-aspect, etc. Similarly, I shall not speak of specified appearances, for example of a frontal pen-appearance, but simply of an unspecified A-appearance, B-appearance, etc. To every aspect-concept there corresponds a co-ostensive appearance-concept. Co-ostensiveness will be indicated by using the same letter so that the concepts 'A-aspect' and 'A-appearance' are co-ostensive.

A concept is an aspect-concept if, and only if, the following conditions are fulfilled: namely, if (1) 'being an aspect' entails 'being fused with other aspects'; if (2) every aspect-concept is dependently co-ostensive with a lower-level concept (which is called an "appearance-concept"); if (3) every concept of an aspect-fusion is dependently co-ostensive with a lower-level concept of an appearance-fusion; and if (4) the difference between an aspect-concept and its co-ostensive appearance-concept lies in their logical content and not, as of course it could not lie, in the ostensive rules governing their use. In particular if 'being an A-aspect' entails 'being fused with a B-aspect' then 'being an A-appearance' does *not* entail 'being fused with a B-appearance'. In the cases which will interest us the relation between the latter two concepts will be found to be one of overlap.

It follows from our definitions that "aspect" and "appearance" are correlative terms; it is self-contradictory to state that an instance of an aspect-concept is not also an instance of the co-ostensive appearance-concept. It is self-contradictory to assert that one of these concepts is and that the other is not descriptively empty. It is self-contradictory to assert the ontological emptiness for some person of the appearance-concept and to deny it of the aspect-concept. The converse is, however, not self-contradictory.

If an A-aspect is fused with a B-aspect we may conveniently speak of an A-B-fusion of aspects. The fusion of appearances co-ostensive with this will be called an A-B-fusion of appearances. In speaking simply of an A-B-fusion, we leave the question open whether the fusion of appearances is also a fusion of aspects.

Some A-B-fusions are given as changes from an A-aspect or A-appearance to a B-aspect or B-appearance. In this case we shall speak of A-B-transitions of aspects, of A-B-transitions of appearances or simply of A-B-transitions. In the last case the question is left open whether the A-B-transition of appearances is also an A-B-transition of aspects. An example of an A-B-transition is the change of a frontal view into a side view of a physical object which is suitably moving relatively to an observer.

Some A-B-transitions are or seem to be the result of deliberate action. I shall call such action an A-B-operation if, and only if, it effects an A-B-transition when performed on an A-aspect. Consequently, though an A-B-operation which is performed on an A-aspect is necessarily successful, an A-B-operation which is performed on an A-appearance may, but need not, be successful. For example, "walking round" a frontal appearance of a chair is an A-B-operation which may but need not effect a transition from a frontal to a side view. The frontal appearance may be a mere appearance which does not happen to be fused with a side appearance of a chair. On the other hand, the same operation on a frontal *aspect* of a chair necessarily leads to a transition from a frontal to a side view.

The concepts 'A-aspect', 'A-appearance', 'A-B-fusion', 'A-B-transition', 'A-B-operation' are familiar from experience, although as a rule the need for naming them does not arise. They are, of course, all ostensive concepts, and to explain their use without resorting to exemplification is impossible. The same applies to their different species, in particular to the different types of fusion which vary from one aspect-continuum to another. The aspects of one and the same aspect-continuum may be fused in different ways. The fusion of visual aspects differs from the fusion of visual and tactual aspects of a physical object.

The ostensive character of these concepts does not preclude the possibility of a morphology of aspect-continua by means of detailed phenomenological descriptions and classifications. As far as the aspect-continua which are physical objects are concerned, much valuable work has been done by philosophers, notably in recent times by Husserl, Moore and Broad. The subject-matter of a morphology of aspect-continua comprises not only physical objects and external processes, but also other aspect-continua with which we, so to speak, do not grow up. Examples of the latter are those which come to be accepted provisionally in consequence of the scientists' co-operative endeavour after the unification of lower-level concepts in the service of prediction and manipulation. The different manner in which concepts of aspect-continua come to be accepted must not blind us to what all such continua have in common. Thus if the question whether aspects of atomic arrangements and aspects of chairs *are real*, means whether the concepts of which these aspects are instances are or are not descriptively empty, both kinds of aspects are equally real. Again, if the question of their reality is the question of their ontological emptiness, there is again no difference between the two kinds of aspects.

No morphology of aspect-continua could be guaranteed to be complete, since no one can ever be sure that all the possibilities of unification of appearances into aspect-continua have been exhausted. Exhaustive classifications are, however, possible. Thus we can distinguish between aspect-continua all of whose aspects cannot conceivably be directly given at the same time; and those all of whose aspects can be so given. To the former belong, for example, physical objects, to the latter photographs which can be seen at a glance.

By defining a "mediated aspect-fusion" as a relation between aspects of the same aspect-continuum which are not immediately fused but are connected by a sequence of aspect-fusions, we can introduce a distinction between closed and open aspect-continua. In a closed aspect-continuum every aspect stands in a mediated aspect-fusion to itself, but in an open aspect-continuum at least one aspect does not stand in this relation to itself. In a strictly open aspect-continuum no aspect is mediately fused with itself. Examples of strictly open aspect-continua and thus also of open aspect-continua are irreversible external processes; examples of closed aspect-continua are physical objects. In order to make this distinction more precise we should have to take into consideration the nature of the aspect-fusions. It might be, for instance, that some aspect-continua which are closed with respect to one type of fusion are open with respect to another. For our purpose it is not necessary to consider these possibilities in detail.

For us it is more important to distinguish operational from non-operational aspect-continua, that is, those between some of whose aspects A-B-transitions can be effected by A-B-operations from those between none of whose aspects such transitions can be effected. Operational aspect-continua can again be distinguished according to the nature of the possible A-B-operation. No sharp lines can be drawn between manipulation, observation by more or less complicated instruments and, lastly, mere contemplation. A merely contemplated aspect-transition can of course no longer be regarded as the result of an A-B-operation. Marxists, pragmatists and operationalists require all aspect-continua to be operational.

Operational aspect-continua play an important role in scientific inquiry. To appreciate it we have to remember that though 'A-B-operation on an A-*aspect*' entails 'A-B-transition', 'A-B-operation on an A-*appearance*' overlaps with 'A-B-transition'. If, consequently, an A-B-operation does not lead to an A-B-transition, we must conclude that it was not performed on an A-aspect, but on a mere A-appearance. This conclusion is, of course, compatible with both the entailment and the overlap.

Let us call the above entailment an "operational entailment", and any statement to the effect that an A-B-operation has not been successful "a statement of operational failure". A statement of operational failure is, of course, an empirical statement, and as such cannot *falsify* the operational entailment. It nevertheless *weakens* it in so far as it records the mistaken application of 'A-aspect' to a mere A-appearance. The greater the danger of this misapplication, the less useful becomes the operational entailment and the corresponding aspect-continuum. The cumulative effect of many statements of operational failure may in the end make it advisable no longer to accept the operational entailment and the concept of the aspect-continuum whose logical content it indicates.

If the criterion of scientific statements is the relevance of experiments and observations to them, then operational entailments are scientific statements. The relevance of experiments and observations to operational entailments lies in their being weakened by statements of operational failure. Empirical laws are, as we have seen (Chapter XI), scientific statements of quite a different structure, and the relevance of experiments and observations to them is also different. There are many types of proposition which satisfy the above general criterion for scientific propositions. It makes little sense to argue which of them are the more scientific, so long as the ways in which they satisfy the criterion are clearly characterised and distinguished.

Examples of operational aspect-continua are given and analysed in Bridgman's *Logic of Modern Physics*[1] and other works on the philosophy of science. Some operational aspect-continua can be compared in respect of their comprehensiveness. Thus, to use a previously given example, we unify aspects of different aspect-continua into one more comprehensive aspect-continuum by stating that an aspect of a chair is at the same time an aspect of an atomic arrangement. The aspects of the latter include the aspects of the material from which it is made and of its ashes after it has been burned. The aspects of the more comprehensive aspect-continuum are instances of a more highly interpretative aspect-concept than are the aspects of the less comprehensive aspect-continuum. Operational aspect-continua can also be compared with regard to the operational success which could be measured by the number of statements of operational failure known to be true.

[1] New York, 1927.

233

Although the general tendency in science seems to be towards the use of more comprehensive, and consequently more highly interpretative, aspect-continua, it may perhaps still be on the whole true that operational aspect-continua above the level of physical objects, and the corresponding operational entailments, are much more common in the physical than in the biological sciences. This may, among other things, explain on the one hand a tendency toward "rationalism" in philosophical physicists, and, on the other hand, a tendency towards an "empiricism" which admits only physical objects and impressions as "real", in philosophical biologists. The classical examples would be, of course, on the one hand Descartes, on the other Locke.

Whatever the type of operation by which their aspect-transitions can be effected (from manipulation to more or less passive observation), it is typical of all operational aspect-continua that some of their aspects are related by operational entailments which can with some degree of success be used for prediction and manipulation. According to our definition of aspect-continua, the aspects of an aspect-continuum may be fused without being related by operational entailments and without there being any possibility of prediction. The biographer, the historian and the literary critic who "see" the life of a person, the history of a nation or the elements of a work of art "as a whole", and who state what they see, apply aspect-concepts whose instances are unified into non-operational aspect-continua. The application of such aspect-concepts distinguishes the historian from the chronicler, and the literary critic and the biographer from the reporter.

The predominant employment of non-operational aspect-continua distinguishes explanations in the humanities from explanations in the sciences (distinguishes the *Geisteswissenschaften* from the *Naturwissenschaften*). Whether such aspect-concepts and concepts of aspect-continua can be called "explanatory", and whether there can be explanation without prediction, are verbal questions which do not call for decision; especially when the similarities and dissimilarities between operational and non-operational aspect-continua are recognised. The employment of the latter in aesthetic judgments and in historical explanation without prediction, is the reason for the close relationship between history and aesthetics which has often been noted. It is also the reason why philosophers who are only interested in predictive explanation, and who repudiate non-operational aspect-continua, have nothing worth while to say about either history or aesthetics. Thus an account of propositions about the past, without an account of the interpretative but non-operational aspect-concepts, is not even the most rudimentary of versions of a philosophy of history. The main tasks of any philosophy of history, as has been pointed out (Chapter xv), are the problems of propositions about the past *and* of historical explanation.

It might be asked whether we are justified in referring appearances to aspect-continua, which is what we are doing when we judge that an instance of an appearance-concept is also an instance of an aspect-concept. We might, in other words, be asked for a "transcendental deduction" of our belief that the aspect-concepts and in general the interpretative concepts which we apply have instances. A concept has instances if, and only if, it is not descriptively empty and if it is accepted (Chapter xxi). The first condition is fulfilled by every ostensive concept. Since the application of a concept entails its acceptance, the second condition also is fulfilled.

CHAPTER XXVII

ON THE INSTRUMENTAL
AND CONTEMPLATIVE APPLICATION OF
OSTENSIVE CONCEPTS

IT is, we have seen, possible that the application of aspect-concepts should serve the purpose of unifying appearances into aspect-continua and that the unification may itself subserve ulterior purposes, in particular manipulation, contemplation and conduct. This does not, of course, imply that we cannot manipulate or contemplate things unless we previously apply aspect-concepts. Yet the application of aspect-concepts can and often does facilitate these activities.

In considering the application of aspect-concepts in the service of manipulation, contemplation and moral conduct one soon finds oneself confronted with philosophical problems. Thus it is clear that in discussing the application of aspect-concepts in the service of contemplation, one is led to questions concerning the nature of aesthetic judgment. It is clear, too, that discussion of the application of concepts in the service of moral conduct is sooner or later likely to lead to questions about the nature of moral judgment. On the other hand, the application of aspect-concepts in the service of manipulation is not to the same extent surrounded by traditional philosophical problems. If, therefore, we discuss this type of the application of concepts first we shall fix our attention the more easily on features common to the different functions of aspect-concepts.

We know what it is to manipulate things; we do it constantly whether we are aided in the activity by applying concepts or not. When turning a chair round we do not necessarily first ask ourselves whether the chair-appearance which we try to shift is a chair-aspect and whether consequently our intended operation is likely to be successful. In other cases, however, we do ask such questions with the express purpose of ensuring the success of our operation. The surgeon in an operating theatre will as a rule apply aspect-concepts, especially when faced with an unusual condition of his patient. In less technical, but also in less precise language, we should say that he will think before acting.

Aspect-concepts belonging to operational aspect-continua (Chapter XXVI) can all be applied in order to facilitate manipulation. They can all, as we may say more briefly, be applied instrumentally. The aspect-concepts whose instrumental application is most familiar to us are concepts of external physical things and processes. Where examples are wanted they may be most conveniently considered. We must not forget, however, that many other aspect-concepts are capable of instrumental application, in particular many which are used in scientific inquiry and have been discovered in the course of it.

An aspect-concept which can be applied instrumentally is not necessarily so applied on all occasions. The same aspect-concept might always be applied instrumentally by one person and never by another. Physical-object concepts are applied by the same person instrumentally at one time, and at another otherwise.

By stating that a person A applies an aspect-concept, say 'chair-aspect', "instrumentally" to a basis b, we are clearly characterising the person's application of 'chair-aspect' in a particular case. We are not indicating the logical content of 'chair-aspect'—as we should be were we, for instance, stating that 'chair-aspect' entails 'aspect of a piece of furniture'. Further, by stating that A applies 'chair-aspect' instrumentally to b we are not indicating that A is also applying, apart from 'chair-aspect', another logically independent concept, say 'instrumentality', to b. Lastly, we are not, by stating that A applies it instrumentally, characterising 'chair-aspect' as we should be characterising it, for example, in saying that it is a physical object or an interpretative concept.

No one is likely to mistake the instrumental application of an aspect-concept to a basis, for a characterisation either of the concept or of the basis. If, however, he does make this mistake, and if in particular he starts looking for a concept of instrumentality among the characteristics of the basis, he will not succeed in

finding it. Such failure may then lead him to one of two conclusions: that "instrumentality" is used for a spurious concept, or
else that it is used for an unanalysable and non-ostensive concept
sui generis. The latter conclusion might then be expanded into
a doctrine of instrumental intuitionism.

An instrumental intuitionist would hold that instrumentality is,
like yellowness, not logically equivalent to a compound of other
characteristics, but that, unlike yellowness, instrumentality is not
an ostensive concept. Since instrumentality is also not a logical
concept, an instrumental intuitionist would be likely to assume
that it is apprehended neither after the fashion of empirical concepts nor after the fashion of logical. Consequently a special kind
of apprehension or intuition of instrumentality would have to be
postulated. I have, of course, assumed that the instrumental
intuitionist is ignorant of our discussion of the relation between
ostensive and non-ostensive concepts and that he does not accept
any theory of incomplete symbols. Neither this nor any of the
other tenets I have been imputing to instrumental intuitionism
need cause disturbance, since, as far as I know, no philosopher holds
this doctrine.

An opponent of instrumental intuitionism might describe the
situation in which a person applies a concept instrumentally to
a basis, by saying that the latter expresses an instrumental attitude
towards it. This would to some extent be true. Yet the person who
applies a concept instrumentally does not merely *express* his attitude to the basis, or his intention of manipulating it. Actually—at
least in many cases—the instrumental application of the concept
does help the manipulation in ways which are different from mere
expressions of attitudes. Thus the person who, before or whilst
manipulating something, judges it to be a specific kind of physical
object, is enabled the better to concentrate on certain features of it.
Rhythmic shouting of meaningless syllables might "express an
instrumental attitude" and yet not serve manipulation in the same
way as the instrumental application of concepts. Moreover, if the
instrumental application of aspect-concepts were only the expression of an instrumental attitude, it would be of little consequence
which of a number of such concepts we applied instrumentally.

This is obviously not the case, as is seen if we consider the scientists' search for such aspect-concepts as will ensure the greatest possible likelihood of operational success.

In thus contrasting a possible intuitionist and a possible attitude theory of instrumentality, neither of which is held by any philosophers, my aim has chiefly been to prepare the ground for a later discussion of intuitionist and attitude theories in ethics. This aim perhaps also justifies some emphasis being placed on the almost unlimited variety of attitudes, and of favourable and unfavourable attitudes. It implies that any account of a situation in conceptual thinking in terms of attitudes, or of favourable or unfavourable attitudes as such, is likely to be so meagre as to be of little use.

It is further advisable to draw attention to the important difference between attitudes which as a matter of anthropological fact are shared by all, or nearly all, human beings, and attitudes which differ from one group of people to another or even from person to person. In this respect the attitude to certain types of action and the attitude to, say, cheese may differ very importantly.

All men are users of tools and apply certain concepts instrumentally. It is, moreover, fair to assume that most people use physical-object concepts instrumentally. Yet it is quite possible that some people should not only at some times but always replace the instrumental application of physical-object concepts by the instrumental application of some interpretative concepts of higher level. If so their instrumental attitudes will be different. It is in any case not of great interest to decide the anthropological question whether certain instrumental attitudes, and if so which of them, are shared by all people or by all "rational beings". On the other hand, in the case of aesthetic and moral attitudes, the question as to whether some of them are shared by everybody is, as we shall see, of the greatest importance.

In the widest sense of the term, the manipulation of things, whether or not aided by the instrumental application of concepts, differs entirely from the contemplation of things. Manipulation excludes contemplation. This does not imply that there are no intermediary activities. Thus the absent-minded or playful handling of things is in many cases an activity which, while being neither manipulation nor contemplation, is sometimes difficult to distinguish from either.

As the manipulation of things is possible without the previous or simultaneous application of concepts, so is their contemplation. Yet our application of concepts can aid our contemplation of a thing just as it can aid our manipulation of it. In the present context our interest in the activities of manipulation and contemplation is only secondary. We are interested in them not for their own sake, but only in so far as conceptual thinking can be subservient to them. To give a phenomenological description of manipulation is thus not necessary, and as regards contemplation a bare minimum is sufficient.

In discussing the borderline between the discursive and the non-discursive use of symbols, and in a digression (Chapter XXIV) on their non-discursive use, the notion of aesthetic "meaning" or aesthetic coherence was briefly considered. It was pointed out that every particular which has parts has aesthetic coherence. To contemplate something is to concentrate solely on its aesthetic coherence, which, as we have seen, may involve a great variety of heterogeneous elements.

In describing contemplation we might thus first of all say, negatively, that in contemplating a thing we shut out, as far as possible, all other attitudes and intentions towards it. In contemplating a basis of 'chair-aspect', whether or not we apply the concept to it, we do in particular shut out any instrumental attitude and any intention of handling it. A positive description of the contemplation of something, which should not merely repeat that it consists in concentrating on its aesthetic coherence, is more difficult. One might feel inclined to say with Schopenhauer that a person who contemplates something "ceases to consider the where, the when, the why and the whither of things, and looks simply and solely at the *what*...". Although this and similar metaphorical expressions may be helpful, they can easily be used to grind the axe of some specific philosophical theory, for example Schopenhauer's own doctrine that aesthetic contemplation reveals to us Platonic Ideas. In the end we must rely on familiarity with the use of ‹contemplation› which, like ‹manipulation›, is used for an ostensive concept.

It is not difficult to give examples of the application of aspect-concepts which subserve and facilitate contemplation. Even the application of 'chair-aspect' to a basis might help us in concentrating on a particular fusion of aspects, and thereby on a feature whose place in an aesthetically coherent whole might easily be overlooked. However, the help which the application of aspect-concepts can give to contemplation is perhaps most apparent if we consider concepts which are solely or primarily used to facilitate concentration on the aesthetic coherence of what is being contemplated. Examples are 'novel', 'tragedy', 'sonnet', 'fugue', 'dactyl', 'impressionistic'.

Of a person who applies an aspect-concept to a basis, with the aim of helping himself or others to concentrate on the aesthetic coherence of a particular, I shall say that he applies the concept contemplatively to the basis, or that he judges the basis as an aesthetic whole. The words ⟨as an aesthetic whole⟩ and more adequately the word ⟨contemplatively⟩ qualify the application of the concept to the basis. They do not indicate the logical content of the contemplatively applied concept: neither do they characterise it as belonging to a certain kind of concept: nor—as before—do they imply that apart from the contemplatively applied concept some further concept is applied to the basis. All this is analogous to what has been said about the instrumental application of concepts.

The contemplative application of a concept, again, does not merely express a contemplative attitude; it may aid the contemplation. Otherwise, the contemplative application of concepts might be replaced without loss by, for example, sighs of admiration or interjections. Moreover, the careful choice between different aspect-concepts, in respect of their power to draw attention to this or that aesthetic feature of the contemplated object, would be pointless. Yet it seems clear, especially when new modes of literary and musical composition are being tried, that the contemplative application of some aspect-concepts is more helpful than that of others.

The great variety of aesthetic theories makes it appear likely that the word ⟨beautiful⟩ and its cognates are not used for one single concept. The preceding discussion of contemplation and the contemplative application of aspect-concepts allows us nevertheless to make some general remarks about concepts of beauty. A person who judges something to be beautiful applies a concept of beauty contemplatively. The statement that something is beautiful is in any case to be explained (1) in terms of the contemplative application of the aspect-concept for which ‹beautiful› is being used in the statement, and (2) by characterising the concept itself.

In characterising the different aspect-concepts for which ‹beautiful› and its cognates are used, one can, I believe, safely point to two features which are common to all of them. First, every concept of beauty is applicable to some instances of every other category. The kind of aesthetic coherence which is exhibited by the application of 'chair' cannot conceivably be exhibited in instances of 'melody'; and the aesthetic coherence which is exhibited by the application of 'fugue' cannot be exhibited by a chair. On the other hand, the kind of aesthetic coherence which is exhibited by the application of a concept of beauty can conceivably be exhibited in instances of every aspect-concept. (However these remarks may need to be qualified, the main distinction—a distinction in range of applicability as between concepts of beauty and other contemplatively applied concepts—must, I think, remain unaffected.)

Secondly, what is beautiful is, in every sense of the term, if contemplated, necessarily accompanied by a feeling of enjoyment of a particular kind. It is hardly possible to describe this feeling. The reason lies in the fact that although aesthetic enjoyment, like a feeling of pain, is exemplifiable, the difficulties of providing other people with reliable examples of aesthetic enjoyment are incomparably greater than those of providing them with reliable examples of pain.

In other respects concepts of beauty may differ widely from person to person. It is, moreover, quite possible that one and the same person accepts different concepts of beauty. The traditional distinction between the beautiful and the sublime is evidence of such aesthetic pluralism.

So far I have said nothing about the controversy between naturalistic and non-naturalistic, or between subjective and objective theories of beauty. The general characterisation of judgments that something is beautiful does not on the whole prejudge these issues, which, however, can now be more clearly formulated. By a naturalistic theory of beauty philosophers seem to mean any theory which implies that ⟨beautiful⟩ is used for an ostensive concept of, at most, the level of physical-object concepts, or of some low interpretative level. If this theory is supplemented by our account of the contemplative function of aspect-concepts, then its definition of beauty is compatible with our general characterisation of concepts of beauty.

Philosophers who hold a non-naturalistic theory of beauty either hold that ⟨beautiful⟩ is used for an ostensive concept of higher interpretative level than is admitted by their naturalistic opponents; or else they imply that it is used for a non-ostensive concept *sui generis*. Thus definitions of 'beauty' as quasi-teleological unity may be put forward in both ways. The controversy as to the admissible interpretative level of ostensive concepts concerns, not the question of their applicability or inapplicability, but the question as to whether they are or are not ontologically empty. The real point at issue, in other words, is whether concepts above a certain interpretative level should be applied or accepted. It will be discussed as a special case of arguments for and against ontological assumptions (Chapter XXXIII).

The view that ⟨beautiful⟩ is used for a non-ostensive concept *sui generis* is obscure. It may be due to the mistaken belief that whenever one applies a concept 'P' contemplatively to a basis, one is necessarily applying to it some further concept 'Q' which is logically independent of 'P'. Failure to find such a concept 'Q' among the ostensive characteristics of the basis may then lead to the postulation of a non-ostensive characteristic *sui generis* of the basis. An analogous mistake was discussed above when the instrumental application of concepts was being considered.

I have given an account of statements to the effect tnat something is beautiful, in terms of the contemplative application of concepts. It might be objected that such an account makes beauty "subjective". The ambiguity of the term—as so often before—makes it difficult to answer the objection. If the objector understands "subjective" as being synonymous with "personal" (Chapter xx), then the objection can be met. The concept 'a person X applies a concept 'Y' contemplatively' is, of course, personal—precisely like the more general concept 'a person X applies a concept 'Y''. But, that the application of any concept in any manner is necessarily personal, does not imply either that the concept applied is itself personal or that it is not. According to our general account a contemplatively applied concept may be either. There are theories of beauty, and other uses of ‹beautiful›, which are evidence that both possibilities are in fact realised.

Aristotle's *Poetics*, Lessing's *Laökoön* and similar works are concerned not only with the nature of aesthetic judgment but also with the discovery and recommendation of rules for the creation of works of art, that is to say, rules governing the making of particulars for contemplation. I shall say that a work of art is, in respect to such rules and a person who accepts them, aesthetically appropriate, if it, or more precisely its making, does not violate these rules. If a work of art does violate these rules, I shall say that with respect to them and their accepter it is aesthetically inappropriate.

Aesthetic appropriateness is in any case a narrower concept than beauty, since only the latter concept is applicable both to works of art and objects of nature. The logical relation between the notions 'aesthetic appropriateness' and 'being a beautiful work of art' will, of course, depend on their logical content. From our general characterisation of the two types, the logical relationship between their particular representatives does not follow. As a rule we shall probably find that ‹being a beautiful work of art› is used for a concept which unilaterally entails a concept for which ‹aesthetically appropriate› or its cognates is used.

There could be an anthropological inquiry into the question whether any particular rules of artistic creation are explicitly or implicitly accepted by all people or by an overwhelming majority of them so that some works of art would be aesthetically appropriate or, at least, some others aesthetically inappropriate for everybody or nearly everybody. Such an inquiry would, I believe, yield a negative result. This conclusion seems to be borne out by what appear to be great changes of taste and aesthetic judgment in relatively short periods of time. Some support for this conclusion might be derived also from the fact that in questions of aesthetics philosophers appeal much more rarely to the constitution of all rational beings than they do in matters of theoretical and moral judgment.

The above account of the contemplative application of aspect-concepts, in particular of concepts of beauty and aesthetic appropriateness, may prove helpful in understanding and, if necessary, in justifying the activities of literary and art critics in general. By appealing to aesthetic standards critics exhibit rules of aesthetic appropriateness, and thus often clarify some otherwise obscure aims of aesthetic creation. This is especially important when we are trying to understand (through its works of art) an epoch whose aesthetic standards we no longer accept, or when we are trying to enjoy works of art which are composed in new ways.

In contemplatively applying aspect-concepts, particularly aspect-concepts invented or discovered for the purpose of contemplative application, critics may reveal features of works of art which otherwise might be overlooked, and thus they may cure a kind of aesthetic "Gestalt-blindness" which is an obstacle to aesthetic enjoyment. In so doing some art critics are the living proof of how conceptual thinking can serve contemplation.

CHAPTER XXVIII

THE PRACTICAL APPLICATION OF OSTENSIVE CONCEPTS

THE key to the understanding of instrumental and aesthetic judgments lies, I have argued, in realising that the former can, but need not, serve manipulation and that the latter can, but need not, serve contemplation. Thus it is unnecessary to postulate the intervention of judgments to account for activities which can occur without them, and further, if instrumental and aesthetic judgments can help manipulation and contemplation in the way described then it is certainly not necessary to assume that these judgments are merely expressions of attitudes. The possibility of aesthetic and instrumental judgments which do not subserve other activities but, for example, merely accompany them, has not been ruled out; but these can be regarded as limiting cases of helpful judgments. Moreover, although not all aesthetic and instrumental statements do in fact facilitate manipulation and contemplation, they are characterised as conceivably so functioning.

Similarly, by recognising that in moral judgments conceptual thinking *can* serve moral conduct, we may avoid some of the philosophical difficulties which make certain standard accounts of moral judgments unacceptable. In speaking of moral conduct, moral judgment, moral characteristics, I am using the term "moral" as referring to a feature common to differing and even opposed moralities. In this use of the term its contradictory is not "immoral", but "amoral". Before we attempt to argue for the acceptance of the *true* moral judgments, whatever this may mean, we must explain the nature of moral judgments in general.

We may begin by considering the type of situation in which a person X, who may be ourselves, states that an action b which is characterised by a conjunction of non-moral characteristics, say 'P', has a moral characteristic 'M'. We might, for example, assume that the action consists in giving money to a needy person or that it is productive of pleasant feelings and is for one of these reasons, or for some similar reason, judged to be good. Now the moral characteristic 'M', say 'good', is clearly not entailed by the non-moral characteristic 'P', say 'productive of pleasant feelings'. It is further not the case that 'M' is, like 'P', an ostensive concept or a compound of such concepts; and consequently if 'M' characterises the action it is quite unlike any empirical or logica characteristic. The failure to find 'M' in the logical content of 'P' or among the obvious characteristics of the action b seems to be the reason why the following ethical theories, in more or less elaborate form, have been advanced with some plausibility.

First, it has been suggested (for example, by Ross) that although the moral characteristic 'M' is not entailed by the empirical characteristic 'P' of the action, 'M' necessitates 'P' in a different way. By calling this necessitation "synthetic *a priori*" we are not clarifying it, but putting it into a class of heterogeneous and often spurious relations (Chapter VI). Secondly, it has been suggested that the moral characteristic 'M' is *sui generis* and unanalysable and that its apprehension is at most analogous to the apprehension of empirical or of logical characteristics. This view is implied by the moral-sense school of ethics and by some modern ethical intuitionists. The first and the second theory can be combined. A third theory deals with the apparent elusiveness of moral characteristics by regarding them as pseudo-concepts and explaining their appearance in terms of favourable attitudes towards actions which only *seem* to possess moral characteristics.

The objections which can be made to ethical intuitionism and attitude theories are analogous to those raised to similar theories about instrumental and aesthetic judgments. The objections to letting non-moral characteristics necessitate moral ones spring mainly from the obscurity of the notion of necessitation. The main argument in favour of the theory seems to be that in no other way can a satisfactory account of moral judgment be given; but it is difficult to believe that all possible alternatives have been exhausted.

Moral as opposed to amoral actions are prompted by desires of a specific kind which will be called "practical". A practical desire is a combination of two, namely, a desire for the performance of a certain type of action and the further desire that *everybody* should try to satisfy the former desire whenever possible.

Moral conduct—we are using the term in the wide sense in which, for example, polygamy and monogamy may both be moral —is not dependent on the intervention of conceptual thinking. Without in all cases applying them, indeed without ever applying them, a person may yet be acting in accordance with his moral principles. A person may be a utilitarian without ever applying the concept 'productive of the greatest possible happiness' to any of his or anybody else's past, present or future actions. Yet no doubt sometimes the concept is applied and its application may facilitate the achievement of the person's practical desire. In such cases we shall speak of the practical application of this concept.

'Productive of the greatest happiness' is not a moral concept. It only, so to speak, becomes one by being practically applied. More precisely, if a person X states that an action b which is productive of the greatest happiness is therefore moral, he applies the concept 'productive of the greatest happiness' practically to b.

A person is a utilitarian, in a not very subtle sense of the term, if he has the practical desire for actions productive of the greatest happiness. In many of the cases in which he applies the concept— judges an action to be productive of the greatest happiness—his judgment does not in fact facilitate the satisfaction of his practical desire, but is only incidental. Incidental moral judgments, as distinguished from such as are facilitating, can be regarded as limiting cases of the practical application of concepts. Moreover, even if, for example, the application of the concept 'productive of the greatest happiness', by a utilitarian in a particular case, does not subserve his practical desire, the concept is, nevertheless, practically accepted. That is to say, its accepter either practically applies it or, at the least, has the intention of applying it in this manner to some actions.

A schematic account of moral judgments, covering such as subserve moral conduct as well as those which are only incidental to it, would be the following. The proposition 'A person X states that an action b which has the non-moral characteristic 'P' is therefore moral' is logically equivalent to the proposition 'A person

X applies 'P' to b and accepts 'P' practically'. The feature which characterises a statement as moral is thus to be found not in the logical content of 'P', nor is it a concept which is logically independent of 'P' and is applicable to b. It is, precisely, as we have argued in considering instrumental and aesthetic judgments, a qualification of the application of 'P' or, if the judgment is only incidental, of the acceptance of this concept.

A person who uses a sentence for a moral judgment may, of course, use this sentence also in other ways. He may in particular use it not only in the service of a practical desire but also in order to express this desire or induce it in other people. Yet a moral statement may serve to satisfy a practical desire without self-expression or propaganda. However interesting a study of the expression of attitudes and of propaganda may be, it is not a study of moral judgments. The latter is concerned with the application of concepts which are practically applied or, at least, accepted. It is the study of conceptual thinking in the service of moral conduct.

The above sketch of a theory of moral judgment cannot be made fully convincing without much elaboration which cannot be undertaken here. A few remarks must, however, be appended. In treating of moral statements I have discussed only the practical application of concepts to actions, more precisely to instances of 'action'. 'Action' is co-ostensive with, and of higher interpretative level than, 'behaviour'. The relation between 'action' and 'behaviour' is thus analogous to the relation between 'physical object' and 'appearance of a physical object'. This is relevant to attempts at "analysing" 'action' in terms of 'pieces of behaviour', which like all attempts to establish the logical equivalence of higher interpretative concepts to compounds of lower interpretative concepts must fail (Chapter XVIII).

While the bases of 'action' are bases of practically applied or accepted concepts, they are not the only bases of them. We speak indeed of moral motives, moral laws, moral purposes, moral states of affairs. All these imply a reference to practical desires or are themselves objects of practical desires. What has been said about moral judgments in their relation to actions can *mutatis mutandis* be applied to other bases of practically applied or accepted concepts.

So far practically applied or accepted concepts have only been characterised negatively as non-moral concepts. We may now add that they are empirical concepts, that is, either ostensive concepts of any level, or self-consistent compounds of such. Some practically applied or accepted concepts may seem at first not to be empirical. An example would be 'approximating to an ideal state of affairs', where we assume that the ideal, whatever else it involves, is unrealisable. Yet '*approximating* to an ideal state of affairs' can, even if 'ideal state of affairs' is non-empirical, be shown to be equivalent to an empirical concept in the same way as we have shown the equivalence of 'approximating to a perfect triangle' to 'physical triangle' (Chapter VII).

In discussing moral judgments, I have intended to draw attention to what is common to all such and have ignored the differences between different moral systems. These differences are mainly due to the different concepts which are practically accepted by different people. It might perhaps be objected that our account involves an infinite regress since, it might be said, the practical acceptance of a concept is itself an action which may be but need not be moral. However, having the intention to apply a concept, practically or in any other fashion, neither is an action nor is necessarily the result of an action. It may be entirely involuntary and caused by circumstances over which we have no control.

From our point of view the controversy between the supporters of a naturalistic and of a non-naturalistic ethics may be interpreted in two ways. On the one hand, it may be a controversy between those who hold that moral concepts are concepts *sui generis* which characterise actions (motives, situations, etc.) and are apprehended in a special way, and those who believe this view to be false. In this sense of "non-naturalism" there is no difference between it and intuitionism. I have rejected this view with the proviso that the denial of ethical intuitionism does not imply the assertion that so-called moral judgments are merely sentences used for the expression and inducement of desires.

On the other hand, the controversy may and, I believe, frequently does concern merely the interpretative level of the practically accepted concepts. In other words, the naturalist declares concepts above a certain level to be empty. The term "empty" in this context cannot refer to logical or descriptive emptiness, since no ostensive concept, whatever its level, is empty in these senses of the term. It can refer only to ontological emptiness. An ostensive concept, however, is ontologically empty only for a person who does not accept it (Chapter XXI). The naturalist's declaration is thus merely a statement of the fact that *he* does not accept concepts above a certain level. This statement is often combined with a metaphysical decree to follow his example. In a logical inquiry such decrees are not anything to be passed, defended or attacked— only understood. It is an argument in favour of our account of moral judgments that it does not decide between the two types of theory, but on the contrary fits both of them.

The controversy between those who assert and those who deny that moral characteristics are "subjective", seems to find its centre in the question whether the characteristics in question—such as 'right' or 'good'—are or are not impersonal. Neither party has, so far as I know, distinguished between the practical acceptance and application of a concept in moral statements and the concept itself. As has been pointed out in the discussion of aesthetic judgments, the concept 'a person X applies a concept 'P' in some particular fashion' is necessarily a personal concept, but the applied concept 'P' may or may not be personal. Whether the concepts which are practically accepted by a person are or are not personal is a question of fact and not of logic. A general account of moral judgments must cover both those in which the practically accepted concepts are, and those in which they are not, personal.

In a similar manner the relationship between moral characteristics and desires can be clarified. If we consider the logical content of a practically accepted impersonal concept, say 'productive of the greatest happiness', it is clear that it does not entail the presence of any desire in its accepter. By emphasising this we may seem to support the often expressed thesis that the characteristic 'moral' does not entail the characteristic 'desired'. It is, on the other hand, equally clear that the *practical acceptance* of a concept entails the presence in its accepter of a practical desire for what are instances of the concept. By drawing attention to this entailment we may seem to be supporting the thesis that what is moral is necessarily in some way desired: but the apparent paradox about the relation between the moral and the desired is resolved by distinguishing between a practically accepted (impersonal) concept which does not, and its practical acceptance which does, entail the presence in the accepter of a practical desire for what are instances of the concept.

Since the chief aim of the discussion of moral judgments was their general characterisation moral disagreements have so far not been considered. Although different kinds of moral disagreement are frequently expressed by the same form of words, it is important to distinguish between them. Failure to do so may easily result in a misunderstanding of the nature of moral judgment. Our main classification of moral disagreements distinguishes those between persons who practically accept different concepts, from those between persons who practically accept the same concepts. The former type of disagreements might be called "essential moral", the latter "accidental moral", since disagreements of the latter type involve no conflict of moral desires.

Essential moral disagreements can again be divided according to the relation between the different concepts which are practically accepted by the disagreeing parties. It may be, for instance, that of the two different concepts one entails the other; or that apart from this relation of unilateral entailment between the concepts they are or are not of different interpretative level. It may further be that the concepts overlap or that they are mutually incompatible. The last is, of course, the strongest kind of essential disagreement.

Accidental moral disagreements concern the applicability or the application in particular cases of a concept which is practically accepted by the disagreeing parties. It may be that one of them asserts the applicability of the concept but the other denies it. It may even be that both parties agree that the concept which they practically accept is applicable, but that one of them nevertheless refuses to apply it. The case is analogous to the situation in which two persons agree about the applicability of the instrumentally accepted concept 'chair-aspect' to a basis of 'chair-appearance', but one of them refuses to undertake the risk of being mistaken by applying the former concept. This risk, as we have seen (Chapter XVI), is involved in the application of all interpretative concepts.

As an example of this type of disagreement in morals assume that two persons who practically accept the ostensive concept 'leading to pleasure' also accept, though not practically, the co-ostensive concept 'apparently leading to pleasure'. Let us further assume that the only available evidence for the applicability of the former concept to a particular basis is the applicability to it of the latter concept. In that case it is quite possible that although the disagreeing parties agree about the applicability of the concept, only one of them does apply it.

It would, I believe, be a mistake to assume that the only method of argument by which essential moral disagreements can be removed is persuasion and propaganda. Factual, logical and combinations of factual and logical arguments are all apposite and frequently used. Thus we may argue that our opponent, who believes himself to be a practical accepter of a certain concept, does in fact practically accept a different one which is identical with or similar to the concept which we ourselves practically accept. This may be done by confronting him with imaginary situations which are particularly apt to shake his conviction that he has practically accepted the concept which he wrongly believes himself to have accepted.

We may next argue that the concepts which are practically accepted by our opponent are internally or mutually inconsistent, or that they are inconsistent with other concepts which he accepts even if his acceptance of them is not practical. We may, for instance, show the inconsistency of his theology or his metaphysics with his ethics. This type of logical argument may be combined with a factual argument to the effect that our opponent does in fact, although not practically, accept concepts of whose acceptance he is not aware. None of these types of argument has anything to do with persuasion or propaganda. The belief that persuasion and propaganda are the only means of removing essential moral disagreements may lead to the view that moral statements are merely ways of expressing and inducing attitudes. It may thus obscure the manner in which the application of concepts can subserve moral conduct, that is, conduct prompted by moral desires.

Writers on ethics often discuss the question whether all moral characteristics can be "analysed" in terms of a single moral characteristic. The question seems to be whether there is one moral characteristic which, alone or in combination with different non-moral characteristics, is logically equivalent to any other moral characteristic. From our point of view it is quite possible that all concepts which are practically accepted by a person are in the described manner reducible to one. It is equally possible that this should not be the case. The issue of ethical pluralism or monism is connected with the controversy concerning another question to which we shall turn presently, namely, whether moral systems are systems of rules or whether they are teleological.

CHAPTER XXIX

MORAL RULES AND ETHICAL "RELATIVITY"

MORAL rules and actions conforming to them have so far not been explicitly considered. What falls to be said on these topics will largely be a translation of the above account of moral judgments into another terminology. The translation, however, will be useful in dealing with two questions: the difference between teleological and non-teleological systems of ethics, and the question of ethical relativity—whether there are or are not some actions which are moral, or immoral, for everybody. We shall see that teleological and non-teleological systems, however else they differ, are not differentiated in terms of the acceptance of rules in one case and that of ends in the other. Their difference is to be explained in terms of the acceptance of different kinds of rule or different kinds of concept. As to ethical relativity, and the venerable problem of alternative moralities, our cue will be found in a comparison between alternative codes of logic and alternative codes of morals.

The acceptance of rules may serve different purposes. It may in particular be practical. Consider schematically a rule, say 'r', to the effect that actions which are instances of a concept 'P' should be performed. We shall say that a person accepts 'r' "practically" if, and only if, he accepts 'P' practically. We shall further say that 'r' is a practical (or moral) rule for every person who accepts 'P' practically. Thus the statement that somebody accepts a moral rule, say, to the effect that actions which are productive of pleasure should be performed, is logically equivalent to the statement that he accepts the concept 'productive of pleasure' practically. The practical acceptance of a rule need not be explicit. In particular, it is not necessary that the accepter of the rule should be able to formulate it clearly.

We can now distinguish between teleological and non-teleological ethics, or at least draw a distinction which will help us to understand the nature of the issue between them. A concept '*P*', whatever the manner of its acceptance, is teleological if, and only if, it entails 'bringing about a desired state of affairs as nearly as is possible in the circumstances'. A teleological concept is not in itself a moral characteristic; but a person who accepts it practically and applies it to an action is making a moral judgment—more precisely a teleological moral judgment.

If a person practically accepts a teleological concept '*P*' then he *ipso facto* also accepts the practical rule to the effect that actions which are instances of '*P*' should be performed by everybody. Such a practical rule is then teleological. On the other hand, to the practical acceptance of a non-teleological concept there corresponds *ipso facto* the acceptance of a practical rule which is non-teleological. We can now clearly distinguish between purely teleological, purely non-teleological or deontological, and partly teleological systems of ethics.

A person "believes in" a purely teleological system of ethics if he practically accepts only teleological concepts or, what amounts to the same, only teleological rules. A person believes in a purely non-teleological or a deontological system of ethics if he practically accepts only non-teleological concepts or rules. Lastly, a person believes in a partly teleological and partly non-teleological system of ethics, or, as we might say, a mixed system, if he accepts practically teleological and non-teleological concepts or rules. It would be a mistake to say that to believe in a deontological system of ethics is to be the practical accepter of rules only; for rules of action may be both teleological and non-teleological. The difference between those who believe in a deontological and those who believe in a teleological system of ethics lies in the kind of rules which they practically accept.

Philosophers who hold mixed ethical theories tend to use ‹morally good› and its cognates for their practically accepted teleological concepts and ‹morally right› and its cognates for their practically accepted non-teleological concepts, in so far as the latter are applicable to actions. That in such systems 'right' and 'good' are not logically equivalent follows from the non-equivalence of teleological and non-teleological concepts in general.

The accepter of a purely teleological system may, as has often been pointed out, practically accept non-teleological rules as rules of thumb. This is possible because certain kinds of action which conform to non-teleological rules are as a matter of fact in "normal" circumstances also instances of teleological concepts. For example, a utilitarian whose only practically accepted concept is 'productive of the greatest possible happiness' may accept a rule of thumb to the effect that charitable actions should be performed by everybody.

Having shown that the transition from the terminology of practically accepted concepts to that of practically accepted rules is no more than a transition from one *façon de parler* to another, we can now turn to the discussion of ethical relativity. We shall find it useful to recall some results of our inquiry into the rules of conceptual thinking as such, that is, these rules considered apart from any specific manner of their acceptance. The points of chief importance for us at the moment concern the logic of rules, the notion of theoretically appropriate and inappropriate statements, and lastly the characterisation of a conceptual thinker and his primitive and non-primitive logical commitments.

We recall that rules are sharply distinguished from empirical and from logical propositions. In particular, we must distinguish a rule from the empirical proposition that it is accepted, or that it is satisfied or violated by somebody's action. A person accepts a rule if he satisfies it intentionally by his action, or if he has the intention to satisfy it. The logic of rules is linked with that of statements, through the notion of the indicative. An action satisfies a rule if, and only if, the proposition describing the action entails the indicative of the rule. An action violates a rule if, and only if, the proposition describing the action is incompatible with the indicative of the rule. To state therefore that an action satisfies or that it violates a rule is to state a logical proposition whose antecedent and consequent are empirical propositions (Chapter III).

The rules which so far have naturally been the centre of our attention are ostensive rules and other rules of conceptual thinking. It is by reference to them that mere utterances are distinguished from theoretical utterances or statements. (We can, of course, in a similar manner distinguish other performances such as the writing down of marks on paper, or the waving of flags, from theoretical performances.) An utterance is a theoretical utterance or a statement if it is theoretically appropriate or inappropriate.

An utterance is theoretically appropriate with respect to a rule or conjunction of rules of conceptual thinking (for example, <b has P> with respect to 'r' governing <P>) if, and only if, an accepter of the rule would not violate it by making the utterance (Chapter IV). We shall say that an utterance is theoretically appropriate with respect to a rule *and a person* if it is theoretically appropriate with respect to a rule which is in fact accepted by this person.[1] By using some schematic abbreviations we can exhibit the relations between persons, rules and utterances more clearly.

Let us write '$m(X, p)$' for the empirical proposition that an unspecified person X utters <p>; and '$i(r)$' for the indicative of a rule or conjunction of rules 'r' of conceptual thinking. The proposition '$i(r)$' is, of course, also empirical.

To state that the utterance <p> is *theoretically* appropriate with respect to a person A and rule 'r' is to state (1) the empirical proposition that A accepts 'r' and (2) the logical proposition that '$m(X, p)$' is compatible with '$i(r)$' (that is, that the action described by '$m(X, p)$' does not violate 'r'). Similarly, to state that the utterance <p> is theoretically inappropriate with respect to A and 'r' is to state (1) the empirical proposition that A accepts 'r' and (2) the logical proposition that '$m(X, p)$' is incompatible with '$i(r)$'. We can thus never ask simply whether an utterance as such is theoretically appropriate or inappropriate, but only whether it is theoretically appropriate or inappropriate with respect to a rule of conceptual thinking or with respect to such a rule *and* a person who accepts it. To ask the latter question is to ask a compound question whose components are an empirical or anthropological question and a logical one.

The last point which we must remember in view of the comparison we are about to institute between ethical relativity and logical, concerns the definition of the notion of a conceptual thinker.

---

[1] When speaking of theoretical appropriateness without qualification we shall as hitherto always mean theoretical appropriateness with respect to rules only.

We have, mainly for the following reasons, characterised a conceptual thinker as an accepter of ostensive rules. First of all, the definition is applicable to all human beings with the possible exception of certain types of mental defectives and very small children. Secondly, the acceptance of ostensive rules is fundamental to the acceptance of all other rules of conceptual thinking. In other words, unless ostensive rules are accepted by a conceptual thinker he cannot accept any other rules of conceptual thinking.

Just as no utterance as such is theoretically appropriate or inappropriate, so no action as such is practically appropriate or inappropriate. To state that an action is practically appropriate is to state a relation between an action, a rule, and a person who accepts this rule practically. More precisely, an action is practically appropriate with respect to a rule and a person if, and only if, (1) the person accepts the rule practically, and if (2) the action would not violate the rule, that is, if a proposition describing the action is compatible with the indicative of the rule. An action is practically inappropriate with respect to a rule and a person if, and only if, (1) the person accepts the rule practically, and if (2) a proposition describing the action is incompatible with the indicative of the rule. We might have defined moral appropriateness more strongly by requiring that the action not only does not violate the rule but actually satisfies it. Yet though the choice between these definitions, including the possibility of adopting both of them, is for our present purpose of little consequence, the weaker definition seems more suitable for the comparison between theoretical and practical appropriateness.

In asking whether an action is *practically* appropriate or inappropriate with respect to a person and a rule we are again asking two questions, namely, an empirical or anthropological question and a logical. In judging actions to be practically appropriate or inappropriate we often assume or pretend that the agent, perhaps contrary to his own beliefs, accepts practical rules which are accepted by ourselves who judge the action. It is thus often advisable to make it clear whether the person with respect to whom an action is practically appropriate or inappropriate is the agent, the judge or perhaps both.

Are there any actions, then, which are morally appropriate or inappropriate for every rational being? The notion of a rational being is, of course, too vague to be properly of service. Those who make use of it seem to imply that a rational being is characterised by the acceptance of certain rules of conceptual thinking and of conduct. A rational being is thus a conceptual thinker and a moral agent. In order to answer our question we must, therefore, give a definition of 'moral agent'. It was similarly necessary to give a definition of 'conceptual thinker' in order to answer the question whether any propositions are theoretically appropriate or inappropriate for every conceptual thinker.

A suitable definition of 'moral agent' would have to satisfy the following requirements. It would first of all have to be applicable to all human beings with the exception of small children who are not yet moral beings, and adults whom we should regard morally, not as misguided, but as moral imbeciles or a-moral. We should secondly require that rules of the type which are characteristic of a moral agent should be fundamental in the sense that unless he accepts some rules of this type a person cannot accept rules of any other type.

The person who practically accepts a concept 'P' does, as we have seen, *ipso facto* practically accept a rule to the effect that actions which are instances of 'P' should be performed by everybody. A person accepts a concept and therefore the corresponding rule practically, if he accepts it in the service of a desire that actions which are instances of the concept should be performed and the further desire that everybody should do his best to satisfy the former desire wherever it is present. I shall characterise a moral agent as a practical accepter of rules, or, in different words, as one who accepts practical rules.

The definition satisfies both requirements. On the one hand, all persons who must fall under an adequate definition of 'moral agent' are, as a matter of anthropological fact, covered by it. On the other hand, the definition satisfies the second requirement for the simple reason that all moral rules are of the type of practical rules.

The analogy between the notion of a conceptual thinker and that of a moral agent should now be clear. Just as the former is characterised by the acceptance of some ostensive rules and not by the acceptance of one or more specific ostensive rules, so the latter is characterised by the acceptance of some practical rules (by the practical acceptance of some concepts or rules of conduct), and not by the acceptance of one or more specific practical rules. Two ostensive rules, if we disregard differences in the labels or signs which are used for ostensive concepts in accordance with these rules, differ in governing the use of different ostensive concepts. Two practical rules differ in prescribing actions which are instances of different concepts.

In consequence of accepting some ostensive rules, which may differ from person to person, every conceptual thinker is committed to primitive propositions of second and higher order, for example, to the proposition that for any three unspecified ostensive concepts 'P', 'Q', 'R', the propositions that 'P' entails 'Q' and that 'Q' entails 'R' entail the proposition that 'P' entails 'R'. In other words, the acceptance of different ostensive rules entails the acceptance of the rule of transitivity. Propositions which do not violate this and the other rules of primitive logic are appropriate, whereas propositions which violate these rules are inappropriate for every conceptual thinker (Chapter VIII). We might call the system of propositions which are theoretically appropriate *or inappropriate* for every conceptual thinker the "common theoretical system". Systems of propositions which are appropriate or inappropriate for some conceptual thinkers as a consequence of their acceptance of specific ostensive rules or of supplementary non-ostensive rules are then "alternative theoretical systems".

In order to answer the question whether some actions are practically appropriate or inappropriate for all moral agents, and therefore with respect to practical rules accepted by all moral agents, we must look for practical rules whose acceptance is entailed by the acceptance of any set of unspecified practical rules. We must, in other words, look for practical rules which, for example, would be analogous to the theoretical rule of transitivity for unspecified ostensive predicates.

The only rule of conduct whose acceptance is entailed by the acceptance of *any* set of practical rules is the rule to the effect that no action should violate any *practical* rule which the agent accepts, that is, any rule which he accepts with the desire that everybody should accept it. We do not regard as immoral the violation of a rule, say of chess or grammar, merely because we have accepted it. But we do regard as immoral the violation of any rule, whatever its content, which we have practically accepted. *If*, unlike Kant himself, we interpret the categorical imperative as a necessary but not as a sufficient condition of practical appropriateness, then there is only one rule to which every moral agent is committed: the categorical imperative.

The actions which are practically *in*appropriate with respect to the categorical imperative and thus with respect to every moral agent constitute what we may call the "common practical system". All practically appropriate and all practically inappropriate actions which do not violate the categorical imperative in the sense of a merely negative condition are appropriate or inappropriate with respect to rules of conduct which are not necessarily accepted by every moral agent. They fall into what might be called "alternative practical systems".

The common practical system is based on the anthropological fact that with negligible exceptions all human beings accept some practical rules. In this respect it is like the much richer common theoretical system which is based on the anthropological fact that with negligible exceptions all human beings accept some ostensive rules. The widespread acceptance of certain alternative practical systems within different communities is again as much an empirical fact as the widespread acceptance of certain alternative theoretical systems or systems of logic.

The reason why the common practical system is poor as compared with the common theoretical system lies in the fact that actions are not arranged in a hierarchy of different orders which would be in any way similar to the hierarchical ordering of propositions into factual propositions, that is, propositions of order zero, and logical propositions, that is, propositions of first, second and higher order. Logical propositions, roughly speaking, relate propositions in such a manner that the theoretical appropriateness of the relating propositions does not depend on the theoretical appropriateness of the related propositions (Chapter IV). There are, on the other hand, no actions which relate other actions in such a way that the practical appropriateness of the relating actions is independent of the practical appropriateness of the related actions.

To sum up: as some theoretical performances are appropriate or inappropriate for all conceptual thinkers, so are some practical performances inappropriate for all moral agents. To assert the theoretical or practical appropriateness or inappropriateness of a performance is to state a logical *and* an anthropological proposition. Practical appropriateness and inappropriateness are in this sense no more "relative" than theoretical appropriateness or inappropriateness.

Before leaving the topic of the practical application of concepts and of practical appropriateness it is necessary to consider the objection that it has nowhere been proved that when "we" speak of moral actions we mean practically appropriate ones. Though I do not claim to have given such a proof, I should point out, first, that the concept of practical appropriateness is employed in people's thinking about conduct and that its clarification is therefore not an idle task; secondly, that the clarification becomes still more significant for all those whose concept of a moral action is such that its practical appropriateness is a necessary, a sufficient or both a necessary and a sufficient condition of its morality. Since in the nature of the case I could expect only the first point to be generally conceded, I have been careful to use the term "practical appropriateness" in a manner which does not make my argument dependent on the second point's being also conceded.

CHAPTER XXX

METAPHYSICAL AND OTHER DIRECTIVE PROPOSITIONS

IN drawing distinctions and discussing relations between ostensive and non-ostensive concepts, between ostensive concepts of different interpretative levels, and between different ways of accepting concepts, the question *why* a conceptual thinker accepts some concepts rather than others has been deliberately avoided. As so often, it is a highly ambiguous question to which the possible answers are inevitably of different kinds. Among them are various causal explanations, and the exhibition of hidden deductive commitments. An answer which, though somewhat obscure, leads straight to the topics of the remaining chapters of this inquiry is given by some historians of ideas. According to them most concepts which in a certain period are accepted by the members of a civilisation, have their root in a common metaphysical background. This they describe by drawing attention to some highly general principles put forward and advocated mostly by philosophers and usually called "metaphysical".

Examples are the proposition that reality is, or is not, ultimately mental or material; that propositions, concepts, numbers and other non-ostensive particulars do, or do not, exist; that the world is, or is not, a causally ordered system. By calling these and similar propositions or systems of propositions the "background" of others which are not metaphysical, one implies that metaphysical propositions are associated with and relevant to non-metaphysical theories. Although the nature of this association will have to be clarified it is evident that every metaphysical theory is associated with some non-metaphysical theories and not with others. It may, moreover, be associated with theories mutually incompatible. We should not expect a person who accepts Aristotle's metaphysical doctrines also to accept, without important reservations, Newtonian physics. Neither should we expect a person who is convinced by the argument of the *Critique of Pure Reason* to accept without reservation Einstein's theory of relativity. We might, however, expect him to accept any of a number of, possibly mutually incompatible, mechanistic physical theories.

The nearest we have come so far to a discussion of metaphysical propositions was in considering the different ways in which concepts may or may not be empty (Chapters XXI and XXII) and in considering alleged proofs of the applicability of concepts of higher interpretative level from the applicability of concepts of lower level (Chapter XVIII). Alleged deductive proofs, we saw, were self-contradictory, alleged probability proofs circular. If we cannot prove in this way that a concept is applicable (not descriptively empty) then *a fortiori* we cannot prove it not to be ontologically empty; for a concept is ontologically not-empty for a person only if it is descriptively not empty and if the person accepts it.

To "believe" that a concept, descriptively not empty, is also ontologically not empty, is to accept the concept. The "belief" or the acceptance may be either blind, or a result of choice between acceptances of different concepts or sets of concepts, or at least between an acceptance and a rejection. Blind "beliefs" would not be regarded as metaphysical except in a rudimentary form. A child or unphilosophical adult who believes as a matter of course in the existence of an external world is not in that entertaining a metaphysical belief. On the other hand, a person who believes that physical objects, but not also sense data, exist, is believing a metaphysical proposition. It is not necessary or possible to distinguish sharply between metaphysical and the corresponding blind "beliefs". It is, however, important to characterise the former and thereby blind "beliefs" deriving from them. The metaphysical "beliefs" of some men tend to become the blind "beliefs" of others. Keeping to our terminology, we shall focus our discussion not on metaphysical "beliefs" but on metaphysical propositions.

It will be useful before attempting to characterise such propositions, or a determinate species of them, to consider an argument which under different forms has been put forward in order to show that metaphysical propositions are meaningless. The argument profits by habitually combining an almost universally accepted distinction and a question-begging definition. The distinction is between metaphysical propositions on the one hand and empirical and logical (logico-mathematical) propositions on the other. According to the definition the term "meaningless" means what is meant by the term "neither empirical nor logico-mathematical".

From the distinction and the definition it follows that metaphysical propositions are meaningless, but only in the sense of the definition. The definition ascribes a meaning to "meaningless" which is far removed from its usual senses. It implies, for instance, that rules, or at least some rules, are meaningless. Indeed, the statement "in the sense of this definition metaphysical propositions are meaningless" is nothing but a restatement of the almost undisputed thesis that metaphysical propositions are neither empirical nor logico-mathematical. After proving the meaninglessness of metaphysical propositions in the harmless sense of "meaningless" given in the definition one may replace the term by "nonsensical" in one of its usual senses. In that event, one is committing one of the standard fallacies against which the elementary text-books warn us.

The argument is frequently fortified by highly technical references to the language of *Principia Mathematica* and similar systems. It is, for instance, assumed that the impossibility of expressing metaphysical propositions in these systems is another test of their meaninglessness, and this not only within these systems but in general. Yet surely if a proposition cannot be expressed in a formal system the reason may lie in a limitation of the system.

It would be ungracious and almost unfair to seem to ignore the great benefits which have been derived by modern philosophy from the argument here criticised. One of them has been the renewed interest in the logical status of metaphysical propositions and another the insistence on a clear distinction between metaphysical and other types of proposition.

If we are to address ourselves to the question about the logical status of metaphysical propositions with any hope of success we must try to be clear, first, about some minimum requirements which an answer would have to satisfy. Only then can we propose an answer and see whether it is in these essentials satisfactory.

First, metaphysical propositions are not empirical. Not only modern positivists and their predecessors, but most metaphysical philosophers, would agree with this requirement. Some of them may seem to disagree and to regard metaphysical propositions as highly general empirical propositions. If so their dissent appears to be due mainly to their use of ‹empirical›. By empirical propositions I shall understand, as before (Chapter XI), the following: ostensive propositions; negations of ostensive propositions; internally consistent conjunctions whose members are ostensive propositions or negations of ostensive propositions; and lastly, propositions which are incompatible with propositions of the preceding types. The argument is not bound up with this particular characterisation of empirical propositions. Others might do equally well.

The proposition, for example, that the world is a causally ordered system is not an ostensive proposition, since in stating it the term "world" is not used to identify a basis of an ostensive concept. Neither has this proposition any of the other alternative characteristics of empirical propositions. It is, in particular, not incompatible with any empirical proposition to the effect that one particular event causes or does not cause another particular event. The same applies to the propositions that the external world is real: for the reality of the external world must be distinguished from the applicability to a particular basis of 'physical object'. If this were not so a Berkeleyan could not at the same time grant that 'physical object' is not descriptively empty and deny that it is ontologically empty (Chapter XXI). Again, a Platonist could not at the same time judge something to be a chair and yet deny the reality of the external world. Our examples lack clarity not because they imply the denial of the empirical character of metaphysical propositions, but because they contain the terms "world" and "reality". The vagueness of these terms has its root in the fact that a satisfactory positive account of metaphysics which would cover different and even mutually incompatible metaphysical theories has so far not been given, at least not in this inquiry.

The *second* requirement which must be satisfied by all metaphysical propositions, if there are to be such propositions, has, like the first one, also been emphasised by the logical positivists. This is the requirement that metaphysical propositions be not logical propositions, that is, propositions of first or higher order (Chapter VIII). Some philosophers would regard metaphysical propositions as logical or logically necessary, but their use of these terms differs from ours. They might at most hold that metaphysical propositions constitute one species of a common genus of necessary propositions, of which our logical propositions constitute another species. This, however, would imply that they agree with our second requirement.

The *third* requirement concerns the relation between metaphysical propositions and others, in particular empirical ones. It is vaguely indicated by those who speak of the metaphysical background of propositions and theories themselves not metaphysical. We formulate this requirement by saying that metaphysical propositions and theories are associated with some non-metaphysical theories and not with others; and that, moreover, mutually incompatible non-metaphysical theories can be associated with the same metaphysical theory. The nature of this association will have to follow from our account of metaphysical propositions. It will have to explain, for example, the nature of the association of the metaphysical theory of mechanism with mutually incompatible mechanistic physical theories.

A *fourth* requirement must be introduced in view of the difference between metaphysical and corresponding blind "beliefs", for example that of a child in the existence of the external world. Since the difference is not sharp the requirement cannot be stated precisely. We formulate it by demanding that any account of metaphysical propositions should do justice to the fact that they are "believed" as the result of a choice between alternative possibilities.

Before proposing a fifth requirement it is convenient to show that the preceding four are sufficient to exclude some accounts of metaphysical propositions which are not lacking in *prima facie* plausibility. It is also convenient to show that the preceding requirements are fulfilled by a class of propositions which comprises not only metaphysical propositions, but also some general scientific or common-sense principles. The need for distinguishing the former from the latter, even if border-line cases are admitted, will lead to the formulation of our fifth requirement, which will be satisfied by metaphysical propositions only.

At least two views of the nature of metaphysical propositions are excluded. On the one hand, we cannot regard a metaphysical theory as an internally consistent set of first principles which are associated with non-metaphysical propositions as are the premises and the conclusions of deductive arguments. If this were so then an internally consistent metaphysical theory could not be associated with mutually incompatible theories which themselves are not metaphysical.

On the other hand, a metaphysical theory cannot, as Whitehead seems to have held, be regarded as an internally consistent propositional function '$\phi(x_1, \ldots, x_n)$' from which non-metaphysical theories result by substituting descriptions of concrete experiences for the variables. It is again by reason of the third requirement that such an account must be excluded. Whatever else descriptions of concrete experiences may be, no two results of the substitution described could be incompatible.

Philosophers who have taken up the antimetaphysical challenge have not, I believe, given sufficient attention to the possibility that a metaphysical system may be associated with mutually incompatible theories. This applies even to the otherwise widely different accounts of L. J. Russell, who regards metaphysical propositions as proposals,[1] and of Collingwood, who regards them as absolute presuppositions. Closer attention to our third requirement would perhaps have led to a more precise account of metaphysical propositions and of their relevance to propositions which are not metaphysical.

The first four requirements are satisfied by any conjunction of two rules of which one is a rule for the use of a concept or a relation between possibly unspecified concepts, and the other a rule to the effect that the former rule be applied to the exclusion of other rules. We should thus interpret the sentence "The world is a causally ordered system" in its metaphysical sense, as a rule governing the concept 'x causes y' together with a further rule to the effect that

[1] 'Science and Philosophy', *Proc. Aristotelian Society*, vol. 25 (1924/25).

some other concept, for example 'x is merely followed by y', be not applied where the former concept can be applied. The acceptance of the second rule, which allows for great variation in the rejected alternatives, indicates that the first rule has been chosen among alternative possibilities. We should similarly interpret the sentence "the world is a coherent system". Here the first rule concerns a relation of coherence between concepts which may not yet have been specified.

It is convenient to call such a conjunction of a rule for the use of a concept or of an interconceptual relation with a rule prescribing the more or less exclusive use of the former rule, "a directive proposition" or more briefly "a directive". It must be emphasised that just as the same sentence can be used both for a logical and a factual proposition, so a sentence which can be used as a directive can also be used for a proposition of a different kind, for example a logical proposition.

Directive propositions satisfy our four requirements. As rules they are not factual and, *a fortiori*, not empirical propositions. For the same reason they are also not logical propositions. Directives, moreover, are satisfied by the statement of propositions and theories in which the concepts whose application is prescribed by the directives are in fact applied. To state that a system of directives is associated with, possibly, mutually incompatible theories, is to state that in holding the theory one is satisfying the directives. The way in which directives are associated with non-metaphysical theories is thus clarified.

So far our notion of directives is wider than the notion of specifically metaphysical directives. A directive for the use of the concept 'dog', or of a concept which belongs to a particular science, would fulfil our requirements. What distinguishes metaphysical from other, and in particular scientific, directives is a higher degree of comprehensiveness. This is indicated by the fact that in formulating directives one uses expressions like "the world", "reality", "experience", and that one often reinforces them by "total", "in all its aspects", etc.

The *fifth* requirement is thus the requirement of a high degree of comprehensiveness. It expresses the need for a distinction between metaphysical and other directives. The distinction again need not, and indeed ought not to, be a sharp one, since, as has been mentioned before, in most senses of the term "metaphysical" it is often doubtful whether some highly general directives are metaphysical or scientific. The requirement of a high degree of comprehensiveness is thus not a very precise one, and might be reasonably satisfied in different ways. This, however, seems to be of little consequence, since it is much more important to recognise that metaphysical principles, or at least a very large species of them, are directives, than to draw a thin demarcation line between them and other directives.

The following is one of the ways in which the fifth requirement can be satisfied. Recall the notion of an ostensive category (Chapter XVII). An ostensive concept which belongs to a set of concepts, in particular to a set consisting of all concepts accepted by the same person, is an ostensive category if, and only if, it is entailed by all concepts of the interpretative level to which it belongs. As regards non-ostensive concepts we cannot in the same way distinguish between interpretative levels. We can, however, divide a set of non-ostensive concepts into subsets, such that each subset contains a concept which is entailed by every member of it. This concept we might call a "non-ostensive category". A metaphysical directive could then be defined as either a directive for the use of a category or as a directive for the use of an inter-conceptual relation between all concepts belonging to the same category. It might be reasonably argued that the definition should be strengthened, for example by requiring directives for inter-conceptual relations to cover more than the concepts belonging to one category. Some directives, for example the principle that the world is a coherent system, whatever this may mean, seem to cover all concepts of a system which has been or is to be accepted. These and similar modifications need not be considered here.

Since scientific propositions or laws in general have not been discussed under any separate heading it may be important to recall that so far we have distinguished three different types of them: empirical laws of nature (Chapter XI), operational entailments (Chapter XXVI), and, in the present chapter, scientific directives. The distinction makes no claim to completeness. Moreover, by distinguishing between scientific propositions of the types mentioned it is not implied that the same sentence as used by the same scientist is always used for a proposition of the same type. Nor is it implied that the user of a sentence may not be in doubt as to the type of the proposition for which he has used it on different occasions.

Although I believe that many so-called "metaphysical propositions" are metaphysical directives, it is more important to see that metaphysical directives are in fact accepted by conceptual thinkers, than to decide whether our account of a large species of metaphysical propositions as directives is correct. Some metaphysical sentences, for example <God exists>, are, I believe, not in general used for directives.

Directives are rules. They may be accepted and imposed for various reasons and purposes. They may be accepted explicitly or implicitly, and their explicit formulation may precede or follow the construction of theories by which they are satisfied. Which of the last two possibilities is realised in any particular case is a historical question and examples of either possibility can be found in the history of conceptual thinking. It may perhaps be not far wrong to say that on the whole in the early periods of scientific thought the formulation of metaphysical directives tended to precede the construction of scientific theories, but in later periods the process tended to be in the opposite direction.

CHAPTER XXXI

ON THE POSSIBLE RELEVANCE OF VARIOUS TYPES OF METAPHYSICAL DIRECTIVES

In the present chapter I shall discuss the possibility of classifying (or of there being a procedure for classifying) metaphysical directives. This may emphasise some features of such directives which they do not share with propositions of other types. It may also show how the acceptance of metaphysical directives can influence thinking in fields which lie outside metaphysics, and thirdly, it may warn against possible and actual misunderstandings of the nature of metaphysical directives.

Every metaphysical directive is, as we have seen, a conjunction of a main rule with a subsidiary rule. The main rule governs the use of a concept or a relation between otherwise not fully specified concepts. The subsidiary rule prescribes the acceptance of the main rule to the exclusion of other more or less clearly determined alternatives. A classification of metaphysical directives will thus naturally proceed by first distinguishing between different kinds of concept and interconceptual relation which are governed by their main rules. When this has been done the directives so classified will subdivide according to differences in their subsidiary rules.

This procedure could be based on a great variety of distinguishing characteristics and would consequently lead to different classifications. The choice would depend on the purpose in hand. For us the most important classification is a threefold division of metaphysical directives into ostensive, whose main rules govern the use of ostensive concepts and of relations between (possibly not fully specified) ostensive concepts; non-ostensive whose main rules govern the use of non-ostensive concepts; and lastly mixed directives, that is, such as are neither ostensive nor non-ostensive. They include directives governing the use of both ostensive and non-ostensive concepts and of relations between (possibly not fully specified) ostensive concepts on the one hand, and non-ostensive concepts on the other.

Ostensive directives can be classified in many ways. A possible *fundamentum divisionis* might be the interpretative level of the concepts governed by their main rules or, as we shall say briefly, their main concepts. Another classification might proceed by first enumerating the most frequently used main concepts such as 'physical thing', 'physical process', 'cause', and then distinguishing the others by their different relations to all or some concepts of the former group. A classification of this kind could not, of course, claim to be exhaustive in the sense of covering all possible systems of metaphysical directives and not only the historically important.

The subdivision of ostensive directives according to their subsidiary rules is again possible in many different ways. We might distinguish between subsidiary rules proscribing the acceptance of all concepts which are co-ostensive with the main concept of the directive; those proscribing the acceptance of some co-ostensive concepts, for example, those of higher interpretative level; those proscribing acceptance of concepts which although not co-ostensive with the main concept of the directive yet stand in certain logical relations to it, etc. The proscription of alternative concepts may be more or less determinate and more or less explicit. The discovery of subsidiary rules belonging to the metaphysical directives which a philosopher or scientist accepts is apt to be difficult, being often better gleaned from his polemical digressions than from the main stream of his argument.

The classification of non-ostensive directives would follow the same pattern, first dividing non-ostensive directives according to differences in the concepts governed by their main rules, and then subdividing them according to differences in their subsidiary rules. Without claiming that the distinction is exhaustive, we have distinguished (in Chapter XXII) between non-ostensive concepts which are simplifying and those which are completable. Simplifying concepts, for example 'perfect triangle' or 'mathematical addition', are, roughly speaking, relata of concept-concept relations which simplify overlaps between ostensive concepts into inclusions or exclusions between non-ostensive. Completable concepts are such non-ostensive concepts as are not simplifying, and, like ostensive concepts, are combinable with ostensive concepts to form other ostensive concepts.

Within the class of completable concepts we have distinguished between ideal-constituent ones such as 'ideal particle', and epistemological concepts, for example 'concept'. The ideal-constituent are unexemplified, but not necessarily unexemplifiable. Epistemological concepts are necessarily unexemplifiable. They can be completed to 'a person applying a concept', or some other ostensive concept whose instances are situations such as are of interest to epistemology.

Non-ostensive directives having been divided into directives whose main rules govern simplifying, ideal-constituent and epistemological concepts, each of these classes would subdivide according to differences in the subsidiary rules. This, however, will not be attempted. As far as directives for completable concepts are concerned, their subsidiary rules would frequently have to refer to ostensive concepts which are permitted or proscribed as completions. On the whole, the discovery of subsidiary rules belonging to accepted non-ostensive directives seems even more difficult than the discovery of subsidiary rules which belong to accepted ostensive directives.

The acceptance or otherwise of metaphysical directives may greatly influence the course of inquiries in different fields. To the course of empirical inquiries the acceptance of directives governing the use of ostensive and ideal-constituent concepts is most important. However, if the mathematisation of empirical theories is desired, then directives governing the use of simplifying concepts may also become relevant; for restrictions on the range of permissible simplifying concepts may narrow down the possibility of simplifying relations between ostensive concepts.

The acceptance of an ostensive directive must not be confused with the discovery of an empirical proposition of great generality. The confusion is often found in books on the social sciences. There the scarcity of empirical laws, together with the great need for knowledge of them in the interest of human happiness, easily give rise to the temptation of mistaking a system of directives governing the use of certain concepts, for a system of empirical laws formulated in terms of these concepts. Thus Hegelian dialectics, which, as a system of directives governing the use of concepts in a projected social science, makes sense, is often considered as being a system of empirical laws constituting part of this science.

Directives are rules and cannot conceivably be incompatible with empirical propositions. They cannot, in other words, be falsified by experiment and observation. This, however, does not imply that experiment and observation are irrelevant to a system of directives. Experiments and observations may or may not falsify a scientific theory associated with a given directive system. In this way they may be indirect evidence for or against a directive system. The appeal by philosophers to scientific theories and consequently to experiments and observations, as evidence for or against a metaphysical system, is therefore not entirely vain. It loses its justification, however, if one confuses the direct support given by empirical evidence to a scientific theory with the indirect support given by this evidence to a metaphysical system associated with the theory. The confusion between direct empirical evidence for a scientific theory and indirect empirical evidence for a metaphysical theory has its root in the mistake that metaphysical directives are highly general empirical propositions. It explains why some philosophers (for example, Brentano) have believed that the proper method of philosophy is the method of the natural sciences.

Similar remarks could be made about directives governing the use of ideal-constituent concepts. The empirical evidence which directly supports the scientific theories of Dalton and his successors, lends indirect support to the theories of Leucippus, Democritus and later metaphysical atomists. This indirect support is mediated by the relation between empirical statements and the metaphysical directives which they satisfy.

Metaphysical directives of the types described are not heuristic principles; for we may decide to use as a heuristic principle a rule which clashes with our accepted directives. On the other hand, if a person accepts a set of metaphysical directives governing the use of certain ostensive and ideal-constituent concepts, he will naturally look for empirical laws, operational entailments and other types of scientific proposition, whose statement satisfies these directives. Metaphysical systems, at least in so far as they contain metaphysical directives, need not be mere verbal ornaments of scientific inquiry. They can give it direction and have often done so.

Just as the acceptance of directives governing the use of certain ostensive and ideal-constituent concepts can direct the course of scientific inquiry, so the acceptance of directives for the use of certain simplifying concepts can influence the course of mathematical research. The controversy between formalist and intuitionist mathematicians is a metaphysical one. In it each party accuses the other, not of logical mistakes, but of a deeply rooted misunderstanding of the nature of mathematics, in the sense of a metaphysical error. This error, it is alleged, finds its expression in the use of certain mathematical concepts rather than others, in particular in the use of set-theoretical concepts which are too wide or too narrow. The metaphysical "belief", for instance, that there are "no infinite sets which are given in their complete totality", is the acceptance of one concept of 'set' to the exclusion of others.

Directives governing the use of ostensive concepts may also influence aesthetic and ethical thinking. To see this we need only assume that a person accepts a directive whose main rule governs the category 'physical process' and whose subsidiary rule proscribes the acceptance of any concept which is co-ostensive with 'physical process' and of higher interpretative level. The accepter of this directive would violate it by the application of any such "non-naturalistic" concept. He would consequently violate the directive by applying it either contemplatively or practically. The aesthetic and moral judgments which he would thus pass would, from the point of view of his metaphysics, be metaphysically faulty judgments.

Philosophers whose main interest is the philosophy of science, which needs no ostensive concepts above the level of physical-object and physical-process concepts, tend to accept a "naturalistic" metaphysics. They tend, in other words, to accept ostensive directives whose subsidiary rules proscribe the acceptance of "non-naturalistic" concepts in general. The scientific outlook, not only on science but on all other fields of thought, is the acceptance for all theorising of directives which originally are satisfied by scientific theorising.

It is not necessary to discuss directives for the use of some epistemological concepts rather than others. We have seen (Chapter XXII) that the "belief" that certain epistemological concepts are not ontologically empty (that they are quasi-applicable) is nothing but the acceptance of the rules governing the concepts. The acceptance of epistemological directives differs from the mere acceptance of epistemological concepts by the additional acceptance of rules which proscribe the acceptance of alternative concepts.

From the point of view of our inquiry the adoption of epistemological directives is incidental. Thus, nothing in it turns on our use of 'concept' and 'proposition' rather than, for example, 'meaningful part of a sentence' and 'meaningful sentence'. Our results can *salva rei substantia* be translated into other schemes of epistemological concepts. For instance, what has been said about the logical relations between ostensive concepts, about their stratification into interpretative levels, and about their relations to non-ostensive concepts is invariant with respect to any change in the epistemological directives which have been adopted for the sake of presentation.

As a kind of mixed directive we may mention rules to the effect that completable, non-ostensive concepts be completed to ostensive concepts of some types rather than others. An example would be the rule to the effect that all ideal-constituent concepts be completed to physical-process and not to physical-object concepts. Another example would be the rule to the effect that all epistemological concepts be completed to 'making a statement' and not, for example, to 'asserting a proposition'.

Epistemological and ideal-constituent concepts are often treated under the name of "synsemantic" or "incomplete" symbols, which stand in need of contextual definitions. Rules permitting or requiring certain completions rather than others are metaphysical directives. Any theory of incomplete (synsemantic) symbols, for example Russell's "no-class" theory, which implies the acceptance of such directives, is consequently not metaphysically neutral.

General or inter-categorial directives are another kind of mixed directives. They prescribe that all concepts, without regard to their being ostensive or non-ostensive, which are accepted by a person, should in some specified manner be interrelated. We have already mentioned the general directive to the effect that a person's accepted concepts should all "cohere" in some sense of this highly ambiguous term (Chapter XXIII).

Some general directives which embody cherished metaphysical ideals are on closer inspection seen to be internally inconsistent. We have seen (Chapter III) that no rule or conjunction of rules 'r' can conceivably be comprehensive in the sense that every proposition describing an action (which may be a statement) either satisfies or violates 'r'. We have similarly seen that no rule or conjunction of rules 'r' can conceivably be perfect in the sense that it can be satisfied only by mutually consistent actions, more precisely by actions whose descriptions are mutually consistent. What applies to every rule applies *a fortiori* to every rule governing the use of concepts. Consequently, the general directives which require that the conjunction of rules which govern a person's accepted concepts should be comprehensive and perfect cannot conceivably be satisfied either separately or jointly.

It has been emphasised earlier that the logical relation between systems or metaphysical directives on the one hand and their associated theories on the other implies nothing about the historical order of their explicit formulation. It similarly implies nothing about the reasons why metaphysical directives begin to be or cease to be accepted. It seems that continuous failure to develop a non-metaphysical theory which conforms to a person's metaphysical directives, will generally wear down his loyalty towards them. However, whether and when this happens depends in addition on a great variety of heterogeneous factors. A person's character or his government's interest or lack of interest in a particular metaphysical system may here be of importance.

Our account of metaphysical directives agrees to some extent with Kant's account of the principles "which make experience possible". It agrees in particular with his rejection of the view that these principles are highly general empirical propositions and the view that they are logical propositions.

His positive account of these principles as synthetic *a priori* propositions is full of difficulties, and his whole doctrine of synthetic *a priori* propositions unsatisfactory. In particular, his twofold criterion of *a priori* propositions, namely, necessity and universality, as formulated and used by him, applies to logical propositions of different kinds and to rules (Chapter VI). His alleged necessary presuppositions of all science are the presuppositions of Newtonian physics. This can be clearly seen in the case of the First Analogy, that is, the principle of the conservation of substance.

If one were to attempt a reconstruction of Kant's critical philosophy on the assumption that his doctrine of synthetic *a priori* propositions is untenable, one might proceed by replacing his synthetic *a priori* propositions by metaphysical directives. His presuppositions of all natural science would, in particular, be transformed into metaphysical directives which are associated only with mechanistic scientific theories. As a result of this reconstruction his distinction between synthetic *a priori* and merely regulative metaphysical principles would have to be abandoned or, at least, greatly modified.

CHAPTER XXXII

THE ADEQUACY OF METAPHYSICAL
DIRECTIVES

THE charge that metaphysics is intellectually useless is generally based on all or some of the following theses: that its propositions are meaningless; that they are irrelevant to non-metaphysical inquiries; that they are incapable of being true or false. Each of these admits, no doubt, of different interpretations. It can, I believe, nevertheless be fairly said that we have already dealt with the first two of them. As regards the alleged meaninglessness it has been shown that metaphysical directives are meaningful in the same sense in which rules of which they are a species are meaningful. As regards the alleged irrelevance it has been shown that metaphysical directives are relevant to non-metaphysical inquiries, in the sense that their acceptance restricts the range of concepts used in such inquiries.

There remains for discussion the third thesis and, more generally, the question how far, if at all, metaphysical directives are capable of being true or false. The result of the discussion of these points may be anticipated in order to make its drift clear at the outset. Roughly speaking, we shall find reasons for rejecting two extreme answers to our question; on the one hand the view that metaphysical directives are true or false in exactly the sense in which empirical or logico-mathematical propositions are; on the other hand, the view that they are no more "true" or "false" than are works of art, for example musical compositions.

The first part of our task is easily accomplished. We remember that on any theory of truth, the truth of a factual or logical proposition entails its theoretical appropriateness. A proposition of either kind is theoretically appropriate if, and only if, an utterance used for it is theoretically appropriate. Again, such an utterance is theoretically appropriate with respect to a person and a rule (or conjunction of rules) if, and only if, the person accepts the rule and if his making the utterance would not violate the rule (Chapters IV and XXIV). Now metaphysical directives are themselves rules. They cannot, therefore, be theoretically appropriate. Consequently they also cannot be true in any of the senses in which 'true' entails 'theoretically appropriate'. Similar remarks apply on the whole also to the question of the falsehood of metaphysical directives.

By rejecting thus the first of the above-mentioned extreme views we are not, of course, committed to the second. It does, however, seem advisable to apply the terms "true" and "false" only to propositions which are theoretically appropriate or inappropriate. As far as metaphysical directives are concerned I shall, therefore, speak not of their truth or falsehood, but of their adequacy or inadequacy. The terminological advantages of this will presently become apparent. One lies in the possibility it opens up of speaking of degrees of adequacy and inadequacy.

The adequacy of a metaphysical directive depends on its relation to non-metaphysical propositions, and on its relation to other metaphysical directives. In order to explain this more clearly I shall introduce first of all a strict sense of "a system of metaphysical directives". A set of metaphysical directives is a system if, and only if, it possesses logical and directive order. A set of metaphysical directives possesses logical order if it is internally consistent and if it contains all its logical consequences. Such a set can be developed in one or more ways as a deductive system. The logical relations between the directives correspond exactly to the logical relations between their indicatives (see Chapter III). I shall consider only sets of metaphysical directives which possess logical order, without stating explicitly that this condition is fulfilled.

The notion of the directive order of a set of metaphysical directives has no obvious analogy in the sphere of factual propositions. It involves reference on the one hand to an accepter of the directives, and on the other hand to non-metaphysical propositions which are associated with the directives, that is, whose statement satisfies the directives. It is, I believe, best to explain the notion of directive order by describing an imaginary but by no means unnatural situation.

Assume that a metaphysical mechanist, that is, a person who accepts a set of mechanistic metaphysical directives m, which need not be specified in detail, is asked to justify his acceptance of m. He does this by first of all appealing to a standard of adequacy which he regards as generally accepted, as self-evident or for some other reason not in need of justification. This standard is again a set of directives, say a. No directive contained in 'a' is also contained in 'm', for if it were the justification would be circular. For a person who shares what is vaguely called "the scientific outlook", the standard of adequacy for any theory will contain directives which require some kind of empirical evidence and predictive usefulness.

Having more or less explicitly appealed to the standard of adequacy embodied in the directives 'a', the defender of metaphysical mechanism will draw attention to certain non-metaphysical theories, say 't_1', ..., 't_n' which are associated with 'a', and show that they are also associated with 'm'; or that these theories are more closely associated with 'a' than their known non-mechanistic alternatives. One theory is associated more closely than another with a set of directives if it conforms to more of these directives. It would be possible to define "closer association with a set of directives" in a more subtle, yet plausible, manner.

The metaphysical mechanist of our example thus justifies his acceptance of 'm' on the ground that certain theories associated with it are associated with 'a'. He does not, however, also justify his acceptance of 'a' by reference to 'm' and non-metaphysical theories associated with it. In this sense 'a' takes for him precedence over 'm'. We shall say that for him 'a' directively precedes 'm'.

In general, for an accepter of two directives or sets of directives 'd_1' and 'd_2', 'd_1' directively precedes 'd_2' if he would in the manner described above justify his acceptance of 'd_2' by reference to 'd_1' and theories associated with it but would not similarly justify his acceptance of 'd_1' by reference to 'd_2' and theories associated with it. It is possible that someone might accept directives 'd_1', 'd_2', ..., 'd_n' in such a manner that every member of the sequence which preceded another preceded it also directively. We shall call a person's primary directives those which for him directively precede all his other directives. In the above sequence 'd_1' is a primary directive or a set of primary directives.

In terms of directive precedence we can define the notion of the directive order of a set of directives. A set of directives which is accepted by anyone has directive order for him if one or more of these directives are primary. Not every set of accepted directives has directive order for its accepter. It may be, for example, that for an accepter of 'd_1', 'd_2' and 'd_3', 'd_1' directively precedes 'd_2', 'd_2' directively precedes 'd_3' and 'd_3' directively precedes 'd_1'. Again, a set of directives may have different directive order for different accepters. It may also have directive order for one person and not for another. A set of directives, all of whose directives are primary, has, according to our definition of the term, directive order. With regard to such a system we could not, of course, distinguish between the directives which embody a standard of adequacy on the one hand and the directives which are justified by reference to this standard on the other. The directives of a directively ordered system which are not primary are, we shall say, its secondary directives. A more detailed distinction between primary, secondary, tertiary directives, etc., will not be needed in the present context.

Before turning to the question of the adequacy or inadequacy of metaphysical directives, I shall briefly consider the nature of some allegedly anti-metaphysical philosophies, in particular pragmatism, "operationalism" and "verificationalism". Once the nature of metaphysical directives has become clear, it is not difficult to see that in holding any of these views one is not rejecting all metaphysical directives. For example, Bridgman's principle of essential connectivity,[1] and the principle of verification in its various forms, are metaphysical directives.

It might be tempting to remark, here, that the anti-metaphysical views mentioned amount to anti-metaphysical systems of metaphysics and are based on a contradiction in terms. Yet this often repeated statement misses an important point. Though these allegedly anti-metaphysical doctrines clearly contain metaphysical directives and are therefore metaphysical, they nevertheless differ

[1] See *Logic of Modern Physics* (New York, 1927), p. 158.

in an important respect from other metaphysical doctrines. This difference can be made clear by means of the notion of directive order.

We may assume that a metaphysical mechanist and a logical positivist or operationalist accept the same primary directives to the effect that every theory should be in some sense verifiable and predictive. The metaphysical mechanist, however, accepts *in addition* certain secondary directives whose main rules govern mechanistic concepts, that is, concepts which are more or less similar to the concepts of Newtonian physics and whose subsidiary rules proscribe the acceptance of alternative concepts. What the allegedly anti-metaphysical philosopher rejects are not metaphysical directives in general but all secondary directives. In other words, though he requires that any theory should conform to certain primary directives, he rejects any further restriction on possible theories by the acceptance of secondary directives. His allegedly "anti-metaphysical" philosophy involves thus the acceptance of certain primary, and the rejection of all secondary, directives.

The word "metaphysical" is frequently used as a term of abuse. In this use it refers to metaphysical directives or systems of such, which the user of the term rejects. A dialectical materialist or logical positivist who calls every system of directives except the one which he accepts "metaphysics", does not thereby cease to be the accepter of metaphysical directives, but merely adds a new burden of meaning to an already heavily overburdened word. In using "metaphysical" in conjunction with "directive" the intention has been to preserve a link with traditional usage while avoiding the dangers of its ambiguity.

As a result of the preceding considerations the following definitions and distinctions suggest themselves. A factual or logical proposition 't' is adequate for an accepter of a metaphysical directive 'd' if it conforms to 'd'. The proposition 't' may be a conjunction of propositions. It may, in particular, be a theory in some sense of the term. Since we are chiefly interested in the adequacy of theories, I shall speak only of adequate theories, although everything said about them applies equally to single propositions or sets of propositions which are not regarded as theories.

A non-metaphysical theory 't_1' is for an accepter of 'd' more adequate than another such theory 't_2' if 't_1' conforms more closely to 'd' than 't_2'. The adequacy of a theory must not be confused with its theoretical appropriateness (Chapters IV and XXIV); for a theoretically appropriate proposition may be adequate with respect to some metaphysical theories and with respect to others inadequate.

The adequacy or comparatively greater adequacy of a non-metaphysical theory must be sharply distinguished from the adequacy or greater adequacy of a metaphysical directive. In the latter case therefore I shall speak of directive adequacy or of greater directive adequacy. These notions are defined for secondary directives only. A secondary directive 'd' is directively adequate with respect to an accepter of a primary directive 'a' and a set of non-metaphysical theories 't_1', ..., 't_n' if, and only if, these theories conform to 'd' and 'a'. A secondary directive 'd' is with respect to an accepter of 'a' and a set of theories 't_1' ... 't_n' directively more adequate than a secondary directive 'e' if, and only if, the theories conforming to 'd' conform more closely to 'a' than the theories conforming to 'e'. According to this definition the directive adequacy of some but not of all secondary directives can be compared.

When people say that from the point of view of modern science one philosophy is more adequate than another—Kant's, say, than Aristotle's—they compare, in the manner described, the metaphysical directives of the one with those of the other, by relating them to their own accepted primary directives on the one hand and to certain contemporary scientific theories on the other.

The above definitions of "directively adequate" and of "directively more adequate" admit of many quite plausible refinements. I confine myself to emphasising that the definientia of the new definitions would involve the notions of primary and secondary metaphysical directives, of non-metaphysical theories, and of the relation which holds between directives and their associated theories.

Whatever definitions of this type we adopt, they would not enable us to compare the directive adequacy of every two sets of secondary directives—not even if we agreed to compare them with respect to the same primary directives and the same non-metaphysical theories. Moreover, if with respect to a primary directive and a set of theories 't_1'...'t_n', a set of secondary directives 'd' is directively less adequate than a set of secondary directives 'e', then the discovery of further theories can always reverse this relation between 'd' and 'e'. This consequence of our definition of 'directive adequacy' and 'greater directive adequacy' is quite apposite if we consider the slow death of some metaphysical theories and the surprising revival of others.

The discussion might be summed up by an analogy. Theories may be compared to maps, primary directives to criteria of the adequacy of maps, secondary directives to instructions for the making of them. A map which is a "true" picture of a countryside need not also be an adequate picture of it in the sense, for example, that it does not show with sufficient clarity certain features which for the user of the map are of special importance. Instructions for the making of maps, which correspond to secondary directives, are justified by appealing to adequate maps, that is, maps conforming to the criteria of adequacy.

If we speak of a map's being adequate, an instruction for the making of maps cannot be regarded as adequate in the same sense as a map devised according to this instruction. Again, if we speak of one map's being more adequate than another, one instruction for the making of maps cannot in the same sense be regarded as more adequate than another. It is, however, possible, plausible and useful to introduce the notions of the adequacy and comparative adequacy of instructions for the making of maps. These notions, which would be defined in terms of the adequacy of maps, that is, of some general criteria of adequacy, and of maps satisfying these criteria, would be analogous to the notions of the directive adequacy and the comparative directive adequacy of secondary metaphysical directives.

The question whether, if at all, metaphysical directives are capable of being true or false in a sense of these terms which resembles their use in connection with empirical and logico-mathematical propositions, is too vague to be answered precisely. The adequacy or inadequacy of metaphysical directives differs both from the truth and falsehood of empirical and logico-mathematical propositions, and from the "truth" or "falsehood" of works of art. By establishing the relations which hold between primary and secondary directives and their associated non-metaphysical propositions, we are assured that the definitions of adequacy and comparative adequacy are not empty. The definitions, on the other hand, help us to fix our attention upon these relations. To exhibit them is more important than to give them ambiguous names, laudatory or derogatory, such as "having cognitive value" or "being intellectually useless".

CHAPTER XXXIII

THE PLACE OF METAPHYSICAL DIRECTIVES IN PHILOSOPHICAL THINKING

THE acceptance of metaphysical directives is relevant in varying degrees to the problems which philosophers impose upon themselves, and to the manner in which they attempt their solutions. There are no sharp dividing lines between philosophical and non-philosophical problems. Just as every man in the ordinary business of life is to some degree an artist and a scientist, so he is also at least a rudimentary philosopher. It is equally impossible to draw sharp distinctions between different species of philosophy. Yet, as we must insist, distinction which admits borderline cases is not necessarily useless.

In the present chapter I shall discuss briefly the relevance of metaphysical directives to what could be called phenomenological, critical, analytical and constructive philosophy. Although my use of these terms only roughly resembles their by no means uniform use by other philosophers, I have thought it advisable not to coin any new terms. The distinction, which is not one between pure types, does not pretend to be exclusive or exhaustive.

The phenomenological philosopher, then, attempts to describe experience, that is, experiencing and what is experienced, with the least possible admixture of interpretation. While the "practical man" and the scientist are content to use concepts of a comparatively high interpretative level, the phenomenological philosopher uses concepts of the lowest possible level. For these he must often coin new words like "sense-datum", or use old words like "impression" in new senses. I should like to emphasise that the above characterisation of phenomenological philosophy does not depend on the possibility of testing whether or not the concepts which it uses are absolutely descriptive (Chapter XVI).

The field of phenomenological philosophy is unlimited, since every kind of experience can be described and interpreted and

289

thus presents us with the task of distinguishing between its description and its interpretation. There are, as has been argued earlier, no unfailing criteria of successful phenomenological description, but it is possible to determine which of two co-ostensive concepts is of lower interpretative level (Chapter XVII) and is thus more suitable for a phenomenological description.

Every phenomenological description depends on a choice between alternative applicable concepts, and may thus be influenced by the explicit or implicit acceptance of metaphysical directives. This can be seen in some disagreements between different phenomenological descriptions of allegedly similar experiences. The extent of the disagreements between various existentialist schools, all of which profess to follow Husserl's phenomenological method, may even start a doubt as to the very possibility of phenomenological philosophy. It seems, however, that the reason for these disagreements lies in the fact that many of the concepts used by the existentialists are of a high interpretative level. But in our sense of the term, the application of such concepts is incompatible with phenomenological philosophy. Indeed Husserl's formulation of the method of phenomenological and eidetic reduction does not, so it seems to me, lay sufficient stress on the requirement that only concepts of low interpretative level be admitted.

If we rule out phenomenologists who do not respect this requirement as something essential, we shall notice much less disagreement in the phenomenological descriptions which have been put forward at different times. The phenomenological descriptions, for instance, of perception, found in the works of such diverse philosophers as Plato, Descartes, Hume and Husserl, differ very little from each other, and are little dependent on the widely different metaphysical directives accepted by them.

The reason for this is implicit in the theory of interpretative levels and hierarchies (Chapters XVI and XVII). From the same absolutely or relatively descriptive concepts, we may ascend to a great variety of co-ostensive concepts of higher level. The possible variety increases with every successive step. The range of concepts opened to our choice increases correspondingly, and with it increases the importance of our metaphysical directives. Conversely, the lower the interpretative level of our concepts, the smaller the range of alternatives and the smaller the effect of the acceptance of one set of metaphysical directives rather than another.

Critical philosophy, as understood here, aims at exhibiting rules of conceptual thinking, their interrelations, and the manner of their acceptance. The rules which it tries to discover are such as either are accepted by all conceptual thinkers or, although accepted only by some, are of philosophical interest. The rules which are of philosophical interest shade, pretty continuously, into those which are not. Perhaps it is best to say that a rule has philosophical interest if its consideration is believed to throw light on problems which are considered traditionally as belonging to philosophy. Critical philosophy includes large parts of logic, of epistemology, and of the philosophy of scientific and common-sense views.

The critical philosopher in choosing concepts for pursuing his task is to some extent dependent on the acceptance of metaphysical directives, in particular those governing the use of epistemological concepts. Yet, as has been argued, the dependence is slight, since the results of critical philosophy can without substantial change be translated from one epistemological terminology into others.

Analytical and constructive philosophy are essentially dependent on metaphysical directives. All their problems could be expressed after the fashion of mathematicians by a formulation beginning with "given a metaphysical directive to the effect that...". This reference to metaphysical directives is essential, in the sense that if in it we replace one such directive by another we *eo ipso* replace one problem by another.

The analytical philosopher tries to analyse defective concepts into others which are not defective. Every problem of analytical philosophy presupposes (1) a concept (or concepts) which is considered in some sense to be defective, that is, the analysed concept or analysandum; (2) a concept itself not defective, by which the defective one is replaced, that is, the analysing concept or analysans; and (3) a certain relation between the analysans and the analysandum, that is, the analysing relation.

Philosophers who practise philosophical analysis frequently do not attempt to explain its nature. Even those who are prepared to explain what they are doing do not as a rule explain with sufficient clarity why the concepts which are supposed to need analysis are considered defective and what the nature of the analysing relation is considered to be. The answer to this question is that there are different notions of the defectiveness of concepts and different analysing relations.

It would be out of the question to try, here, to compile a list of the various analysing relations used by analytical philosophers. They range from relations of logical equivalence of decreasing strictness, over truth-functional equivalence, to various relations of greater or less resemblance between analysans and analysandum.

A similarly wide variety of notions of defectiveness could be found in the writings of analytical philosophers. Self-contradictory concepts are regarded as defective by all of them. Apart from this the notion varies with the analytical philosopher's accepted metaphysical directives. A concept is defective with respect to a conceptual thinker if its application (or, in the case of non-ostensive concepts, its quasi-application) would violate the metaphysical directives which he accepts. Analytical philosophers are frequently unaware of their accepted metaphysical directives; yet these determine for them the concepts which are to be regarded as in need of analysis.

If, as seems reasonable, one defines the defectiveness in concepts which can be cured by analysis, in terms of metaphysical directives, then the belief that analytical philosophy and metaphysics are strictly separate branches of philosophy becomes untenable. The opposite view, that philosophical analysis presupposes metaphysical commitments, comes nearer the truth. The view, however, is often connected with obscure theories of the nature of metaphysics which leave the nature of the alleged metaphysical commitments in the dark.

The dependence of analytical philosophy on the acceptance of metaphysical directives can be illustrated by examples of different notions of defective concepts. For the accepter of a general metaphysical directive to the effect that no ostensive concepts above a certain level should be accepted, all concepts of higher level will be defective. If his analysing relation allows this, he will analyse all concepts above the permissible level into concepts of this level or below it. If, however, his analysing relation is mutual entailment it is logically impossible for such an analysis to succeed (Chapter XVIII). Analysis of the sort just described might be called "analysis by reduction of interpretative level". Examples are various analyses of physical-object concepts into sense-datum concepts, of causal relations into relations of contiguous succession, of non-naturalistic into naturalistic concepts. Analyses by reduction of interpretative level or repudiations of such analyses fill many pages of books on the theory of knowledge and ethics by authors who do not stop at all—or do not stop long enough—to explain the type of analysis on which they are engaged.

Another species of philosophical analysis might be called "exactification". It serves, though in a dubious way, the ideal of philosophical exactitude, not by exhibiting accepted concepts, whether exact or inexact, exactly, but by replacing inexact concepts by exact ones. The notion of defective concepts is here defined by a general metaphysical directive to the effect that all accepted concepts, or a specified group of them, should stand only in exact logical relations, each to another. This metaphysical directive calls for an elimination of inclusion-or-overlaps and exclusion-or-overlaps by overlaps, inclusions or exclusions. It can be achieved by the acceptance of supplementary rules or by replacing ostensive concepts by non-ostensive ones (Chapters VI and VII).

The analysis of ostensive and empirical predicates into Boolean classes is an example of what we are here calling exactification. In itself it is quite harmless, and for many purposes may be extremely useful. If, however, it be accompanied by the mistaken belief that the analysing relation is mutual entailment, it can lead to much philosophical confusion.

Lastly, we may consider the type of philosophical analysis which perhaps most obviously of all depends on the acceptance of metaphysical directives. Its purpose is the adaptation of non-philosophical theories to accepted metaphysical directives. A person may accept a set of metaphysical directives to which certain scientific or other theories, which he regards as otherwise valuable, do not conform. He then finds it natural to modify the concepts of these theories so as to make them conform to his metaphysical directives while in other respects changing them as little as possible. If he does not reflect on what he is doing, he may easily convince himself that he is freeing a fundamentally sound theory from "the handicap of a false metaphysics" or even from "all metaphysics".

These examples could be multiplied. Any systematic classification of them would first divide them according to the analysing relation used and then subdivide them according to the metaphysical directives in terms of which the notion of defective concepts was defined. That the analytical philosopher is often faced with very difficult problems is known to everybody who has any acquaintance with philosophical writing. Our account of philosophical analysis does not contribute a great deal towards the solution of its specific problems. Yet seeing the nature of a problem more clearly may, at least sometimes, prove useful in attempts to solve it.

All problems of analytical philosophy can be schematically formulated as follows: Given a concept (or set of concepts) 'P', a metaphysical directive or conjunction of such directives 'd' with respect to which 'P' is defective, and an analysing relation 'R'; to find a concept 'Q' which is not defective with respect to 'd' and which stands to 'P' in the relation 'R'.

The critical and the analytical philosophers do not put forward any new metaphysical directives. The critical make explicit accepted rules of conceptual thinking. These may be either rules governing the use of concepts or metaphysical directives, which in addition to governing the use of concepts proscribe the use of more or less determinate alternatives. The analytical philosophers replace concepts which do not conform to accepted metaphysical directives by concepts which do conform to them. The constructive philosopher differs from both by laying down metaphysical directives which hitherto have not been accepted.

The recommendation of new metaphysical directives may to different degrees depend on the results of a critical inquiry into commonly held scientific and common-sense views. It may indeed be almost entirely independent of it. A philosopher might, for example, as a result of a mystical experience or of his belief in its occurrence in some other person, lay down a general metaphysical directive to the effect that all concepts must be rejected which are incompatible with those by whose application he describes this experience. The general directive might be laid down as a primary metaphysical directive, that is, as a directive to which every adequate theory must conform. In the history of mankind religious experience has often led, in this way, from the belief in religious dogmas to the acceptance of primary metaphysical directives.

Again it is possible that a critical inquiry into a group of theories should lead to the discovery of rules governing the use of certain concepts, to which there correspond no subsidiary rules proscribing the acceptance of alternatives. By the recommendation of such subsidiary rules, the limits of a merely critical philosophy are overstepped. In practice it can be very difficult to discern such a transition from critical to constructive philosophy.

Critical inquiry into a group of theories may lead to the discovery of certain primary directives, and as a result of this, secondary directives may be laid down which are directively adequate with respect to the theories and the primary directives. It may even be that the primary metaphysical directives refer only to very generally characterised secondary directives which have yet to be found. In these cases the primary directives and the theories constitute a constructive programme which is to be implemented by laying down new secondary directives.

Not only critical philosophy but also analysis may precede the constructive task. This happens when the theories and metaphysical directives which constitute the constructive programme make its implementation impossible because the theories do not conform to the directives. Philosophical analysis may then modify the theories by replacing their defective concepts by concepts conforming to the directives.

The problems of constructive philosophy, whether or not they arise from critical inquiries and whether or not they are preceded by philosophical analysis, are unlimited in number and variety. If the constructive philosopher accepts certain primary directives, then his problems can be schematically formulated as follows:

Given certain primary metaphysical directives (or certain primary and secondary directives) and certain theories, to find further metaphysical directives which are directively adequate with respect to the given primary directives and theories.

In conclusion, it should perhaps be emphasised again that these kinds of philosophy—phenomenological, critical, analytical and constructive—do not cover everything that has traditionally been called by the name. I have, in particular, said nothing about the type of philosophy which claims to express a vision of the universe as a whole and to be incapable of being conveyed by the mere statement of propositions. Synoptic philosophy, as it is often called, claims to embody non-conceptual thinking. In this it resembles poetry, from which, however, it differs by presupposing conceptual thinking as a necessary preliminary to the apprehension of the insight which it offers. An examination of its claims and nature transcends the scope of a critical inquiry into conceptual thinking.

INDEX

Philosophy, Religion

GUIDE TO PHILOSOPHY, C. E. M. Joad. A modern classic which examines many crucial problems which man has pondered through the ages: Does free will exist? Is there plan in the universe? How do we know and validate our knowledge? Such opposed solutions as subjective idealism and realism, chance and teleology, vitalism and logical positivism, are evaluated and the contributions of the great philosophers from the Greeks to moderns like Russell, Whitehead, and others, are considered in the context of each problem. "The finest introduction," BOSTON TRANSCRIPT. Index. Classified bibliography. 592pp. 5⅜ x 8.
T297 Paperbound **$2.25**

HISTORY OF ANCIENT PHILOSOPHY, W. Windelband. One of the clearest, most accurate comprehensive surveys of Greek and Roman philosophy. Discusses ancient philosophy in general, intellectual life in Greece in the 7th and 6th centuries B.C., Thales, Anaximander, Anaximenes, Heraclitus, the Eleatics, Empedocles, Anaxagoras, Leucippus, the Pythagoreans, the Sophists, Socrates, Democritus (20 pages), Plato (50 pages), Aristotle (70 pages), the Peripatetics, Stoics, Epicureans, Sceptics, Neo-platonists, Christian Apologists, etc. 2nd German edition translated by H. E. Cushman. xv + 393pp. 5⅜ x 8.
T357 Paperbound **$1.85**

ILLUSTRATIONS OF THE HISTORY OF MEDIEVAL THOUGHT AND LEARNING, R. L. Poole. Basic analysis of the thought and lives of the leading philosophers and ecclesiastics from the 8th to the 14th century—Abailard, Ockham, Wycliffe, Marsiglio of Padua, and many other great thinkers who carried the torch of Western culture and learning through the "Dark Ages": political, religious, and metaphysical views. Long a standard work for scholars and one of the best introductions to medieval thought for beginners. Index. 10 Appendices. xiii + 327pp. 5⅜ x 8.
T674 Paperbound **$2.00**

PHILOSOPHY AND CIVILIZATION IN THE MIDDLE AGES, M. de Wulf. This semi-popular survey covers aspects of medieval intellectual life such as religion, philosophy, science, the arts, etc. It also covers feudalism vs. Catholicism, rise of the universities, mendicant orders, monastic centers, and similar topics. Unabridged. Bibliography. Index. viii + 320pp. 5⅜ x 8.
T284 Paperbound **$1.85**

AN INTRODUCTION TO SCHOLASTIC PHILOSOPHY, Prof. M. de Wulf. Formerly entitled SCHOLASTICISM OLD AND NEW, this volume examines the central scholastic tradition from St. Anselm, Albertus Magnus, Thomas Aquinas, up to Suarez in the 17th century. The relation of scholasticism to ancient and medieval philosophy and science in general is clear and easily followed. The second part of the book considers the modern revival of scholasticism, the Louvain position, relations with Kantianism and Positivism. Unabridged. xvi + 271pp. 5⅜ x 8.
T296 Clothbound **$3.50**
T283 Paperbound **$2.00**

A HISTORY OF MODERN PHILOSOPHY, H. Höffding. An exceptionally clear and detailed coverage of western philosophy from the Renaissance to the end of the 19th century. Major and minor men such as Pomponazzi, Bodin, Boehme, Telesius, Bruno, Copernicus, da Vinci, Kepler, Galileo, Bacon, Descartes, Hobbes, Spinoza, Leibniz, Wolff, Locke, Newton, Berkeley, Hume, Erasmus, Montesquieu, Voltaire, Diderot, Rousseau, Lessing, Kant, Herder, Fichte, Schelling, Hegel, Schopenhauer, Comte, Mill, Darwin, Spencer, Hartmann, Lange, and many others, are discussed in terms of theory of knowledge, logic, cosmology, and psychology. Index. 2 volumes, total of 1159pp. 5⅜ x 8.
T117 Vol. 1, Paperbound **$2.50**
T118 Vol. 2, Paperbound **$2.25**

ARISTOTLE, A. E. Taylor. A brilliant, searching non-technical account of Aristotle and his thought written by a foremost Platonist. It covers the life and works of Aristotle; classification of the sciences; logic; first philosophy; matter and form; causes; motion and eternity; God; physics; metaphysics; and similar topics. Bibliography. New Index compiled for this edition. 128pp. 5⅜ x 8.
T280 Paperbound **$1.00**

THE SYSTEM OF THOMAS AQUINAS, M. de Wulf. Leading Neo-Thomist, one of founders of University of Louvain, gives concise exposition to central doctrines of Aquinas, as a means toward determining his value to modern philosophy, religion. Formerly "Medieval Philosophy Illustrated from the System of Thomas Aquinas." Trans. by E. Messenger. Introduction. 151pp. 5⅜ x 8.
T568 Paperbound **$1.25**

LEIBNIZ, H. W. Carr. Most stimulating middle-level coverage of basic philosophical thought of Leibniz. Easily understood discussion, analysis of major works: "Theodicy," "Principles of Nature and Grace," "Monadology"; Leibniz's influence; intellectual growth; correspondence; disputes with Bayle, Malebranche, Newton; importance of his thought today, with reinterpretation in modern terminology. "Power and mastery," London Times. Bibliography. Index. 226pp. 5⅜ x 8.
T624 Paperbound **$1.35**

CATALOGUE OF DOVER BOOKS

THE SENSE OF BEAUTY, G. Santayana. A revelation of the beauty of language as well as an important philosophic treatise, this work studies the "why, when, and how beauty appears, what conditions an object must fulfill to be beautiful, what elements of our nature make us sensible of beauty, and what the relation is between the constitution of the object and the excitement of our susceptibility." "It is doubtful if a better treatment of the subject has since been published," PEABODY JOURNAL. Index. ix + 275pp. 5⅜ x 8.
T238 Paperbound **$1.00**

PROBLEMS OF ETHICS, Moritz Schlick. The renowned leader of the "Vienna Circle" applies the logical positivist approach to a wide variety of ethical problems: the source and means of attaining knowledge, the formal and material characteristics of the good, moral norms and principles, absolute vs. relative values, free will and responsibility, comparative importance of pleasure and suffering as ethical values, etc. Disarmingly simple and straightforward despite complexity of subject. First English translation, authorized by author before his death, of a thirty-year old classic. Translated and with an introduction by David Rynin. Index. Foreword by Prof. George P. Adams. xxi + 209pp. 5⅜ x 8.
T946 Paperbound **$1.60**

AN INTRODUCTION TO EXISTENTIALISM, Robert G. Olson. A new and indispensable guide to one of the major thought systems of our century, the movement that is central to the thinking of some of the most creative figures of the past hundred years. Stresses Heidegger and Sartre, with careful and objective examination of the existentialist position, values—freedom of choice, individual dignity, personal love, creative effort—and answers to the eternal questions of the human condition. Scholarly, unbiased, analytic, unlike most studies of this difficult subject, Prof. Olson's book is aimed at the student of philosophy as well as at the reader with no formal training who is looking for an absorbing, accessible, and thorough introduction to the basic texts. Index. xv + 221pp. 5⅜ x 8½.
T55 Paperbound **$1.65**

SYMBOLIC LOGIC, C. I. Lewis and C. H. Langford. Since first publication in 1932, this has been among most frequently cited works on symbolic logic. Still one of the best introductions both for beginners and for mathematicians, philosophers. First part covers basic topics which easily lend themselves to beginning study. Second part is rigorous, thorough development of logistic method, examination of some of most difficult and abstract aspects of symbolic logic, including modal logic, logical paradoxes, many-valued logic, with Prof. Lewis' own contributions. 2nd revised (corrected) edition. 3 appendixes, one new to this edition. 524pp. 5⅜ x 8.
S170 Paperbound **$2.00**

WHITEHEAD'S PHILOSOPHY OF CIVILIZATION, A. H. Johnson. A leading authority on Alfred North Whitehead synthesizes the great philosopher's thought on civilization, scattered throughout various writings, into unified whole. Analysis of Whitehead's general definition of civilization, his reflections on history and influences on its development, his religion, including his analysis of Christianity, concept of solitariness as first requirement of personal religion, and so on. Other chapters cover views on minority groups, society, civil liberties, education. Also critical comments on Whitehead's philosophy. Written with general reader in mind. A perceptive introduction to important area of the thought of a leading philosopher of our century. Revised index and bibliography. xii + 211pp. 5⅜ x 8½.
T996 Paperbound **$1.50**

WHITEHEAD'S THEORY OF REALITY, A. H. Johnson. Introductory outline of Whitehead's theory of actual entities, the heart of his philosophy of reality, followed by his views on nature of God, philosophy of mind, theory of value (truth, beauty, goodness and their opposites), analyses of other philosophers, attitude toward science. A perspicacious lucid introduction by author of dissertation on Whitehead, written under the subject's supervision at Harvard. Good basic view for beginning students of philosophy and for those who are simply interested in important contemporary ideas. Revised index and bibliography. xiii + 267pp. 5⅜ x 8½.
T989 Paperbound **$2.00**

MIND AND THE WORLD-ORDER, C. I. Lewis. Building upon the work of Peirce, James, and Dewey, Professor Lewis outlines a theory of knowledge in terms of "conceptual pragmatism." Dividing truth into abstract mathematical certainty and empirical truth, the author demonstrates that the traditional understanding of the a priori must be abandoned. Detailed analyses of philosophy, metaphysics, method, the "given" in experience, knowledge of objects, nature of the a priori, experience and order, and many others. Appendices. xiv + 446pp. 5⅜ x 8.
T359 Paperbound **$2.25**

SCEPTICISM AND ANIMAL FAITH, G. Santayana. To eliminate difficulties in the traditional theory of knowledge, Santayana distinguishes between the independent existence of objects and the essence our mind attributes to them. Scepticism is thereby established as a form of belief, and animal faith is shown to be a necessary condition of knowledge. Belief, classical idealism, intuition, memory, symbols, literary psychology, and much more, discussed with unusual clarity and depth. Index. xii + 314pp. 5⅜ x 8.
T235 Clothbound **$3.50**
T236 Paperbound **$1.75**

LANGUAGE AND MYTH, E. Cassirer. Analyzing the non-rational thought processes which go to make up culture, Cassirer demonstrates that beneath both language and myth there lies a dominant unconscious "grammar" of experience whose categories and canons are not those of logical thought. His analyses of seemingly diverse phenomena such as Indian metaphysics, the Melanesian "mana," the Naturphilosophie of Schelling, modern poetry, etc., are profound without being pedantic. Introduction and translation by Susanne Langer. Index. x + 103pp. 5⅜ x 8.
T51 Paperbound **$1.25**

CATALOGUE OF DOVER BOOKS

AN ESSAY CONCERNING HUMAN UNDERSTANDING, John Locke. Edited by A. C. Fraser. Unabridged reprinting of definitive edition; only complete edition of "Essay" in print. Marginal analyses of almost every paragraph; hundreds of footnotes; authoritative 140-page biographical, critical, historical prolegomena. Indexes. 1170pp. 5⅜ x 8.

T530 Vol. 1 (Books 1, 2) Paperbound **$2.50**
T531 Vol. 2 (Books 3, 4) Paperbound **$2.50**
2 volume set **$5.00**

THE PHILOSOPHY OF HISTORY, G. W. F. Hegel. One of the great classics of western thought which reveals Hegel's basic principle: that history is not chance but a rational process, the realization of the Spirit of Freedom. Ranges from the oriental cultures of subjective thought to the classical subjective cultures, to the modern absolute synthesis where spiritual and secular may be reconciled. Translation and introduction by J. Sibree. Introduction by C. Hegel. Special introduction for this edition by Prof. Carl Friedrich. xxxix + 447pp. 5⅜ x 8.

T112 Paperbound **$2.25**

THE PHILOSOPHY OF HEGEL, W. T. Stace. The first detailed analysis of Hegel's thought in English, this is especially valuable since so many of Hegel's works are out of print. Dr. Stace examines Hegel's debt to Greek idealists and the 18th century and then proceeds to a careful description and analysis of Hegel's first principles, categories, reason, dialectic method, his logic, philosophy of nature and spirit, etc. Index. Special 14 x 20 chart of Hegelian system. x + 526pp. 5⅜ x 8.

T254 Paperbound **$2.75**

THE WILL TO BELIEVE and HUMAN IMMORTALITY, W. James. Two complete books bound as one. THE WILL TO BELIEVE discusses the interrelations of belief, will, and intellect in man; chance vs. determinism, free will vs. determinism, free will vs. fate, pluralism vs. monism; the philosophies of Hegel and Spencer, and more. HUMAN IMMORTALITY examines the question of survival after death and develops an unusual and powerful argument for immortality. Two prefaces. Index. Total of 429pp. 5⅜ x 8.

T291 Paperbound **$2.00**

THE WORLD AND THE INDIVIDUAL, Josiah Royce. Only major effort by an American philosopher to interpret nature of things in systematic, comprehensive manner. Royce's formulation of an absolute voluntarism remains one of the original and profound solutions to the problems involved. Part One, Four Historical Conceptions of Being, inquires into first principles, true meaning and place of individuality. Part Two, Nature, Man, and the Moral Order, is application of first principles to problems concerning religion, evil, moral order. Introduction by J. E. Smith, Yale Univ. Index. 1070pp. 5⅜ x 8.

T561 Vol. 1 Paperbound **$2.75**
T562 Vol. 2 Paperbound **$2.75**
Two volume set **$5.50**

THE PHILOSOPHICAL WRITINGS OF PEIRCE, edited by J. Buchler. This book (formerly THE PHILOSOPHY OF PEIRCE) is a carefully integrated exposition of Peirce's complete system composed of selections from his own work. Symbolic logic, scientific method, theory of signs, pragmatism, epistemology, chance, cosmology, ethics, and many other topics are treated by one of the greatest philosophers of modern times. This is the only inexpensive compilation of his key ideas. xvi + 386pp. 5⅜ x 8.

T217 Paperbound **$2.00**

EXPERIENCE AND NATURE, John Dewey. An enlarged, revised edition of the Paul Carus lectures which Dewey delivered in 1925. It covers Dewey's basic formulation of the problem of knowledge, with a full discussion of other systems, and a detailing of his own concepts of the relationship of external world, mind, and knowledge. Starts with a thorough examination of the philosophical method; examines the interrelationships of experience and nature; analyzes experience on basis of empirical naturalism, the formulation of law, role of language and social factors in knowledge; etc. Dewey's treatment of central problems in philosophy is profound but extremely easy to follow. ix + 448pp. 5⅜ x 8.

T471 Paperbound **$2.00**

THE PHILOSOPHICAL WORKS OF DESCARTES. The definitive English edition of all the major philosophical works and letters of René Descartes. All of his revolutionary insights, from his famous "Cogito ergo sum" to his detailed account of contemporary science and his astonishingly fruitful concept that all phenomena of the universe (except mind) could be reduced to clear laws by the use of mathematics. An excellent source for the thought of men like Hobbes, Arnauld, Gassendi, etc., who were Descarte's contemporaries. Translated by E. S. Haldane and G. Ross. Introductory notes. Index. Total of 842pp. 5⅜ x 8.

T71 Vol. 1, Paperbound **$2.00**
T72 Vol. 2, Paperbound **$2.00**

THE CHIEF WORKS OF SPINOZA. An unabridged reprint of the famous Bohn edition containing all of Spinoza's most important works: Vol. I: The Theologico-Political Treatise and the Political Treatise. Vol. II: On The Improvement Of Understanding, The Ethics, Selected Letters. Profound and enduring ideas on God, the universe, pantheism, society, religion, the state, democracy, the mind, emotions, freedom and the nature of man, which influenced Goethe, Hegel, Schelling, Coleridge, Whitehead, and many others. Introduction. 2 volumes. 826pp. 5⅜ x 8.

T249 Vol. I, Paperbound **$1.75**
T250 Vol. II, Paperbound **$1.50**

THE ANALYSIS OF MATTER, Bertrand Russell. A classic which has retained its importance in understanding the relation between modern physical theory and human perception. Logical analysis of physics, prerelativity physics, causality, scientific inference, Weyl's theory, tensors, invariants and physical interpretations, periodicity, and much more is treated with Russell's usual brilliance. "Masterly piece of clear thinking and clear writing," NATION AND ATHENAE-UM. "Most thorough treatment of the subject," THE NATION. Introduction. Index. 8 figures. viii + 408pp. 5⅜ x 8.   S231 Paperbound **$1.95**

CONCEPTUAL THINKING (A LOGICAL INQUIRY), S. Körner. Discusses origin, use of general concepts on which language is based, and the light they shed on basic philosophical questions. Rigorously examines how different concepts are related; how they are linked to experience; problems in the field of contact between exact logical, mathematical, and scientific concepts, and the inexactness of everyday experience (studied at length). This work elaborates many new approaches to the traditional problems of philosophy—epistemology, value theories, metaphysics, aesthetics, morality. "Rare originality . . . brings a new rigour into philosophical argument," Philosophical Quarterly. New corrected second edition. Index. vii + 301pp. 5⅜ x 8.   T516 Paperbound **$1.75**

INTRODUCTION TO SYMBOLIC LOGIC, S. Langer. No special knowledge of math required — probably the clearest book ever written on symbolic logic, suitable for the layman, general scientist, and philosopher. You start with simple symbols and advance to a knowledge of the Boole-Schroeder and Russell-Whitehead systems. Forms, logical structure, classes, the calculus of propositions, logic of the syllogism, etc., are all covered. "One of the clearest and simplest introductions," MATHEMATICS GAZETTE. Second enlarged, revised edition. 368pp. 5⅜ x 8.   S164 Paperbound **$1.85**

LANGUAGE, TRUTH AND LOGIC, A. J. Ayer. A clear, careful analysis of the basic ideas of Logical Positivism. Building on the work of Schlick, Russell, Carnap, and the Viennese School, Mr. Ayer develops a detailed exposition of the nature of philosophy, science, and metaphysics; the Self and the World; logic and common sense, and other philosophic concepts. An aid to clarity of thought as well as the first full-length development of Logical Positivism in English. Introduction by Bertrand Russell. Index. 160pp. 5⅜ x 8.   T10 Paperbound **$1.25**

ESSAYS IN EXPERIMENTAL LOGIC, J. Dewey. Based upon the theory that knowledge implies a judgment which in turn implies an inquiry, these papers consider the inquiry stage in terms of: the relationship of thought and subject matter, antecedents of thought, data and meanings. 3 papers examine Bertrand Russell's thought, while 2 others discuss pragmatism and a final essay presents a new theory of the logic of values. Index. viii + 444pp. 5⅜ x 8.
                                                                        T73 Paperbound **$2.25**

TRAGIC SENSE OF LIFE, M. de Unamuno. The acknowledged masterpiece of one of Spain's most influential thinkers. Between the despair at the inevitable death of man and all his works and the desire for something better, Unamuno finds that "saving incertitude" that alone can console us. This dynamic appraisal of man's faith in God and in himself has been called "a masterpiece" by the ENCYCLOPAEDIA BRITANNICA. xxx + 332pp. 5⅜ x 8.
                                                                        T257 Paperbound **$2.00**

HISTORY OF DOGMA, A. Harnack. Adolph Harnack, who died in 1930, was perhaps the greatest Church historian of all time. In this epoch-making history, which has never been surpassed in comprehensiveness and wealth of learning, he traces the development of the authoritative Christian doctrinal system from its first crystallization in the 4th century down through the Reformation, including also a brief survey of the later developments through the Infallibility decree of 1870. He reveals the enormous influence of Greek thought on the early Fathers, and discusses such topics as the Apologists, the great councils, Manichaeism, the historical position of Augustine, the medieval opposition to indulgences, the rise of Protestantism, the relations of Luther's doctrines with modern tendencies of thought, and much more. "Monumental work; still the most valuable history of dogma . . . luminous analysis of the problems . . . abounds in suggestion and stimulus and can be neglected by no one who desires to understand the history of thought in this most important field," Dutcher's Guide to Historical Literature. Translated by Neil Buchanan. Unabridged reprint in 4 volumes. Vol I: Beginnings to the Gnostics and Marcion. Vol II & III: 2nd century to the 4th century Fathers. Vol IV & V: 4th century Councils to the Carlovingian Renaissance. Vol VI & VII: Period of Clugny (c. 1000) to the Reformation, and after. Total of cii + 2407pp. 5⅜ x 8.

T904 Vol I	Paperbound	**$2.50**
T905 Vol II & III	Paperbound	**$2.75**
T906 Vol IV & V	Paperbound	**$2.75**
T907 Vol VI & VII	Paperbound	**$2.75**
	The set	**$10.75**

THE GUIDE FOR THE PERPLEXED, Maimonides. One of the great philosophical works of all time and a necessity for everyone interested in the philosophy of the Middle Ages in the Jewish, Christian, and Moslem traditions. Maimonides develops a common meeting-point for the Old Testament and the Aristotelian thought which pervaded the medieval world. His ideas and methods predate such scholastics as Aquinas and Scotus and throw light on the entire problem of philosophy or science vs. religion. 2nd revised edition. Complete unabridged Friedländer translation. 55 page introduction to Maimonides's life, period, etc., with an important summary of the GUIDE. Index. lix + 414pp. 5⅜ x 8.   T351 Paperbound **$2.00**

Orientalia

ORIENTAL RELIGIONS IN ROMAN PAGANISM, F. Cumont. A study of the cultural meeting of east and west in the Early Roman Empire. It covers the most important eastern religions of the time from their first appearance in Rome, 204 B.C., when the Great Mother of the Gods was first brought over from Syria. The ecstatic cults of Syria and Phrygia — Cybele, Attis, Adonis, their orgies and mutilatory rites; the mysteries of Egypt — Serapis, Isis, Osiris, the dualism of Persia, the elevation of cosmic evil to equal stature with the deity, Mithra; worship of Hermes Trismegistus; Ishtar, Astarte; the magic of the ancient Near East, etc. Introduction. 55pp. of notes; extensive bibliography. Index. xxiv + 298pp. 5⅜ x 8.
T321 Paperbound **$2.00**

THE MYSTERIES OF MITHRA, F. Cumont. The definitive coverage of a great ideological struggle between the west and the orient in the first centuries of the Christian era. The origin of Mithraism, a Persian mystery religion, and its association with the Roman army is discussed in detail. Then utilizing fragmentary monuments and texts, in one of the greatest feats of scholarly detection, Dr. Cumont reconstructs the mystery teachings and secret doctrines, the hidden organization and cult of Mithra. Mithraic art is discussed, analyzed, and depicted in 70 illustrations. 239pp. 5⅜ x 8.
T323 Paperbound **$2.00**

CHRISTIAN AND ORIENTAL PHILOSOPHY OF ART, A. K. Coomaraswamy. A unique fusion of philosopher, orientalist, art historian, and linguist, the author discusses such matters as: the true function of aesthetics in art, the importance of symbolism, intellectual and philosophic backgrounds, the role of traditional culture in enriching art, common factors in all great art, the nature of medieval art, the nature of folklore, the beauty of mathematics, and similar topics. 2 illustrations. Bibliography. 148pp. 5⅜ x 8.
T378 Paperbound **$1.50**

TRANSFORMATION OF NATURE IN ART, A. K. Coomaraswamy. Unabridged reissue of a basic work upon Asiatic religious art and philosophy of religion. The theory of religious art in Asia and Medieval Europe (exemplified by Meister Eckhart) is analyzed and developed. Detailed consideration is given to Indian medieval aesthetic manuals, symbolic language in philosophy, the origin and use of images in India, and many other fascinating and little known topics. Glossaries of Sanskrit and Chinese terms. Bibliography. 41pp. of notes. 245pp. 5⅜ x 8.
T368 Paperbound **$1.75**

BUDDHIST LOGIC, F.Th. Stcherbatsky. A study of an important part of Buddhism usually ignored by other books on the subject: the Mahayana buddhistic logic of the school of Dignaga and his followers. First vol. devoted to history of Indian logic with Central Asian continuations, detailed exposition of Dignaga system, including theory of knowledge, the sensible world (causation, perception, ultimate reality) and mental world (judgment, inference, logical fallacies, the syllogism), reality of external world, and negation (law of contradiction, universals, dialectic). Vol. II contains translation of Dharmakirti's Nyayabindu with Dharmamottara's commentary. Appendices cover translations of Tibetan treatises on logic, Hindu attacks on Buddhist logic, etc. The basic work, one of the products of the great St. Petersburg school of Indian studies. Written clearly and with an awareness of Western philosophy and logic; meant for the Asian specialist and for the general reader with only a minimum of background. Vol. I, xii + 559pp. Vol. II, viii + 468pp. 5⅜ x 8½.
T955 Vol. I Paperbound **$2.50**
T956 Vol. II Paperbound **$2.50**
The set **$5.00**

THE TEXTS OF TAOISM. The first inexpensive edition of the complete James Legge translations of the Tao Te King and the writings of Chinese mystic Chuang Tse. Also contains several shorter treatises: the T'ai Shang Tractate of Actions and Their Retributions; the King Kang King, or Classic of Purity; the Yin Fu King, or Classic of the Harmony of the Seen and Unseen; the Yu Shu King, or Classic of the Pivot of Jade; and the Hsia Yung King, or Classic of the Directory for a Day. While there are other translations of the Tao Te King, this is the only translation of Chuang Tse and much of other material. Extensive introduction discusses differences between Taoism, Buddhism, Confucianism; authenticity and arrangement of Tao Te King and writings of Chuang Tse; the meaning of the Tao and basic tenets of Taoism; historical accounts of Lao-tse and followers; other pertinent matters. Clarifying notes incorporated into text. Originally published as Volumes 39, 40 of SACRED BOOKS OF THE EAST series, this has long been recognized as an indispensable collection. Sinologists, philosophers, historians of religion will of course be interested and anyone with an elementary course in Oriental religion or philosophy will understand and profit from these writings. Index. Appendix analyzing thought of Chuang Tse. Vol. I, xxiii + 396pp. Vol. II, viii + 340pp. 5⅜ x 8½.
T990 Vol. I Paperbound **$2.25**
T991 Vol. II Paperbound **$2.25**

CATALOGUE OF DOVER BOOKS

EPOCHS OF CHINESE AND JAPANESE ART, Ernest T. Fenollosa. Although this classic of art history was written before the archeological discovery of Shang and Chou civilizations, it is still in many respects the finest detailed study of Chinese and Japanese art available in English. It is very wide in range, covering sculpture, carving, painting, metal work, ceramics, textiles, graphic arts and other areas, and it considers both religious and secular art, including the Japanese woodcut. Its greatest strength, however, lies in its extremely full, detailed, insight-laden discussion of historical and cultural background, and in its analysis of the religious and philosophical implications of art works. It is also a brilliant stylistic achievement, written with enthusiasm and verve, which can be enjoyed and read with profit by both the Orientalist and the general reader who is interested in art. Index. Glossary of proper names. 242 illustrations. Total of 704 pages. 5⅜ x 8½.
T364-5 Two vol. set, paperbound **$5.00**

THE VEDANTA SUTRAS OF BADARAYANA WITH COMMENTARY BY SANKARACHARYA. The definitive translation of the consummation, foremost interpretation of Upanishads. Originally part of SACRED BOOKS OF THE EAST, this two-volume translation includes exhaustive commentary and exegesis by Sankara; 128-page introduction by translator, Prof. Thibaut, that discusses background, scope and purpose of the sutras, value and importance of Sankara's interpretation; copious footnotes providing further explanations. Every serious student of Indian religion or thought, philosophers, historians of religion should read these clear, accurate translations of documents central to development of important thought systems in the East. Unabridged republication of Volumes 34, 38 of the Sacred Books of the East. Translated by George Thibault. General index, index of quotations and of Sanskrit. Vol. I, cxxv + 448pp. Vol. II, iv + 506pp. 5⅜ x 8½.
T994 Vol. I Paperbound **$2.00**
T995 Vol. II Paperbound **$2.00**

THE UPANISHADS. The Max Müller translation of the twelve classical Upanishads available for the first time in an inexpensive format: Chandogya, Kena, Aitareya aranyaka and upanishad, Kaushitaki, Isa, Katha, Mundaka, Taittiriyaka Brhadaranyaka, Svetarasvatara. Prasna — all of the classical Upanishads of the Vedanta school—and the Maitriyana Upanishad. Originally volumes 1, 15 of SACRED BOOKS OF THE EAST series, this is still the most scholarly translation. Prof. Müller, probably most important Sanskritologist of nineteenth century, provided invaluable introduction that acquaints readers with history of Upanishad translations, age and chronology of texts, etc. and a preface that discusses their value to Western readers. Heavily annotated. Stimulating reading for anyone with even only a basic course background in Oriental philosophy, religion, necessary to all Indologists, philosophers, religious historians. Transliteration and pronunciation guide. Vol. I, ciii + 320pp. Vol. II, liii + 350pp.
T992 Vol. I Paperbound **$2.25**
T993 Vol. II Paperbound **$2.25**
The set **$4.50**

Dover publishes books on art, music, philosophy, literature, languages, history, social sciences, psychology, handcrafts, orientalia, puzzles and entertainments, chess, pets and gardens, books explaining science, intermediate and higher mathematics, mathematical physics, engineering, biological sciences, earth sciences, classics of science, etc. Write to:

Dept. catrr.
Dover Publications, Inc.
180 Varick Street, N.Y. 14, N.Y.

DATE DUE